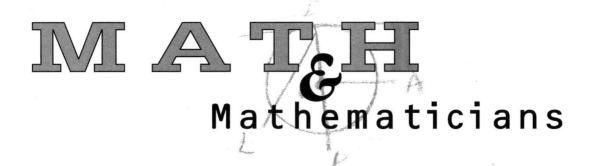

MATH &

Mathematicians

MATH & Mathematicians:

The History of Math Discoveries Around the World

Volume 1 A-H

Leonard C. Bruno

Lawrence W. Baker, Editor

AN IMPRINT OF THE GALE GROUP

DETROIT · SAN FRANCISCO · LONDON
BOSTON · WOODBRIDGE, CT

Math and Mathematicians: The History of Math Discoveries Around the World
Leonard C. Bruno

Staff

Lawrence W. Baker, *U•X•L Senior Editor*
Carol DeKane Nagel, *U•X•L Managing Editor*
Thomas L. Romig, *U•X•L Publisher*

Meggin Condino, *Senior Analyst, New Product Development*

Margaret Chamberlain, *Permissions Specialist (Pictures)*

Rita Wimberley, *Senior Buyer*
Evi Seoud, *Assistant Production Manager*
Dorothy Maki, *Manufacturing Manager*

Eric Johnson, *Page Designer*
Tracey Rowens, *Page Designer*
Martha Schiebold, *Cover Designer*
Cynthia Baldwin, *Product Design Manager*

Pamela Reed, *Imaging Coordinator*
Robert Duncan, *Senior Imaging Specialist*
Randy A. Bassett, *Image Database Supervisor*
Barbara J. Yarrow, *Graphic Services Manager*

Marco Di Vita, Graphix Group, *Typesetting*

Copyright © 1999
U•X•L, an imprint of The Gale Group
27500 Drake Rd.
Farmington Hills, MI 48331-3535

Library of Congress Catalog-in-Publication Data

Bruno, Leonard C.
    Math and mathematicians : the history of math discoveries around the world / Leonard C.
Bruno ; Lawrence W. Baker, editor.
      p.   cm.
    Includes index.
    Contents: v. 1. A-H – v. 2. I-Z.
    Summary: Compilation of fifty biographies of mathematicians from throughout history and
approximately thirty-five articles describing math concepts and principles.
    ISBN 0-7876-3812-9 (set). – ISBN 0-7876-3813-7 (vol. 1). – ISBN 0-7876-3814-5 (vol. 2).
    1. Mathematicians—Biography, Juvenile literature. 2. Mathematics–History Encyclopedias,
Juvenile. [1. Mathematicians Encyclopedias. 2. Mathematics Encyclopedias.] I. Baker,
Lawrence W. II. Title.
QA28.B78 1999
510'.92'2–dc21
[B]
                99-32424
                CIP

32222000247579

Printed in the United States of America
10 9 8 7 6 5 4 3 2 1

Contents

Contents

Contents

Contents

Entries by Mathematical Field

Boldface type indicates volume number; regular type indicates page numbers.

Entries by Mathematical Field

Entries by
Mathematical Field

Number theory

Probability and ratio

Set theory

Statistics

Time

Entries by
Mathematical Field

Biographical Entries by Ethnicity

Boldface type indicates volume number; regular type indicates page numbers.

Biographical
Entries by
Ethnicity

Reader's Guide

Unlike many other fields of science, mathematics has only a few really well-known individuals whose names most people easily recognize. Although by high school we all know something of the contributions of Euclid, Pythagoras, and Isaac Newton, the history of mathematics contains a far greater number of individuals whose accomplishments were nearly as important and whose lives may have been even more interesting, but about whom most of us know very little. *Math and Mathematicians: The History of Math Discoveries Around the World* is intended therefore not only to summarize and describe the lives of those better-known achievers, but to tell the stories of those other greats and near-greats whose contributions have not become an integral part of our popular mathematical knowledge. This two-volume set covers the early life, influences, and career of each individual.

Altogether, fifty such individuals have been selected on the basis not only of their mathematical contributions, but also with the intent of offering young readers a sampling of just how rich the history of mathematics is and how diverse are its contributors. The biographies in *Math and Mathematicians* include representatives from every major part of the world—ancient and modern—as well as

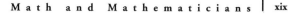

Reader's Guide

mathematicians who were and are young and old, male and female. If there is one common thread that links all these biographies, it is that genius, hard work, determination, inspiration, and courage are multicultural, multiracial, and totally ignorant of gender.

Surveyed as a group, the fifty biographies in *Math and Mathematicians* include fourteen people who either were born or did their major work in the twentieth century—six of whom are still living. This should suggest that not all the great mathematicians are musty names found in old history books. The oldest historical figure included here, Thales of Miletus, harks back to seventh century B.C., while the youngest living mathematician in this book, Andrew Wiles, was born in 1953. Ranging over the entire history of mathematics and selecting only fifty individuals obviously suggests that many more mathematicians were excluded than included, and it should not be surprising that some truly deserving individuals were left out. But with the help of an advisory board, we selected a solid core of mathematicians that spans the centuries: seven were born before the sixteenth century, six in the sixteenth century, five in the seventeenth century, ten in the eighteenth century, eleven in the nineteenth century, and eleven in the twentieth century.

Besides the mathematical accomplishments that earned these individuals a high place in the history of mathematics, there are many fascinating personal stories that make them extremely interesting from a human perspective. While the number of child prodigies like Carl Friedrich Gauss, William Rowan Hamilton, John von Neumann, Norbert Wiener, and others may not be surprising, the number of what might be called martyrs to mathematics certainly is. Archimedes and Hypatia were in fact killed because of their work, and the number of shortened and wrecked lives (Niels Abel, René Descartes, Évariste Galois, Sofya Kovalevskaya, and Alan Turing, among others) is truly shocking. The eccentric or "nutty" professors are also represented here, with the likes of Charles Babbage, Girolamo Cardano, Paul Erdös, Joseph Fourier, Kurt Gödel, John Napier, and Srinivasa A. Ramanujan doing their best to uphold the stereotype of the misfit or oddball scientist.

In addition to the fifty biographical essays, *Math and Mathematicians* also contains thirty-four essays describing math concepts and principles important to the middle school curriculum. These concepts, again chosen with the assistance of our advisory board, are arranged and interfiled alphabetically with the biographies to form one encyclopedic set. Each essay describes, when relevant, the time period, culture, and circumstances in which the concept or theory evolved or was discovered. Each entry also explains the concept in nontechnical language and offers examples.

All entries are easy to read and written in a straightforward style. Difficult words are defined within the text. Each of the thirty-four concept entries also includes a "Words to Know" sidebar that defines technical words and scientific terms. This enables students to learn vocabulary appropriate to mathematics without having to consult other sources for definitions.

Added features

Math and Mathematicians: The History of Math Discoveries Around the World includes a number of additional features that help make the connection between math concepts and theories, the people who discovered and worked with them, and common uses of mathematics.

- Three tables of contents—alphabetically by mathematician or concept, by mathematical field, and by mathematician's ethnicity—provide varied access to the entries.

- A timeline at the beginning of each volume provides a chronology of highlights in the history of mathematics.

- A cumulative "Words to Know" section gives definitions of key mathematical terms.

- More than one hundred photographs and illustrations bring to life the mathematicians, concepts, and ways in which mathematics is commonly used.

- Sidebars provide fascinating supplemental information about important terms, mathematicians, and theories.

- Extensive cross references make it easy to refer to other mathematicians and concepts covered in both volumes; cross references to other entries are boldfaced upon the first mention in an entry.

- Sources for more information are found at the end of each entry so students know where to delve even deeper.

• A comprehensive index quickly points readers to the mathematicians, concepts, theories, and organizations mentioned in *Math and Mathematicians*.

Special thanks

The author wishes to thank his wife, Jane, and children Nat, Ben, and Nina, for their patience, understanding, and actual help when I often needed something explained in a simple, direct manner. The excellent index was prepared by Michelle B. Cadoree, whose knowledge, ability, and professionalism made that part of the book a worry-free experience for the author. Thanks also to copyeditor Theresa Murray and proofreader Mya Nelson for their adept work.

Additional appreciation goes to the folks at U•X•L. Thanks to senior market analyst Meggin Condino for selecting the author and for her work early on, and to publisher Tom Romig for being so pleasant a negotiator. Finally, all praise should go to senior editor Larry Baker, who not only worked long and hard on every aspect of this book, but who actually made the author look forward to each and every contact with him, whether by phone or by email. His wit, "simpatico" for writers, high standards, and simple pride in hard work (not to mention encyclopedic baseball knowledge) made him the perfect editor for me.

Comments and suggestions

We welcome your comments on *Math and Mathematicians* as well as your suggestions for biographies and concepts to be featured in future volumes. Please write: Editors, *Math and Mathematicians*, U•X•L, 27500 Drake Rd., Farmington Hills, Michigan, 48331-3535; call toll-free: 1-800-877-4253; fax to 248-699-8097; or send e-mail via www.gale.com.

Advisory Board

Elaine Ezell
Library Media Specialist
Bowling Green Junior High School
Bowling Green, Ohio

Marie-Claire Kelin
Library Media Teacher
Lincoln Middle School
Santa Monica, California

Eric Stromberg
Mathematics Teacher
Riley Middle School
Livonia, Michigan

Words to Know

A

Abacus a manual computing device consisting of a frame holding parallel rods or wires strung with movable, bead-like counters

Abstract something thought of or stated without reference to anything specific; theoretical rather than practical

Abstraction something that is general and not particular; an idea or concept that is theoretical rather than practical

Acute triangle a triangle in which the measure of every angle is less than 90 degrees

Addend one of a set of numbers to be added; in 4 + 1 = 5, 4 and 1 are the addends

Adjoining touching or having a common point

Algorithm any systematic method of doing mathematics that involves a step-by-step procedure

Analog clock an instrument that indicates the time of day by its moving hands on a numbered dial

Analog computer an early type of computer that converts numbers or quantities into another model or form, such as the column of mercury in a thermometer

Analogy a form of reasoning that assumes if two things are alike in some ways, then they are probably alike in other ways as well

Angle what is formed inside a triangle by two sides meeting at the vertex

Arbitrary something not determined by a reason or necessity but by individual preference

Area the amount of space a flat geometrical shape occupies; the region inside a given boundary

Arithmetic operations the four fundamental actions or processes—addition, subtraction, multiplication, and division—that are performed in a specified sequence and in accordance with specific rules

Associative a property that applies to addition and multiplication (but not subtraction or division) in which addends or factors can be grouped in any order without changing the sum or product

Avoirdupois weight a system of weights and measures based on a pound containing 16 ounces

Axes the intersecting lines of a coordinate system; made up of the horizontal axis (x-axis) and the vertical axis (y-axis)

Axiom a statement that is accepted without proof; something self-evident

B

Bank note a note or piece of paper issued by a bank that represents its promise to pay a certain amount upon demand to the holder of the note; acceptable as money

Barter to trade goods or services instead of using money

Base the number being raised to a certain power or being repeatedly multiplied by itself

Binary a numeral system used by modern computers that contains only two digits, 0 and 1; any number is represented by some sequence of the two

Binary operation an operation that is performed on exactly two numbers at a time

Boundary a line that separates a figure into its interior and its exterior

C

Capacity the ability to receive, hold, or contain; a measure on content

Certified the confirmation that something is genuine; a guarantee that something is worth what it says it is

Chord a line segment that joins any two points on a circle and does not go through its center

Circadian rhythm the daily rhythm or cycle of activity that many organisms exhibit during a single 24-hour period

Circumference the distance completely around the outside of a circle; its perimeter

Clepsydra an ancient timekeeping device that marked the passage of time by the regulated flow of water through a small opening; a water clock

Commutative a property that applies to addition and multiplication (but not subtraction or division) in which the order in which the numbers are added or multiplied does not change the sum; for example, $1 \times 2 = 2 \times 1$

Component an element or part that makes up some sort of system

Composite number a whole number that is not a prime number; any number that can be obtained by multiplying two whole numbers other than itself and 1; the first ten composites are 4, 6, 8, 9, 10, 12, 14, 15, 16, 18

Computation the act or method of carrying out a mathematical process

Compute to carry out a mathematical process; to calculate

Concave polygon a polygon with at least one interior angle that measures more than 180 degrees; at least one straight line can intersect more than two sides

Convex polygon a polygon whose every interior angle measures less than 180 degrees; any straight line intersects no more than two sides

Concentric two or more circles of different size that have the same point as their center; circles that are inside one another

Conversion the exchange of one type of money for another

Cross-multiplication rule the product of the means equals the product of the extremes; for example, in the proportion 1:3 = 2:6, the means (3 and 2) can be multiplied and will equal the product of the extremes (1 and 6)

D

Decimal fraction a fractional number expressed in decimal form; one in which the denominator is some power of ten; for example, .3 is the decimal version of $\frac{3}{10}$

Decimal system a number written using the base of 10

Deductive reasoning or **deduction** a type of reasoning in which a conclusion follows necessarily from a set of axioms or givens; it proceeds logically from the general to the specific

Denomination a particular value, size, or kind of money

Denominator in a fraction, the numeral written below the bar or line; it tells how many parts the whole has

Descriptive statistics the science of collecting, organizing, and summarizing data that characterize a particular group

Diameter a line segment that joins two points on a circle and passes through its center; the longest chord possible in a circle

Difference the result of subtraction

Digital clock an instrument that indicates the time of day by giving its reading in actual digits or numbers

Digital computer a modern type of computer that processes information in the form of numbers or digits

Distributive in multiplying one number times a sum of two other numbers, the sum may be taken first and then the multiplication performed, or each of the numbers to be summed can first be multiplied by the common factor and the results added together; for example, with $3 \times (3 + 4)$, 3 and 4 are added and their sum (7) multiplied by 3 equals 21; or 3 and 4 can each be multiplied by 3 and their products (9 and 12) can then be added to get 21

Dividend the number that is to be divided by another number

Divisor the number by which the dividend is to be divided

E

Electromechanical a mechanical device or system that is controlled by electricity

Equation a mathematical sentence with an equal sign (=) between two expressions; a statement of equality; for example, $3 + x = 10$ and $a + b = b + a$ are both equations

Equator the imaginary circle drawn around the center of the Earth's surface; a line equidistant from the North and South poles

Equiangular polygon a polygon in which every interior angle measures the same number of degrees

Equilateral polygon a polygon in which every side measures the same length

Equilateral triangle a triangle in which all three sides are of equal length

Equivalent something that is essentially equal to something else

Equivalent fraction fractions that are of equal value; for example $\frac{5}{10}$ is the same as $\frac{1}{2}$

Evolution the theory that groups of organisms change with the passage of time as a result of natural selection

Exchange rate the cost of changing one country's currency into that of another; costs or rates fluctuate daily

Exponential increase and decrease when something grows or declines at a particular rate or designated power; often at a massive or dramatic rate

Extract to determine or calculate the root of a number

Extremes the first and fourth terms in a proportion; for example, in the proportion 1:3 = 2:6, 1 and 6 are the extremes

F

Factor in a given number, that which divides that number evenly; for example, the factors of the number 12 are 1, 2, 3, 4, 6, and 12

Factors the numbers multiplied to form a product; both the multiplier and the multiplicand

Force strength, energy, or power that causes motion or change

Formula a general answer, rule, or principle stated in a mathematical way (with an equal sign between two expressions)

Fractional divided into smaller parts or pieces of a whole

G

Genetics the branch of biology that deals with heredity, especially the transmission of characteristics

Gravitation the natural phenomenon of attraction between massive celestial bodies

Grid a pattern of regularly spaced horizontal and vertical lines forming squares, as on a map or chart

H

Hardware the physical equipment or machinery of a computer; its processor, monitor, and other devices

Heretical characterized by a radical departure from traditional standards

Hierarchy a series in which each element is graded or ranked

Hypotenuse the longest side in a right triangle

I

Improper fraction a fraction in which the numerator is equal to or greater than the denominator; the value of the fraction is always equal to or larger than 1; for example, ⅝ is an improper fraction

Incertitude uncertainty or doubt about something

Index the number in the upper left-hand corner of the radical sign that tells which root is to be extracted

Indigenous people who are original to a certain area or environment; native

Inductive reasoning or **induction** a type of reasoning conducted first by observing patterns of something and then by predicting answers for similar future cases; it proceeds logically from the specific to the general

Inertia the tendency of a body to resist being moved and to remain at rest

Inference the act of reasoning or making a logical conclusion based on evidence or something known to be true

Inferential statistics the science of making inferences or predictions about a group based on characteristics of a sample of that group

Infinite set a set whose elements cannot be counted because they are unlimited

Integers a set of numbers that includes the positive numbers, negative numbers, and zero

Integrated circuit a tiny piece of material on which is imprinted a complex series of electronic components and their interconnections; a computer chip

Interaction the state or process of two things acting upon each other; mutual influence

Intersect to cut across or through; to cross or overlap

Intersection two lines that have a common point and necessarily cross each other

Intuition the act or faculty of knowing or sensing something without having any rational thought or doing any reasoning

Irrational number a number that is expressed as a nonrepeating decimal fraction and which, when carried out, simply goes on forever; contrasted to a rational number, which has either a terminating decimal (it comes out even with no remainder) or a repeating decimal (as .33333333...)

Isosceles triangle a triangle with at least two sides of equal length

L

Latitude the angular distance north or south of the Earth's equator; indicated by horizontal lines on a map

Least common denominator in the case of two fractions, it is the smallest multiple common to both denominators; for example, with the fractions ⅚, ¼, and ½, the least common denominator is 12 (the lowest number into which 6, 4, and 2 can be divided)

Legs the sides of a right triangle perpendicular to each other; they have a common point of intersection and are adjacent to the right angle

Length the measure of a line segment or an object from end to end

Like fractions fractions with the same denominator; for example, 2/7 and 4/7 are like fractions

Line a set of points joined together and extending in both directions; it has no thickness and is one-dimensional

Longitude the angular distance east or west from the prime meridian at Greenwich, England; indicated by vertical lines on a map

Linear equation also called a first-degree equation since none of its terms is raised to a power of 2 or higher, it is graphed as a straight line; $y = x + 1$ is a linear equation

Logic the study of the principles of proper or correct reasoning

M

Mass the measure of the quantity of matter that a body contains

Means the second and third terms in a proportion; for example, in the proportion 1:3 = 2:6, 2 and 3 are the means

Memory the part of a computer that stores and preserves information and programs for retrieval

Mercantile of or relating to merchants or trade

Minuend in subtraction, the larger number from which a smaller number is taken away; in $10 - 5$, 10 is the minuend

Minute a measure of time equal to $\frac{1}{60}$th of an hour

Mixed number a number consisting of an integer and a proper fraction; for example, $1\frac{3}{4}$ is a mixed number

Mortality tables statistical tables based on death data compiled over a number of years

Multiplicand the number that is being multiplied by another number; for example, in $3 \times 4 = 12$, 3 is the multiplicand

Multiplier the number that does the multiplying; for example, in $3 \times 4 = 12$, 4 is the multiplier

N

Natural numbers all the cardinal numbers or counting numbers $(1, 2, 3, \ldots)$ except 0

Natural selection the process in nature by which only those organisms best suited to their environment survive and transmit their genetic characteristics to succeeding generations

Negative number a number less than 0; a minus (–) sign is always written before the numeral to indicate it is to the left of 0 on a number line

Number theory a branch of mathematics concerned generally with the properties and relationships of integers

Numeral a symbol or name that stands for a number

Numerator in a fraction, the numeral written above the bar or line; it tells how many parts are being considered

O

Obtuse triangle a triangle with one angle that measures greater than 90 degrees

P

Papyrus an early form of writing paper made by the Egyptians from the stems of the papyrus plant

Parallelogram a quadrilateral in which both pairs of opposite sides are parallel

Parchment the treated skin of a goat or sheep that in ancient times was treated so that it could be written on

Pentagon a polygon with five sides

Perimeter the distance around a polygon, obtained by adding the lengths of its sides; the perimeter or distance completely around a circle is called its circumference

Perpendicular when lines intersect and form a right angle

Perspective the technique of representing three-dimensional objects and depth relationships on a two-dimensional surface

Pi (π) a number defined as the ratio of the circumference to the diameter of a circle; it cannot be represented exactly as a decimal, but it is between 3.1415 and 3.1416

Place value (positional notation) the system in which the position or place of a symbol or digit in a numeral determines its value; for example, in the numeral 1,234, the 1 occupies the 1000 place, the 2 is in the 100 place, the 3 is in the 10 place, and the 4 is in the unit (1) place

Polygon a geometric figure composed of three or more line segments (straight sides) that never cross each other

Population all of the individuals, events, or objects that make up a group

Positive number a number greater than 0 (and to the right of 0 on a number line)

Prime factorization the process of finding all the prime factors of a given number

Prime meridian the zero meridian (0 degrees) used as a reference or baseline from which longitude east or west is measured; by international agreement, it passes through Greenwich, England

Probability likely to happen or to be true; likelihood

Probability theory the branch of mathematics that studies the likelihood of random events occurring in order to predict the behavior of defined systems

Product the result in a multiplication problem

Projection the image of a figure reproduced atop a grid of intersecting lines

Proper fraction a fraction in which the numerator is less than the denominator; for example, ⅔ is a proper fraction

Property a characteristic of something that is assumed

Proposition a statement that makes an assertion; something that is stated as either true or false

Q

Qualifier a word or phrase that limits or modifies the meaning of another word

Quotient the result when one number is divided by another; for example, 2 is the quotient when 10 is divided by 5

R

Radicand the number under a radical sign

Radioactive decay the natural disintegration or breakdown of a radioactive substance that allows it to be dated

Radius a line drawn from the center of a circle to some point on the circle's boundary or edge; it is half the length of the diameter

Words to Know

Random something done unsystematically, without purpose, pattern, or method

Ratio the relationship between two quantities, which is obtained by dividing two things; for instance, the ratio of 3 to 2 is written 3:2 or ³⁄₂

Rational consistent with or based on reason; logical; reasonable

Rectangle a parallelogram whose angles are all right angles

Regular polygon a polygon in which all sides have equal length and all interior angles have equal measure; a polygon that is both equilateral and equiangular

Remainder the number left over when division does not come out evenly; for example, 2 is the remainder when 17 is divided by 5

Renaissance the period between the fourteenth and sixteenth century in Europe characterized by the revival of classical art, architecture, and literature

Rhombus a parallelogram whose four sides are of equal length

Right angle an angle of 90 degrees

Right triangle a triangle in which one of its angles measures 90 degrees (a right angle)

Rigor strict precision or exactness

S

Sample a number of individuals, events, or objects chosen from a given population that are representative of the entire group

Scalene triangle a triangle in which each side is of a different length

Scientific notation writing a number as the product of a number between 1 and 10 and a power of 10; used to represent very large or very small numbers

Secant any straight line that intersects a circle at two points or cuts through its outer edges

Second a measure of time equal to ¹⁄₆₀th of a minute

Set a collection or group of particular things

Sexagesimal a numeration system using 60 as a base; used by the Babylonians

Side one of the line segments of a polygon; also called "legs" for a triangle

Sieve a device with holes or mesh that allows liquid or only particles of a very small size to pass through but which captures larger particles

Simulation representation or imitation of an event, process, or system

Slide rule a device operated by hand that uses sliding logarithmic scales to reduce complex computations to addition and subtraction; replaced by the hand-held calculator

Software all of the programs, routines, and instructions that control a computer's hardware and direct its operation

Spherical having the shape of a sphere; round; globular

Square a rectangle whose four sides are the same length

Square of a number a number raised to the second power or multiplied by itself

Statistics the branch of mathematics consisting of methods for collecting, organizing, and summarizing data in order to make predictions based on these data

Storage the memory system of a computer that keeps information for later retrieval

Subtrahend in subtraction, the smaller number being taken away from a larger number; in $10 - 5$, 5 is the subtrahend

Sum in addition, the result of adding two or more numbers or addends; for example, in $4 + 1 = 5$, 5 is the sum

Subset a set contained within a set

Sundial an instrument that indicates solar time by the shadow cast by its central pointer onto a numbered dial

Words to Know

Surface in terms of area, the region that is inside a given boundary

Syllogism a logical argument that involves three propositions, usually two premises and a conclusion, whose conclusion necessarily is true if the premises are true

Symbolic logic a system of mathematical logic that uses symbols instead of words to solve problems, and whose symbols can be manipulated much like an equation

Symbolic notation a mathematical shorthand in which a sign is used to represent an operation, element, quantity, or relationship

Symmetry the exact correspondence of a form or shape on opposite sides of a center dividing line

T

Tangent a straight line that intersects a circle at only one point or touches its outer edge at only one point

Terms the numerator and denominator of a fraction

Theorem a statement or generalization that can be demonstrated to be true

Transistor a small electronic device containing a semiconductor that acts as an amplifier, detector, or switch; it replaced old, glass vacuum tubes and was itself replaced by silicon chips

Trapezium a quadrilateral with no pairs of opposite sides parallel

Trapezoid a quadrilateral with only two sides parallel

Triangulation the location of an unknown point by forming a triangle whose two points are known

Troy weight a system of weight in which a pound contains 12 ounces

V

Vertex the point at which any two sides of a polygon meet or intersect; plural is "vertices"

Volume a number describing the three-dimensional amount of a space; a measure of the capacity or how much something will hold; the number of cubic units in a solid figure

W

Whole numbers the set of natural or counting numbers (1, 2, 3, . . .) plus 0

Z

Zero a real number that separates positive and negative numbers on a number line; it also functions as an empty set and as a place holder

Milestones in the History of Mathematics

50,000 B.C. Primitive humans leave behind evidence of their ability to count. Paleolithic people in central Europe make notches on animal bones to tally.

c. 15,000 B.C. Cave dwellers in the Middle East make notches on bones to keep count and possibly to track the lunar cycle.

c. 8000 B.C. Clay tokens are used in Mesopotamia to record numbers of animals. This eventually develops into the first system of numeration.

75,000 B.C.
Neanderthal man
can communicate
by speech.

38,000 B.C.
Homo sapiens
species evolves from
Neanderthal man.

12,000 B.C.
The dog is
domesticated from
the Asian wolf.

8000 B.C.
Earth's human
population soars to
5.3 million.

50,000 B.C.   40,000 B.C.   30,000 B.C.   20,000 B.C.   8000 B.C.

Milestones in the History of Mathematics

3500 B.C. The Egyptian number system reaches the point where they now can record numbers as large as necessary by introducing new symbols.

c. 2400 B.C. Mathematical tablets dated to this period are found at Ur, a city of ancient Sumer (present-day Iraq).

c. 2000 B.C. Babylonians and Egyptians use **fractions** as a way to help them tell **time** and measure angles.

c. 1800 B.C. The Babylonians know and use what is later called the **Pythagorean theorem,** but they do not yet have a proof for it.

c. 1650 B.C. The Rhind papyrus (also known as the Ahmes papyrus) is prepared by Egyptian scribe Ahmes, which contains solutions to simple equations. It becomes a primary source of knowledge about early Egyptian mathematics, describing their methods of **multiplication, division,** and **algebra.**

876 B.C. The first known reference to the usage of the symbol for zero is made in India.

c. 585 B.C. Greek geometer and philosopher **Thales of Miletus** converts Egyptian **geometry** into an abstract study. He removes mathematics from a sole consideration of practical problems and proves mathematical statements by a series of logical arguments. Doing this, Thales invents deductive mathematics.

3500 B.C.
Human civilization begins as the Sumerian society emerges.

3000 B.C.
The Sahara Desert has its beginnings in North Africa.

2485 B.C.
The Great Sphinx carved from rock at Giza.

776 B.C.
First recorded Olympic games in Greece are held.

625 B.C.
Metal coins are introduced in Greece.

| 3500 B.C. | 2750 B.C. | 2000 B.C. | 1250 B.C. | 500 B.C. |

c. 500 B.C.	Greek geometer and philosopher **Pythagoras of Samos** formulates the idea that the entire universe rests on numbers and their relationships. He deduces that the square of the length of the hypotenuse of a right **triangle** is equal to the sum of the squares of the lengths of its sides. It becomes known as the **Pythagorean theorem**.
c. 300 B.C.	Greek geometer **Euclid of Alexandria** writes a textbook on **geometry** called the *Elements*. It becomes the standard work on its subject for over 2,000 years.
c. 240 B.C.	Greek geometer **Archimedes of Syracuse** calculates the most accurate arithmetical value for **pi (π)** to date. He also uses a system for expressing large numbers that uses an exponential-like method. Archimedes also finds **areas** and **volumes** of special curved surfaces and solids.
c. 230 B.C.	Greek astronomer Eratosthenes develops a system for determining **prime numbers** that becomes known as the "sieve of Eratosthenes."
c. 100 B.C.	Negative numbers are used in China.
A.D. c. 250	Greek algebraist Diophantus of Alexandria is the first Greek to write a significant work on **algebra**.
c. 320	Greek geometer Pappus of Alexandria summarizes in a book all acquired knowledge of

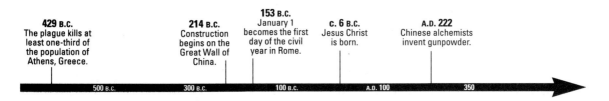

429 B.C.
The plague kills at least one-third of the population of Athens, Greece.

214 B.C.
Construction begins on the Great Wall of China.

153 B.C.
January 1 becomes the first day of the civil year in Rome.

c. 6 B.C.
Jesus Christ is born.

A.D. 222
Chinese alchemists invent gunpowder.

500 B.C. 300 B.C. 100 B.C. A.D. 100 350

Greek mathematics, making it the best source for Greek mathematics. French number theorist **Pierre de Fermat** later restores and studies Pappus's work.

c. 400   Greek geometer, astronomer, and philosopher **Hypatia of Alexandria** writes commentaries on Greek mathematicians Apollonius of Perga and Diophantus of Alexandria. She is the only woman scholar of ancient times and the first woman mentioned in the history of mathematics.

499   Hindu mathematician and astronomer Aryabhata the Elder describes the Indian numerical system. He also uses **division** to popularize a method for finding the greatest common divisor of two numbers.

700   Negative numbers are introduced by the Hindus to represent a negative balance.

820   Arab algebraist and astronomer **al-Khwārizmī** writes a mathematics book that introduces the Arabic word *al-jabr,* which becomes transliterated as **algebra.** His own name is distorted by translation into "algorism," which comes to mean the art of calculating or arithmetic. Al-Khwārizmī also uses Hindu numerals, including zero, and when his work is translated into Latin and published in the West, those numerals are called "Arabic numerals."

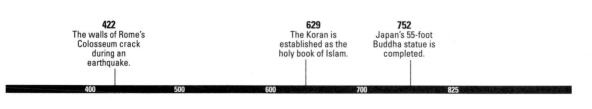

422
The walls of Rome's Colosseum crack during an earthquake.

629
The Koran is established as the holy book of Islam.

752
Japan's 55-foot Buddha statue is completed.

400   500   600   700   825

c. 825	Arab algebraist and astronomer **al-Khwārizmī** recommends the use of a **decimal** system.
1202	Italian number theorist **Leonardo Pisano Fibonacci** writes about the abacus, the use of zero and Arabic (Hindu) numerals, the importance of positional notations, and the merits of the **decimal** system.
1225	Italian number theorist **Leonardo Pisano Fibonacci** writes *Liber Quadratorum* in which he uses **algebra** based on the Arabic system.
1299	A law is passed in Florence, Italy, forbidding the use of Hindu-Arabic numbers by bankers. Authorities believe such numbers are more easily forged than Roman numerals.
1482	The first printed edition of Greek geometer **Euclid of Alexandria**'s **geometry** book, *Elements,* is published in Venice, Italy.
1489	The plus (+) and minus (−) symbols are first used in a book by German mathematician Johannes Widmann. They are not used as symbols of operation but merely to indicate excess and deficiency.
1535	Italian mathematician Niccolò Tartaglia demonstrates in a public forum his correct solution to the cubic equation. He later discloses in confidence his secret methods to another Italian mathematician, **Girolamo Car-**

Milestones in the History of Mathematics

850
Coffee is discovered in East Africa.

1139
Civil war breaks out in England.

1254
Explorer Marco Polo is born.

1492
Christopher Columbus discovers America.

825   1000   1200   1400   1550

dano, who later publishes the solution after learning that another Italian mathematician, Scipione dal Ferro, had discovered the solution as early as 1515. Cardano's paper correctly gives credit to both Tartaglia and dal Ferro.

1557   English mathematician Robert Recorde is the first to use the modern symbol for equality (=) in a book.

1570   The first complete English translation of *Elements,* by Greek geometer **Euclid of Alexandria,** appears.

1581   Italian mathematician **Galileo** discovers that the amount of **time** for a pendulum to swing back and forth is the same, regardless of the size of the arc. Dutch astronomer and mathematical physicist **Christiaan Huygens** would later use this principle to build the first pendulum clock.

1585   Dutch mathematician **Simon Stevin** writes about the first comprehensive system of **decimal fractions** and their practical applications.

1594   Scottish mathematician **John Napier** first conceives of the notion of obtaining exponential expressions for various numbers, and begins work on the complicated formulas for what he eventually calls **logarithms.**

1559
Mary, Queen of
Scots, becomes
queen of England.

1585
Walter Raleigh
founds first colony
in Virginia.

1590
William
Shakespeare
begins writing
plays.

1550   1565   1580   1590   1600

| 1609 | German astronomer and mathematician **Johannes Kepler** advances the development of the **geometry** of the ellipse as he attempts to prove that planets move in elliptical orbits. |

| 1609 | Italian mathematician **Galileo** improves upon the invention of the telescope by building a version with a magnification of about thirty times. |

| 1614 | Scottish mathematician **John Napier** invents "Napier's bones." This calculating machine consists of sticks with a **multiplication** table on the face of each stick. Calculations can be done by turning the rods by hand. He also publishes a book on **logarithms**. |

| 1619 | German astronomer and mathematician **Johannes Kepler** shows that a planet's revolution is proportional to the cube of its average distance from the Sun. |

| 1622 | English mathemetician William Oughtred invents the straight logarithmic slide rule. |

| 1629 | French number theorist **Pierre de Fermat** pioneers the application of **algebra** to **geometry**. Although French algebraist and philosopher **René Descartes** is credited with the invention and full development of analytic geometry, Fermat develops it earlier but does not publish his findings. |

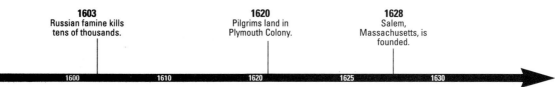

1603
Russian famine kills tens of thousands.

1620
Pilgrims land in Plymouth Colony.

1628
Salem, Massachusetts, is founded.

1600   1610   1620   1625   1630

Milestones in the History of Mathematics

1631 English mathematician William Oughtred includes a large amount of mathematical symbolism in a book he publishes, including the notation "×" for multiplication and "::" for proportion.

1632 Italian mathematician **Galileo** discounts the theory of an Earth-centered universe. As a result, the Roman Inquisition sentences him to life imprisonment.

1636 French number theorist **Pierre de Fermat** introduces the modern theory of numbers. His work includes theories on **prime numbers.**

1637 French algebraist and philosopher **René Descartes** introduces analytic **geometry** by demonstrating how geometric forms may be systematically studied by analytic or algebraical means. He is the first person to use the letters near the beginning of the alphabet for constants and those near the end for variables. He also includes a notation system for expressing **exponents.**

c. 1637 French number theorist **Pierre de Fermat** writes in the margin of a book a reference to what comes to be known as "Fermat's last theorem." This theorem remains the most famous unsolved problem in mathematics until it is solved in 1993 by **Andrew J. Wiles.** Fermat says he has a proof for the particular problem

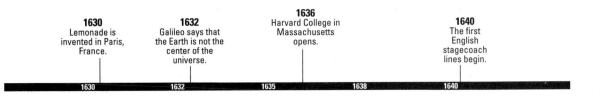

1630
Lemonade is invented in Paris, France.

1632
Galileo says that the Earth is not the center of the universe.

1636
Harvard College in Massachusetts opens.

1640
The first English stagecoach lines begin.

1630   1632   1635   1638   1640

posed, but that the margin is too small to include it there.

1642   French mathematician Blaise Pascal invents the first automatic calculator. It performs **addition** and **subtraction** by means of a set of wheels linked together by gears.

1644   French number theorist Marin Mersenne suggests a formula that will yield **prime numbers.** These "Mersenne numbers" are not always correct, but they stimulate research into the theory of numbers.

1654   French number theorist **Pierre de Fermat** exchanges letters with French mathematician Blaise Pascal in which they discuss the basic laws of **probability** and essentially found the theory of probability.

1657   Dutch astronomer and mathematical physicist **Christiaan Huygens** writes about **probability.**

1659   Swiss mathematician Johann Heinrich Rahn is the first to use today's division sign ($\div$) in a book. Later, English mathematician John Wallis adopts it and popularizes it through his works.

1662   English statistician John Graunt is the first to apply mathematics to the integration of vital **statistics.** As the first to establish life expectancy and to publish a table of demographic data,

Milestones in the History of Mathematics

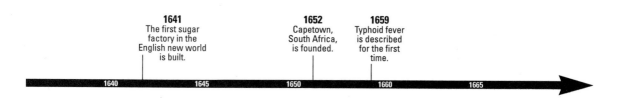

1641
The first sugar factory in the English new world is built.

1652
Capetown, South Africa, is founded.

1659
Typhoid fever is described for the first time.

1640   1645   1650   1660   1665

Graunt is considered the founder of vital statistics.

Milestones in the History of Mathematics

1666   German logician **Gottfried Leibniz** begins the study of symbolic **logic** by calling for a "calculus of reasoning" in mathematics.

1668   German mathematician and astronomer Nicolaus Mercator is the first to calculate the **area** under a curve using the newly developed analytical **geometry.**

1673   German logician **Gottfried Leibniz** begins his development of differential and integral calculus independently of English physicist **Isaac Newton.**

1674   Japanese mathematician **Seki Kōwa** publishes his only book, in which he solves 15 supposedly "unsolvable" problems.

1684   German logician **Gottfried Leibniz** publishes an account of his discovery of calculus. He discovers it independently of English physicist **Isaac Newton,** although later than him. Newton, however, publishes his discovery after Leibniz in 1687. The timing of the discovery produces a feud between the two men.

1687   English physicist **Isaac Newton** introduces the laws of motion and universal gravitation and his invention of calculus.

1667
The first recorded blood transfusion is performed.

1670
Minute hands appear on watches for the first time.

1682
Philadelphia, Pennsylvania, is founded.

1665   1670   1675   1680   1690

1690	Massachusetts is the first colony to produce paper **currency.**

1693	English astronomer Edmund Halley compiles the first set of detailed mortality tables, making use of **statistics** in the study of life and death.
1706	English geometer William Jones is the first to use the sixteenth letter of the Greek alphabet, **pi** (π), as the symbol for the **ratio** of the circumference to the diameter of a **circle.**
1713	The first full-length treatment of the theory of **probability** appears in a work by Swiss mathematician Jakob Bernoulli.
1737	Swiss geometer and number theorist **Leonhard Euler** formally adopts the sixteenth letter of the Greek alphabet (π) as the symbol for the **ratio** of the circumference to the diameter of a **circle.** The ratio itself becomes known as **pi.** Following his adoption and use, it is generally accepted.
1748	Italian mathematician **Maria Agnesi** publishes *Analytical Institutions,* a large, two-volume work that surveys elementary and advanced mathematics. Agnesi is best known for her consideration of the cubic curve or what comes to be translated as the "witch of Agnesi."

1704
America's first regular newspaper begins publication.

1705
Thomas Newcomen invents the steam engine.

1714
Daniel Fahrenheit builds a mercury thermometer.

1725
Antonio Vivaldi composes *The Four Seasons.*

1732
Benjamin Franklin revolutionizes the colonial postal service.

| 1690 | 1705 | 1720 | 1735 | 1750 |

| 1755 | Nineteen-year-old French algebraist **Joseph-Louis Lagrange** sends a paper to Swiss geometer and number theorist **Leonhard Euler** concerning Lagrange's "calculus of variations." Euler is so impressed with the young man's work that he holds back his own writings on the subject, thus allowing Lagrange priority of publication. |

1767   German geometer Johann Heinrich Lambert proves that the number for **pi (π)** is irrational.

1791   African American mathematician **Benjamin Banneker** assists in the surveying process of the new city of Washington, D.C.

1792   African American mathematician **Benjamin Banneker** publishes his first *Almanac*.

1792   The United States establishes its first monetary system, making the dollar its basic unit of **currency.**

1795   France adopts the metric system.

1797   German mathematician **Carl Friedrich Gauss** gives the first wholly satisfactory proof of the fundamental theorem of **algebra.**

1813   English mathematician **Charles Babbage** cofounds The Analytical Society, whose general purpose is to revive mathematical analysis in England.

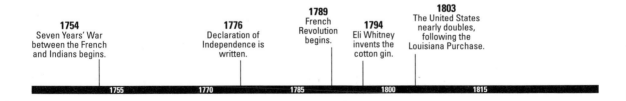

1754
Seven Years' War between the French and Indians begins.

1776
Declaration of Independence is written.

1789
French Revolution begins.

1794
Eli Whitney invents the cotton gin.

1803
The United States nearly doubles, following the Louisiana Purchase.

1755   1770   1785   1800   1815

1816   French mathematician **Sophie Germain** receives an award for her paper on the mathematical theory of elasticity.

1820   English mathematician **Charles Babbage** conceives of the idea of calculation "by machinery." Over the next fifty years, he works on developing the "difference engine," but never succeeds. The technical requirements for such a machine turn out to be beyond the engineering ability of his time.

1821   French mathematician **Augustin-Louis Cauchy** publishes the first of three books on calculus.

1825   Norwegian mathematician **Niels Abel** first proves the impossibility of solving the general quintic equation by means of radicals. This problem had puzzled mathematicians for two and a half centuries.

1829   Russian geometer **Nicolay Lobachevsky** describes his discovery of non-Euclidean **geometry.** This system includes the concept that an indefinite number of lines can be drawn in a plane parallel to a given line through a given point.

1830   French algebraist and group theorist **Évariste Galois** is the first to use the word "group" in the technical sense and to apply groups of sub-

1818
Russian socialist leader Karl Marx is born.

1827
Contact lenses are invented.

1829
George Stephenson develops the railroad.

1815   1818   1821   1825   1830

stitutions to the question of reducibility of algebraic equations.

1832 Hungarian geometer János Bolyai announces his discovery of non-Euclidean **geometry**, which he makes at about the same time as Russian geometer **Nikolay Lobachevsky**. His discovery is totally independent of Lobachevsky's, and when Bolyai finally sees Lobachevsky's work, he thinks it has been plagarized from his own.

1833 Irish algebraist **William Rowan Hamilton** makes one of the first attempts at analyzing the basis of irrational numbers. His theory views both **rational and irrational numbers** as based on algebraic number couples.

1847 English logician **George Boole** maintains that the essential character of mathematics lies in its form rather than in its content. His work focuses on mathematics as symbolic rather than only "the science of measurement and number."

1854 English logician **George Boole** establishes both formal **logic** and Boolean **algebra**.

1854 German geometer **Bernhard Riemann** offers a global view of **geometry**. He develops further the ideas of Russian geometer **Nikolay Lobachevsky** and Hungarian geometer János Bolyai and introduces a new, non-Euclidean system of geometry.

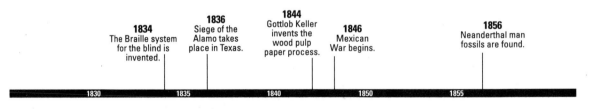

1834
The Braille system for the blind is invented.

1836
Siege of the Alamo takes place in Texas.

1844
Gottlob Keller invents the wood pulp paper process.

1846
Mexican War begins.

1856
Neanderthal man fossils are found.

1830   1835   1840   1850   1855

1860	German geometer **Bernhard Riemann** uses the complex number theory to form the basis for most of the research in **prime numbers** for the next century.
1874	German mathematician **Georg Cantor** begins his revolutionary work on set theory and the theory of the infinite and creates a whole new field of mathematical research.
1874	Russian mathematician **Sofya Kovalevskaya** writes two papers on differential equations.
1884	Greenwich, England, is chosen as the site where the world's 24 **time** zones begin.
1888	Russian mathematician **Sofya Kovalevskaya** receives an award for her paper on the problem of how Saturn's rings rotate the planet.
1905	German American physicist and mathematician **Albert Einstein** writes five landmark papers that cover Brownian motion, the photoelectric effect, and his theory of relativity. It was with relativity that he devised his famous formula, $E = mc^2$.
1913	Indian number theorist **Srinivasa A. Ramanujan** begins a five-year collaboration with English mathematician Godfrey Harold Hardy during which Ramanujan works on and solves many mathematical problems.

Milestones in the History of Mathematics

1859 Charles Darwin publishes his theory of evolution.

1865 U.S. president Abraham Lincoln is assassinated.

1876 Alexander Graham Bell invents the telephone.

1903 Wright Brothers take first airplane flight.

1908 Henry Ford introduces the Model T.

1860   1875   1890   1905   1920

Milestones in the History of Mathematics

1921   German algebraist **Emmy Noether** publishes her studies on abstract rings and ideal theory which become important in the development of modern **algebra.**

1931   Austrian American mathematician **Kurt Gödel** publishes a paper whose incompleteness theorem startles the mathematical community. It states that within any rigidly logical mathematical system there are propositions that cannot be proved or disproved on the basis of the axioms within that system.

1933   Hungarian number theorist **Paul Erdös** discovers a proof for Chebyshev's theorem, which says that for each **integer** greater than one, there is always at least one **prime number** between it and its double.

1936   Chinese American geometrist **Shiing-Shen Chern** begins working with French number theorist Elie-Joseph Cartan on differential **geometry.**

1937   American mathematician **Claude E. Shannon** arrives at a connection between a **computer**'s relay circuit and Boolean **algebra.**

1937   English algebraist and logician **Alan Turing** envisions an imaginary machine that would solve all computable problems and help prove the existence of undecidable mathematical statements.

1914 World War I begins.

1917 V. I. Lenin leads communist takeover of Russia.

1923 Edwin Hubble identifies galaxies beyond the Milky Way.

1928 Alexander Fleming discovers penicillin.

1933 Nazis take control of Germany.

1939 The Baseball Hall of Fame is established.

1920   1925   1930   1935   1940

1943	American computer scientist **Grace Hopper** joins the U.S. Navy, with whom she serves for 43 years.

1943	English algebraist and logician **Alan Turing** helps the World War II allies crack German codes.

1944	Harvard scientists, including American computer scientist **Grace Hopper,** build the Mark I, the world's first digital **computer.**

1944	Hungarian American number theorist **John von Neumann** and Austrian American economist Oskar Morgenstren develop a mathematical theory of games that comes to be known as game theory.

1945	Hungarian American number theorist **John von Neumann** presents the first description of the concept of a stored **computer** program.

1947	African American statistician **David Blackwell** describes "sufficiency," the process of simplifying a statistical problem by summarizing data.

1946	The Electronic Numerical Integrator and Computer (ENIAC), the first fully electronic **computer,** is invented.

1948	American logician **Norbert Wiener** produces a landmark paper that marks the beginning of cybernetics.

1939
World War II
begins.

1941
Japanese attack
U.S. naval base
Pearl Harbor in
Hawaii.

1945
U.S. president
Franklin Roosevelt
dies during his
fourth term.

1948
Jews in
Palestine
form the State
of Israel.

1949
Mao Zedong
becomes first
leader of People's
Republic of China.

1940   1942   1944   1946   1948

1949   University of Michigan students **Evelyn Boyd Granville** and Marjorie Lee Browne become the first African American women to receive Ph.D.'s in mathematics.

1949   American mathematician **Claude E. Shannon** formulates basic information theory, upon which much of today's **computer** and communications technology is based.

1951   Fifteen nations found the International Mathematical Union to promote cooperation among the world's mathematicians and to more widely disseminate the results of mathematical research.

1953   American mathematician **Claude E. Shannon** publishes his pioneering work on artificial intelligence.

1956   African American mathematician **Evelyn Boyd Granville** begins working at IBM as a **computer** programmer.

1960   The metric system is adopted by nearly every country in the world.

1982   Polish-born Lithuanian mathematician **Benoit B. Mandelbrot** founds fractal **geometry,** a new branch of mathematics based on the study of the irregularities in nature.

1993   English-born mathematician **Andrew J. Wiles** announces his proof of "Fermat's last theo-

1954
Elvis Presley makes
his first commercial
recording.

1963
U.S. president John
F. Kennedy is
assassinated.

1978
John Paul II
becomes pope.

1985
Microsoft releases
Windows.

1989
Berlin Wall is
torn down.

| 1948 | 1958 | 1970 | 1980 | 1993 |

rem." His 200-page paper is the result of a seven-year study on a problem left unsolved by French number theorist **Pierre de Fermat** 325 years earlier. Over the years, many mathematicians had declared it unsolvable.

1994   English-born mathematician **Andrew J. Wiles** publishes a corrected, improved version of his proof of "Fermat's last theorem."

1999   The euro becomes legal tender throughout Europe, beginning a three-year transition to January 1, 2002, when the euro becomes common **currency** throughout most of Europe.

Milestones in the History of Mathematics

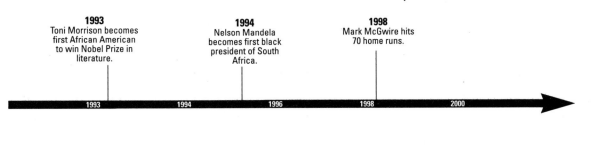

1993
Toni Morrison becomes first African American to win Nobel Prize in literature.

1994
Nelson Mandela becomes first black president of South Africa.

1998
Mark McGwire hits 70 home runs.

1993   1994   1996   1998   2000

Born August 5, 1802
Finnöy, Norway

Died April 6, 1829
Froland, Norway

Norwegian algebraist

Niels Abel

A s Norway's greatest mathematician, Niels Abel might have been one of the best mathematicians of the entire nineteenth century had he not died of tuberculosis at the age of 26. During his short life, however, he solved a problem—called the "quintic equation"—that had baffled mathematicians for three centuries.

Early life and education

Niels Henrik Abel (pronounced NEELS AH-bell) was born in Finnöy, a tiny island on the southwestern coast of Norway. He was the second of seven children born to Sören Georg Abel, a Lutheran pastor, and Anne Marie Simonson, the daughter of a wealthy merchant. Finnöy was the first parish for Abel's father, an ambitious minister who was educated at the University of Copenhagen, in Denmark. In 1804, he received a new parish and moved his family to Gjerstad, near Risor in southern Norway.

All the Abel children received their early education from their father, who was also very active in the political movement for an independent Norway (one that was free of Sweden). Once a union with Sweden was accepted, however, Abel's father had a role in

> *"[Niels Abel was one of] the foremost analysts of our times."*
>
> *—French mathematician Adrien-Marie Legendre*

Niels Abel

revising the new constitution (a country's set of laws). As was common, Niels Abel and his older brother were sent to the Cathedral School in Oslo in 1815. Although this school had formerly been an excellent institution, it lost many of its best teachers when a new university opened the same year that Abel entered. Consequently, many of the people the school hired were better at maintaining discipline than they were at teaching. Abel's grades were at first satisfactory, but they soon began to decline. His brother fared even worse and had to return home when he showed signs of a mental illness. Things at school got very bad when a particularly harsh mathematics instructor named Bader was hired. Not only did he hit the boys with a stick if they had trouble understanding but in 1817 he was so brutal with one boy that the child died eight days later. When Bader was dismissed, the school hired a young man, Bernt Michael Holmboe (1795–1850), who would change Abel's life.

Love of mathematics

Holmboe was as different from the horrible Bader as a person could be, and since he was only seven years older than Abel, he was perhaps more sensitive to the young man than most. It was not long before Holmboe discovered in Abel what he realized was an extraordinary mathematical ability. At first Holmboe gave Abel special problems to do. Then he recommended books that were outside the school's curriculum. Abel made such rapid progress that soon Holmboe suggested that together they study the works of mathematicians **Leonhard Euler** (1707–83), **Joseph-Louis Lagrange** (1736–1813), and Pierre Simon Laplace (1749–1827). Before long, Holmboe realized that their roles had reversed, and Abel was leading him along. More reading and study served only as further fuel to Abel's fiery passion for mathematics. By the time he had finished school in 1821, Abel had read and become familiar with nearly the entire available body of mathematical literature and had begun his own original research.

Hardships of a university education

Growing up at home must have been painful at times for Abel and his siblings, since both his parents were alcoholics. In 1818 his father was elected as a representative, but his political career ended suddenly when he behaved in a violent and bizarre way toward other representatives. His unproven charges against them and his drunkenness made him the butt of jokes. He left office in disgrace and died in 1820. It was now up to the 18-year-old Niels Abel to help his mother take care of his family.

Abel had planned to get a university education, and felt that he could provide for his family better if he had a degree. He thus began studying for the entrance exam at the same time he earned money by tutoring. His good friend Holmboe had informed the university about Abel's exceptional mathematical gifts. When Abel arrived at the University of Oslo penniless, not only was he given a free room to stay in but some of the professors actually contributed their own money to support him. Once Abel had completed the requirements for his philosophy degree, he was free to study what he wished. That the school had no advanced courses in mathematics did not seem to matter, since it is said that Abel read practically everything written in mathematics—good and mediocre, important and unimportant.

Solves quintic problem

In his final year at the Cathedral School, Abel felt bold enough to take on a challenge that had beaten some of the best mathematical minds since the sixteenth century. Called the "quintic equation," or the general equation of the fifth degree, this algebra problem was difficult and complex, yet tantalizing. When Abel believed he had arrived at a solution, he gave his paper to Holmboe, who forwarded it to Danish mathematician Ferdinand Degen. When Degen had trouble figuring out all of Abel's logic, he asked the young man to give him actual examples of his general solution. This, in turn, led Abel to even more hard work and, eventually, to his major discovery in 1823 that a solution to fifth or higher-degree equations was impossible. Although he managed to publish this discovery himself, he had to make his paper very brief in order to cut costs. Sadly, few could understand it and no one took notice.

Crelle's Journal

By 1825, Abel had finished school and become engaged to a Danish governess named Christine Kemp. With few prospects in Norway, he applied for and received a government grant that allowed scholars to travel and to study foreign languages. Abel went first to

Berlin, Germany, where he had the good luck to meet an influential engineer named August Leopold Crelle (1780–1855). Crelle had a strong interest in mathematics. Impressed with Abel's obvious talent, Crelle got to know him and his work, and they became lifelong friends and colleagues. Crelle had plans to start a regular mathematical journal, and he asked Abel for help in getting it going. Abel agreed and contributed his own paper on the quintic equation. This was published in 1825 in the first edition of the *Journal for Pure and Applied Mathematics.* Commonly known as *Crelle's Journal,* it would become the leading German mathematical periodical during the nineteenth century.

In early 1826, Abel continued on to Paris, France, as part of his travel grant. After preparing another paper (which would eventually result in what is called "Abel's theorem") and submitting it to the French Academy, he was informed that it had been rejected for publication because it was "illegible" (hard to read). Deeply disappointed, he returned to Oslo during May 1827 with no job but many debts. He soon took up tutoring and substituting.

Tragic end

As winter fell on Oslo, Abel was literally shut off from the rest of the world. With no mail coming in during the winter months, he was totally unaware that his article in *Crelle's Journal* had slowly begun to get noticed in Europe. By 1828, Abel had already caught tuberculosis—a then-incurable disease of the lungs that would eventually take all his strength and kill him. During that year, Crelle was hard at work in Berlin, trying to find a position for his good friend, but things moved too slowly for the worsening Abel. After traveling for several days in intense cold to be with his fiancée at Christmas, Abel suffered a major attack in January 1829 and died in April of that year. He was buried during a blizzard.

Recognition and a job offer came too late for Abel. In fact, Crelle wrote to him, joyously informing him that he had secured a position for Abel at the University of Berlin—unaware that Abel had died two days earlier. The following year, the French Academy awarded him its Grand Prix (grand prize). Today, a number of useful concepts are named after him. Crelle may have remembered him best, however, when he wrote in 1829 that his great friend was distinguished "by the purity and nobility of his character and by a rare modesty which made his person cherished to the same unusual degree as was his genius."

For More Information

Biographical Dictionary of Mathematicians. New York: Charles Scribner's Sons, 1991.

MacTutor History of Mathematics Archive. "Neils Hendrik Abel" http://www-groups.dcs.st-and.ac.uk/~history/Mathematics/abel.html (accessed on March 2, 1999).

Reimer, Luetta, and Wilbert Reimer. *Mathematicians Are People, Too: Stories from the Lives of Great Mathematicians.* Palo Alto, CA: Dale Seymour Publications, 1995.

Simmons, George F. *Calculus Gems: Brief Lives and Memorable Mathematics.* New York: McGraw-Hill, 1992.

Stillwell, John. *Mathematics and Its History.* New York: Springer-Verlag, 1989.

Young, Robyn V., ed. *Notable Mathematicians: From Ancient Times to the Present.* Detroit: Gale Research, 1998.

Niels Abel

Addition

Addition can be described as a method of combining two or more things to find out how many there are all together. One of the four basic arithmetic operations (addition, **subtraction**, **multiplication**, and **division**) and therefore fairly simple, addition nonetheless has its share of properties and rules.

Description and use

Addition, or finding the sum of two or more objects, probably has its origins with primitive man realizing that there was some sort of connection between counting things one at a time and the fact that he had ten fingers to use. It is easy to imagine a very early human being picking four apples from a tree and, knowing that he already had "five fingers" worth of apples stored at home, holding up five fingers on one hand and four on the other and obtaining some sort of idea of a sum or a total number of apples. He might then raise one finger for each person in his group and compare to see if he has enough apples for everyone.

Probably a great deal of time passed in mankind's history between this breakthrough and the realization that certain numbers or

Addition

quantities could be given names ("one" and "two") and that the *idea* of a certain quantity could be added to the idea of another without having to have the actual things present or even represented by fingers or pebbles. This latter type of addition is the most primitive and is called addition by counting. It got its name because the total of two groups (like 5 and 4) is reached by starting to count from the beginning of the first group (1 through 5) and continuing to count to the end of the second group (6, 7, 8, 9) or by starting with the total of the first group (5) and picking up from there and counting to the end of the second (6, 7, 8, 9). This would be how very young children begin to add today.

But simple counting is not really addition. The faster and best way to add two sets of like things or to find their sum is by computing (sometimes also called addition by thinking). This is a process humans do automatically, but by breaking it down to its essentials, it is possible to examine some of the properties of addition. The number obtained by joining two groups or sets of things is their sum or total. Thus, addition shows the joining of two sets to find an answer, which is called a sum. The parts or numbers that are added are called addends. Thus, in 5 + 4 = 9, the 5 and the 4 are both addends.

One interesting property of addends (and therefore addition) is that they are commutative. This simply means that it does not matter in what order one finds the addends (thus 4 + 5 gives the same sum as 5 + 4). Another property of addition is that it is associative. This means that when three or more numbers are to be added, the way in which the addends are grouped does not affect the sum. Thus, to find the sum of 4 + 4 + 5, one can add the 4's (equaling 8) and then add the 8 to 5 or do the reverse and arrive at the same sum (13). To add larger numbers, the addition algorithm is used in which the idea of place value becomes important. A large number (like 423) can be added to another large one by using column addition and knowing that a number's place determines its value. Thus starting from the right for 423, the 3 equals 3 single units, the 2 equals 2 tens units, and the 4 equals 4 hundreds units. So 3 + 20 + 400 = 423.

Addition symbol

With the invention of mechanical printing around 1450, the symbols used in early printed works on arithmetic and **algebra** were usually only abbreviations or sometimes just the first letter of a key word (such as a "P," taken from the Italian word *piu* for "plus"). This simply continued the system that copyists had long used when each book was a hand-written manuscript. (Long before photocopy machines were in existence, copyists reproduced works by copying by hand—word for word—the original documents.) Eventually, other more simple symbols were suggested, as mathematics started to move from the old, ancient ways to more modern means of expression. The plus (+) symbol is of German origin and first appeared in print in a 1489 book written by German mathematician Johannes Widmann (c. 1462–c. 1498). He used "+" to indicate a surplus (more) and "−" to indicate a deficit (less). The plus sign is believed to come from a shorthand form of the Latin word *et,* meaning "and." It is thought that the shorthand version of *et* was simply a "t" and therefore led to the "+" sign. (See sidebar on mathematical symbols in the **multiplication** entry.)

For More Information

Groza, Vivian Shaw. *A Survey of Mathematics: Elementary Concepts and Their Historical Development.* New York: Holt, Rinehart and Winston, 1968.

Heddens, James W., and William R. Speer. *Today's Mathematics: Concepts and Classroom Methods.* Upper Saddle River, NJ: Merrill, 1997.

Julius, Edward H. *Arithmetricks: 50 Easy Ways to Add, Subtract, Multiply, and Divide Without a Calculator.* New York: John Wiley and Sons, 1995.

Math in Action: Addition. Belmont, CA: Fearon/Janus/Quercus, 1991.

Rogers, James T. *The Pantheon Story of Mathematics for Young People.* New York: Pantheon Books, 1966.

West, Beverly Henderson, et al. *The Prentice-Hall Encyclopedia of Mathematics.* Englewood Cliffs, NJ: Prentice-Hall, 1982.

Addition

WORDS TO KNOW

Property a characteristic of something that is assumed

Set a collection or group of particular things

Sum in addition, the result of adding two or more numbers or addends; for example, in $4 + 1 = 5$, 5 is the sum

Born May 16, 1718
Milan, Habsburg Empire (present-day Italy)

Died January 9, 1799
Milan, Habsburg Empire (present-day Italy)

Italian algebraist, geometer, and logician

Maria Agnesi

Maria Agnesi has been called not only one of the great figures of Italian mathematics but also one of the most extraordinary woman scholars of all time. Considered the first major female mathematician of modern times, she also produced what is the first surviving mathematical work by a woman. She also has the distinction of being the first woman to become a professor of mathematics on a university faculty.

Women in eighteenth-century European society

Born into a family of privilege and intelligence, Maria Gaëtana Agnesi (pronounced on-YAY-zee) benefited from her father's wealth, position, and broad-mindedness. Her father, Pietro, came from a family of wealthy merchants in Milan, Italy. He was both a cultured nobleman and a mathematics professor at the University of Bologna. Maria was his first child, and once he recognized the amazing natural talents she possessed, he arranged for her early education.

At the beginning of the eighteenth century, when she was born, most of Europe thought little of educating women. Often,

> *"It is marvelous to see a person of [Agnesi's] age so conversant with such abstract subjects."*
>
> *—Author C. De Brosses*

Maria Agnesi

wealthy families sent their young daughters to convents, not necessarily to be taught to read, but to acquire religion, social graces, and maybe a skill like dressmaking in preparation for an arranged marriage. Women were supposed to be attractive and natural, and it was commonly thought that an education would make them much less natural. Some parts of upper-class Italian society, however, were unusual for this time: They allowed and even encouraged bright young women to obtain a higher education and sometimes even to lecture at a university.

Early life and achievements

When Pietro Agnesi recognized that his daughter was not only a very bright child with an excellent memory but actually a child prodigy (an extremely smart individual), he took steps to cultivate her talents. As a gifted youngster, she quickly mastered languages other than her native Italian. By the age of 13, she could speak Greek, Hebrew, French, Spanish, and Latin (which was then the common language of scholars). Her tutors also emphasized philosophy and science as well as languages and mathematics.

Soon, Agnesi's father was showing how accomplished his young daughter was by having her speak to gatherings of intellectuals at his home. Agnesi and her younger sister, Teresa (who would become a gifted composer and famous musician), would perform for these groups. When she was as young as nine years old, Agnesi would recite speeches she had written for those assemblies, and by 13 she was debating her father's foreign guests in their own native languages as well as in perfect Latin. Although Agnesi was a dutiful daughter, she always felt uncomfortable at these events, since she was basically a shy, private person. It took her until she was 20 years old to eventually persuade her father to let her stop performing for his friends. Agnesi's teen years were spent in private study, acting as "hostess" for her father's groups, and tutoring her younger brothers. After her mother died, her father married two more times, and she eventually found herself as the oldest of 21 children.

Mathematical work

The great mathematical publication for which she would become internationally famous began when she was about 20 years old. When her mother died, Agnesi's father naturally looked to her as the oldest daughter to oversee the raising of his huge family, and Agnesi took this job very seriously. She was especially concerned with the education of her brothers, and in 1738 she began to prepare a textbook that would help them to understand the mathematics of their time. This work eventually would require ten years of hard work to complete. It would not be her first publication, however, for in 1738 she put together 190 of the essays she had prepared for her father's gatherings and published them with the Latin title *Propositiones philosophicae (Philosophical Propositions).* These far-ranging essays showed how broad her knowledge was. She discussed at a mature level important topics like gravitation, elasticity, and celestial mechanics and touched upon such fields as **logic,** mechanics, chemistry, botany, zoology, and mineralogy.

Great work of mathematical synthesis

Despite her ability to handle many subjects, Agnesi's greatest talent was in mathematics. Once she had begun what eventually would become a major, two-volume work titled in Italian *Instituzioni Analitiche (Analytical Institutions),* she devoted her complete intellectual attentions to her subject. A story is often told that after exhausting herself by concentrating long and hard on a problem she was unable to solve, she would sometimes arise from her bed in a sleep-walking state, sit down at her desk, work it out correctly, and return to bed. In the morning she would awake and discover her work all done perfectly.

After ten years of work, her book was published in 1748. Although it took up two volumes and totaled 1,070 pages, she had remained true to her original plan and wrote a text that would instruct young students. Her book essentially represents a course in elementary and advanced mathematics that is geared especially to young minds. The first volume deals with arithmetic, **algebra,** trigonometry, analytic **geometry,** and calculus. The second volume deals with the more complicated infinite series and differential equations.

Her book caused an immediate sensation in the academic world. Despite being intended for youngsters, it was recognized as the first comprehensive textbook on calculus. Scholars also saw that it pulled together the new and different calculus methods of **Isaac Newton** (1642–1727) and **Gottfried Leibniz** (1646–1716)—both of whom were her contemporaries—and made them much more

Maria Agnesi

Maria Agnesi

understandable. The book also collected and explained the work of other important mathematicians from several different countries— a task made easier for her by her skills with languages. In addition, Agnesi performed the valuable but very difficult task of integrating the work of many mathematicians. She made significant contributions by discovering and explaining hidden connections between and among the mathematicians that no one had ever seen.

Agnesi began her project with her brothers in mind, so she naturally wrote in Italian. Translations quickly followed once foreign scientists and mathematicians realized the importance of her book. In fact, Cambridge mathematics professor John Colson learned Italian fairly late in life so that he would be able to translate her work into English himself. In recognition of her great accomplishments, Agnesi received valuable gifts from Empress Maria Theresa of Austria (1717–80) (Austria ruled Italy at that time) and was appointed to the chair of mathematics and natural philosophy in 1750 at the University of Bologna by Pope Benedict XIV (1675–1758).

Witch of Agnesi

English mathematics professor John Colson was responsible for misnaming a particular mathematical problem after Agnesi. He mistook the Italian word for "curve," or "turn," for a similar word meaning "wife of the devil," or "witch." In her book, Agnesi had presented students with the problem of finding a mathematical equation for a certain geometric or bell-shaped curve. When Colson gave this curve problem the unusual name of the "witch of Agnesi" (instead of the "curve of Agnesi"), its dramatic name simply stuck.

Withdraws from mathematics and devotes life to the poor

It is ironic that Agnesi's name should be associated with that of a witch or a devil's wife, since throughout her long life she was an extremely devout and religious person. Soon after her father died in 1752, she turned away from her mathematics forever. It is not known for certain whether she ever accepted the pope's appointment and actually taught at Bologna. She may have been only an honorary professor. But once she put that part of her life behind her, she never returned. Rather, she devoted all her energy and money to helping the poor and the sick. By 1759, she had moved into a rented house and offered shelter to the poor. She eventually sold the gifts she had received from the empress and the pope.

In 1783, she was made director of women in a home for the aged, and there she spent the rest of her life. When she died at the age of 81, her mathematical achievements were far behind her, and since she died with no money of her own, she was buried in a pauper's grave. Modern-day Milan has since honored her publicly.

For More Information

Burton, David M. *Burton's History of Mathematics*. Dubuque, IA: Wm. C. Brown Publishers, 1995.

MacTutor History of Mathematics Archive. "Maria Gaetana Agnesi." http://www-groups.dcs.st-and.ac.uk/~history/Mathematicians/Agnesi.html (accessed on March 3, 1999).

Morrow, Charlene, and Teri Perl, eds. *Notable Women in Mathematics: A Biographical Dictionary*. Westport, CT: Greenwood Press, 1998.

Ogilvie, Marilyn Bailey. *Women in Science: Antiquity through the Nineteenth Century*. Cambridge, MA: MIT Press, 1986.

Osen, Lynn M. *Women in Mathematics*. Cambridge, MA: MIT Press, 1974.

Young, Robyn V., ed. *Notable Mathematicians: From Ancient Times to the Present*. Detroit: Gale Research, 1998.

Algebra

Algebra is one of the major branches of mathematics. It has been described as a way of doing arithmetic when unknown quantities are involved. In fact, every time one works with an equation or formula that includes an unknown quantity, the process being used is algebra.

Although algebra uses the same basic operations with numbers as arithmetic—**addition**, **subtraction**, **multiplication**, and **division**—it uses letters to represent some of the numbers. A simple example would be $x + 2 = 5$. For this statement to be correct, x must be 3 because $3 + 2 = 5$. The power of algebra is that it can solve problems that could not be figured out by arithmetic alone (such as a rate, **time**, or distance word problem).

Background

History suggests that the ancient Egyptians and Babylonians, as well as the Chinese, Persians, and Hindus, used algebra thousands of years ago. However, the earliest evidence of its use is contained in the Rhind papyrus, one of the oldest known mathematical manuscripts. (See accompanying sidebar for more information.)

The Rhind papyrus

The Rhind papyrus, one of the oldest mathematical documents in existence, is an Egyptian papyrus written around 1700 B.C. by a scribe named Ahmes (pronounced AH-mace) (c. 1680–c. 1620 B.C.). A papyrus is an early form of paper made in Egypt from the papyrus plant, a water grass growing along the Nile River. The paper was made by stripping thin coats from the stalk of the plant, spreading them out in a sheet, and placing another sheet of strips crosswise to form a thicker sheet that was pressed and dried.

Ahmes's document is named after Scottish collector Alexander Henry Rhind, who bought it in 1858 at a Nile resort.

This document has become an important source of information about Egyptian mathematics. As a practical handbook telling how to solve everyday problems, it indicates how Egyptians counted and measured. The Rhind papyrus contains 85 problems and shows the use of fractions, some geometry, and how to measure area and volume.

This document was found in 1858 and suggests that as early as 1700 B.C. people were dealing with the same kind of problems that are now solved with algebra. That is, they were trying to solve a mathematical problem that involved an unknown number.

Much later, Greek mathematician Diophantus (c. 200–c. 284) solved problems using what would now be called algebra, and even worked out a symbolism of his own. Some call him the "father of algebra," since his work inspired Arab scholar **al-Khwārizmī** (c. 780–c. 850), who many also call the father of algebra. Although al-Khwārizmī wrote many books in different fields (such as geography), one of his works dealt with the development of solutions to mathematical problems in which there was an unknown quantity. Land surveyors, then, were an example of people who were able to use al-Khwārizmī's theories. Al-Khwārizmī was the mathematician who was the best at summarizing the teachings of his time.

It was through the title of al-Khwārizmī's math book that algebra got its European name. The book's title contained the Arabic word *al-jabir;* since the title was quite long, translators would often simply shorten it to the words *al-jabir*. Mathematicians in the West first learned about the new techniques of algebra from al-Khwārizmī's book, so they began describing any aspect of the mathematics of solving for unknown quantities as *al-jabir*. Eventually, *al-jabir* was transliterated (spelled out) using the characters of the Latin alphabet. The word became "algebra." Following these translations, algebra was studied seriously in Europe during the 1500s, and by the end of the seventeenth century, it was a fairly sophisticated mathematical tool.

Description and use

As a problem-solving tool, algebra uses what is called an equation. An equation is described as a statement of what equals what, or as a mathematical sentence that says two things are equal. Thinking of an equation as a balanced see-saw sometimes helps to understand the idea. The rules or procedures of algebra sound simpler than they really are, however. First, since algebra is all about trying to find out what the unknown quantity of something is, the problem is written down as an equation in which x is the unknown number. Second, all the terms involving x should be arranged systematically on one side of the equation. Next, these terms are combined and reduced using regular arithmetic until a single x is left on one side of the equation and a known number remains on the other. That is the answer.

The most basic form of algebra (and fortunately that of most of the everyday problems in algebra) involves equations that are

Race car drivers use linear equations to determine how much distance can be covered, given the rate of speed and the car's miles-per-gallon ratio.

Algebra

called linear or first degree equations. They have this name because any graph made of them always results in a straight line. Things become more complicated when certain problems involve not just x, but x to a higher power, such as x^2 (x times itself) or x^3 (x times itself twice). The simpler linear equations of algebra come into play quite often. Banks use them to compute the interest on a savings account. Corporations use them to figure when to replace a machine that is worth less and less each year it gets older. Race car drivers use them to determine whether they can cover a certain distance at a certain rate of speed given how many miles per gallon a car gets. Cooks use them to convert a recipe meant for four people into a recipe for five.

The simple power and usefulness of algebra comes from it being able to show exactly what needs to be known. Besides its broad range of applications in science and industry, algebra is used whenever people are confronted with a problem that has an unknown quantity. Looking at algebra as a helpful, everyday tool makes it a much more friendly and useful subject to study.

For More Information

Bergamini, David. *Mathematics*. Alexandria, VA: Time-Life Books, 1980.

Green, Gordon W., Jr. *Helping Your Child to Learn Math*. New York: Citadel Press, 1995.

West, Beverly Henderson, et al. *The Prentice-Hall Encyclopedia of Mathematics*. Englewood Cliffs, NJ: Prentice-Hall, 1982.

Miller, Charles D., et al. *Mathematical Ideas*. Reading, MA: Addison-Wesley, 1997.

Born 287 B.C.
Syracuse, Sicily

Died 212 B.C.
Syracuse, Sicily

Greek geometer

Archimedes of Syracuse

Archimedes is not only considered one of the greatest intellects of ancient times but also is ranked as one of the three greatest mathematicians in history, alongside **Isaac Newton** (1642–1727) and **Carl Friedrich Gauss** (1777–1855). In addition to his contributions to physics and his sometimes spectacular engineering achievements and inventions, Archimedes' greatest contributions were in the field of **geometry.**

> *"Give me a place to stand*
> *and I will move the earth."*

Early life and education

Although he was born in Syracuse, a Greek settlement on the southeastern coast of Sicily, Archimedes (pronounced ar-ka-MEED-eez) was educated in Alexandria, Egypt, which was then the intellectual center of the world. It was in Alexandria that Alexander the Great (356–323 B.C.)—world conqueror, but also a pupil of philosopher Aristotle (384–322 B.C.)—had earlier established the city named after him. It was also there that the later Ptolemies built a great library and museum. Greek geometer Euclid (c. 325–c. 270 B.C.) himself taught at Alexandria before Archimedes arrived. There Archimedes was trained by astronomers Conon (c. 280–220 B.C.) and Eratosthenes (c. 276– c. 194 B.C.) and studied with some of the

Archimedes of Syracuse

best minds in the Greek world. (See sidebar on Eratosthenes in the **Euclid of Alexandria** entry.) As the son of Phidias, a wealthy astronomer and mathematician, it is thought that Archimedes also was related to the king of Syracuse, Hieron II.

Archimedes was a true genius and a highly original individual who was skilled at both thinking and doing. As a very young man, for example, he invented and built a planetarium that reproduced the movements of the planets. This ability to excel at both the theoretical and the practical (thinking and doing) marked him as a uniquely gifted person as much at home with deep ideas as with complicated tools or mechanisms. After completing his formal studies in Alexandria, he returned to Syracuse where he remained the rest of his life.

Practical inventiveness

Some of the actual technical achievements of Archimedes are so spectacular, especially for the times in which he lived, that it is not surprising that many legends have grown up around his life story. Of the many dramatic legends that depict his skills, one involves the familiar tale of a giant mirror that he built to set enemy ships' sails on fire. Another story, maybe even less believable, tells of his building a huge crane to lift a ship entirely out of the water. Finally, it is not known with any certainty that he ran naked through the streets of Syracuse shouting "Eureka," meaning "I have found it," after discovering a principle of physics while taking a bath. It was in his tub that Archimedes is said to have realized that every substance has its own special density, and that therefore different substances of the same **weight** would displace different amounts of water.

The reality of his genuine technical accomplishments is impressive enough, however. One of the simplest yet most useful devices he created is called the water snail, or Archimedean screw. This device consisted of a corkscrew enclosed in a long cylinder (tube) that was turned by a hand crank. When one end of the tube was placed under water and the crank was turned, the screw spiraled upward and carried water with it and pushed it out the upper end. Just as the threads of a screw remove pieces of wood when removed or unscrewed, so each groove on the water snail would carry a small amount of water with it and eventually deposit the water in a container. Similar primitive but very effective and simple-to-use devices are used today for irrigation in the Nile Delta of Egypt.

Probably the best known of Archimedes' inventions were those he devised to help defend his native Syracuse against the ships of the Roman Empire. Greek biographer Plutarch (c. 46–119) wrote that during the long battle, the population of Syracuse "merely provided the manpower to operate Archimedes' inventions" and relied upon his genius alone. Using levers and pulleys, Archimedes devised catapults, long metal-tipped movable poles, and grappling cranes against enemy ships. All of these were so successful that Plutarch wrote, if the Romans "saw so much as a length of rope or a piece of timber appear over the top of the wall, it was enough to make them cry out, 'Look, Archimedes is aiming one of his machines at us,'" and they would flee. Roman general Marcellus (c. 268–208 B.C.) eventually took the city while the inhabitants were drunkenly celebrating the feast of Artemis, goddess of the moon. It was during this sack of Syracuse that a Roman soldier killed Archimedes with a sword or a lance. Legend has it that he was killed because he refused to stop working on a mathematical diagram. Another version says he was killed on the spot when he ordered a Roman soldier not to disturb the mathematical figures he was drawing in the sand. Marcellus had ordered that Archimedes be spared, and he sadly buried him at the gate of the city with honors.

A sixteenth-century engraving shows Archimedes about to leap out of his bathtub after making a discovery about density.

Mathematical contributions

It is significant that Archimedes died while engaged in his beloved mathematics. Sitting peacefully outside and drawing geometrical figures or equations in the sand was a common practice for mathematicians in the ancient world of the Mediterranean. Archimedes was also known to quickly sketch a geometrical problem in the cool ashes of a fire or even to use his finger to trace a problem on his own oil-covered body when he stepped from a bath.

Among his many major contributions to mathematics—and one of the best known—is his method for finding a good approximation of the value of pi. **Pi** (pronounced PIE) is the name given to the **ratio** between the diameter of a **circle** and its circumference. Diameter is a line drawn completely through a circle's center. Circumference is the distance around a circle. In modern times, this ratio became known as pi since the Greek letter *p* was short for the word "periphery," meaning the outermost edge of a circle. Archimedes determined the ratio, or relationship, between these two parts of a circle: A circle's circumference is roughly three times its diameter (3.14), no matter how big or little the circle. In ancient times, this knowledge was useful to builders, but today the notion of pi occurs more often in higher forms of mathematics like calculus and **probability** theory.

From his work with pi, Archimedes also was able to devise a formula to find the **area** under a curve or the amount of space enclosed by the curve. The sophisticated methods he developed for this complicated theoretical problem are today recognized as having been very close to a discovery of the highly useful branch of mathematics called calculus (which had to wait nearly 2,000 years to be invented).

Another of Archimedes' mathematical achievements was to work out a way of writing extremely large numbers. Although the Greeks were a sophisticated people, the number system they used was very clumsy. Their system used the letters of the Greek alphabet for numbers, so that α (alpha) was number 1, β (beta) was number 2, and so on throughout the alphabet. Following number 9, the letter ι (iota) was 10, κ (kappa) was 20, and so on in increments of ten. Using all twenty-four letters plus three other symbols, the Greeks were barely able to write even small numbers. Very large numbers were out of the question.

Archimedes rose to the challenge of large numbers and attempted to solve it by posing a hypothetical problem and then trying to solve it: How many grains of sand would it take to fill the universe, he asked himself. To the Greeks, the universe consisted of the space between the sun, the moon, and the five known planets. Archimedes began with a known fact—how many grains of sand would equal the diameter of a poppy seed—and began to extrapolate (to project something that is known into an area that is unknown). Going from smaller to larger, he worked out how many poppy seeds would equal the width of a finger, and then how many finger widths would fill a stadium. He kept going until he came up with an answer that was derived from a new system of numbering based on the Greek concept of "myriad." Before him, myriad meant simply "a countless number," but he gave it a value of 10,000. Using that, he was able to go up to a myriad of myriads (100 million) or beyond to his final estimation of the number 1 followed by 80 million billion (or 80 quadrillion) zeroes.

That's a lot of zeroes!

Archimedes devised a way of counting that used powers of ten. "Powers of ten" refers to the number of zeroes in a number. (For instance, 10^1, or "ten to the first power," means there is one zero following the number 1.) Archimedes' method eliminated the clumsy use of the Greek alphabet in the counting system. What follows are numbers to the power of ten in the American system of numeration.

Number	Value in powers of ten	Number of zeroes
ten	10^1	1
hundred	10^2	2
thousand	10^3	3
million	10^6	6
billion	10^9	9
trillion	10^{12}	12
quadrillion	10^{15}	15
quintillion	10^{18}	18
sextillion	10^{21}	21
septillion	10^{24}	24
octillion	10^{27}	27
nonillion	10^{30}	30
decillion	10^{33}	33
undecillion	10^{36}	36
duodecillion	10^{39}	39
tredecillion	10^{42}	42
quattuordecillion	10^{45}	45
quindecillion	10^{48}	48
sexdecillion	10^{51}	51
septendecillion	10^{54}	54
octodecillion	10^{57}	57
novemdecillion	10^{60}	60
vigintillion	10^{63}	63
centillion	10^{303}	303

There was one mathematical discovery of which Archimedes was so proud that he asked that a symbol of it be placed on his tombstone. This was his method for calculating the **volume** of a sphere. A round object like a globe or a basketball is a sphere, and deter-

Archimedes of Syracuse

mining its volume is another way of figuring out how much it will hold. The answer he came up with is, like pi, both simple and pleasing, and it works every time.

Archimedes discovered that a sphere's volume is equal to two-thirds the volume of the smallest cylinder in which the particular sphere will fit (a drinking glass is shaped like a cylinder, as is anything tube-shaped). Thus, for a sphere's volume, there is a constant sphere-to-cylinder ratio of 2 to 3. When the great Roman orator and scholar Cicero (106–43 B.C.) discovered a neglected, overgrown grave in Sicily in 75 B.C., he knew he had found the one he was seeking when he noticed "a small column arising a little above the bushes, on which there was the figure of a sphere and a cylinder." It was Archimedes' grave

The mathematical writings of Archimedes served to inspire the scientific revolution that would change the western world 2,000 years after Archimedes lived. An excellent example of his substantial and lasting influence is the great **Galileo** (1564–1642), who made reference to the ideas of Archimedes more than one hundred times.

For More Information

Abbott, David, ed. *The Biographical Dictionary of Scientists: Mathematicians.* New York: Peter Bedrick Books, 1986.

Bendick, Jeanne, and Laura M. Berquist. *Archimedes and the Door to Science.* Minot, ND: Bethlehem Books, 1997.

Ibsen, D. C. *Archimedes: Greatest Scientist of the Ancient World.* Springfield, NJ: Enslow Publishers, 1989.

MacTutor History of Mathematics Archive. "Archimedes of Syracuse." http://www-groups.dcs.st-and.ac.uk/~history/Mathematicians/Archimedes.html (accessed on March 3, 1999).

Lafferty, Peter. *Pioneers of Science: Archimedes.* New York: Bookwright Press, 1991.

Morgan, Bryan. *Men and Discoveries in Mathematics.* London: John Murray Publishers, 1972.

Rogers, James T. *The Pantheon Story of Mathematics for Young People.* New York: Pantheon Books, 1966.

Young, Robyn V., ed. *Notable Mathematicians: From Ancient Times to the Present.* Detroit: Gale Research, 1998.

Area

Area is a concept in **geometry** that represents the amount of space a flat geometrical shape will occupy. It can also be described as a surface or region that is inside a given boundary. Area is always expressed by a number value that is measured in square units (like square feet or square inches).

Background

Area is derived from the Latin word *area,* meaning "vacant piece of ground." In time, the meaning shifted from the piece of ground itself to the size of the two-dimensional piece of ground. Eventually it came to apply to the size of any particular flat shape whether it was real or not. Long before the Romans, however, both the Babylonians and the Egyptians had very practical reasons for learning how to calculate how much space was contained in a plot of land that had certain, fixed-shape boundaries. One of the oldest known maps is a hand-sized clay tablet that depicts a row of riverfront lots bordering the Euphrates river. Just like today, the property lines or boundaries of these lots were very important to their owners as well as to the government that taxed them. Being able to calculate easily and quickly the area or the amount of space each lot occu-

Area

pied was also a primary concern. The Egyptians had the same practical concerns with their land bordering the Nile, except each year they would have to redraw these boundaries after the spring floods had receded.

Both the Babylonians and the Egyptians probably first measured the area of a rectangular lot by counting how many same-sized squares could fit inside the rectangle. After doing this many times, someone made the generalization that multiplying the number of squares on each adjoining side was exactly the same operation as counting all the squares inside. For a rectangle, the rule then became length times width (adjoining sides were multiplied). For a square, it was one side times any other one side.

The ancients eventually developed rules for finding the area of **triangles** and **circles** and for less symmetrical shapes such as parallelograms and trapezoids. Many Egyptian papyri (ancient writing material made from the papyrus plant) still exist that contain prescription-like rules for determining areas of different shapes, and it is believed that they were the result of ages of trial-and-error experience. (See sidebar on papyrus in the **Algebra** entry.) Although some of these formulas were only partially correct, most were good enough to meet the practical needs of everyday life. The standard technique for dealing with these odd-shaped figures was to subdivide the shape into sections or shapes for which the area could easily be calculated. Thus if they are broken up into rectangles, squares, triangles, or even circles (whose areas are easily calculated using known formulas) and their individual areas added together, the area of an irregular figure can be determined.

Applications

The usefulness and practical application of finding the area of something is obvious to most people. One of the most common examples is calculating how much carpeting or tile is needed to cover the floor of a room. If the floor is a rectangular shape, one need only multiply the long side of the room by the short side to arrive at its area in square feet.

Another example is when a consumer buys paint according to how many square feet one gallon will cover. If, for instance, one gallon of paint will cover an area totaling 200 square feet, and the area to be painted (four walls and a ceiling) equals 300 square feet, an additional half-gallon of paint will be needed.

Other uses of area include fertilizer bags that contain application instructions that tell how many pounds per square feet of grass on which to apply the fertilizer. Property taxes are usually based on the quantity of square feet in a home, and the cost of building a home is often calculated by square feet. It should be remembered that area is the measure of the surface covered by a figure or shape and is not the same as **perimeter,** which is the sum of its borders or the distance around a figure.

For More Information

Beaumont, Vern, et al. *How to . . . Teach Perimeter, Area, and Volume.* Reston, VA: National Council of Teachers of Mathematics, 1986.

Miller, Charles D., et al. *Mathematical Ideas.* Reading, MA: Addison-Wesley, 1997.

Smoothey, Marion. *Let's Investigate Area and Volume.* New York: Marshall Cavendish, 1993.

Wheeler, Ruric E. *Modern Mathematics.* Pacific Grove, CA: Brooks/Cole Publishing, 1995.

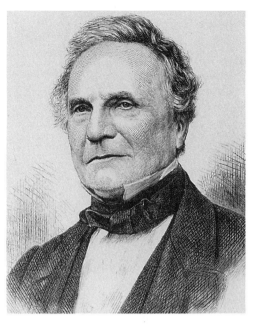

Born December 26, 1791
London, England

Died October 18, 1871
London, England

English mathematician and inventor

Charles Babbage

A pioneer of mechanical computation, Charles Babbage is considered by many to be the grandfather of modern **computers**. The first person to construct a computing machine that went beyond simple arithmetic calculations, he also designed but never completed a highly ambitious steam-powered calculating machine whose complexity was far ahead of its time. His plans and designs accurately foreshadowed modern computing equipment and suggest that he was aware of all of the basic principles upon which modern computers are based.

> *"Errors using inadequate data are much less than those using no data at all."*

Early life and education

Charles Babbage (pronounced BABB-ij) was born in London, England, the son of a wealthy banker, Benjamin Babbage. As a youngster he was unusually curious and obviously very bright. Since illness often interfered with his education, his father placed him in the care of a clergyman whose job it was to educate the boy without tiring him out. By his early teens, Babbage was able to attend boarding school in London. There he developed a strong interest in **algebra,** which led him to pursue the study of mathe-

Charles Babbage

matics in his free time. The young Babbage actually learned so much mathematics on his own that when he entered Cambridge University in 1810, he found that he knew more mathematics than his instructors.

Amazed and shocked at what he considered to be the sad state of British higher education in mathematics, the 18-year-old Babbage decided to do something about it and founded, with John Herschel (1792–1871), the Analytical Society. Herschel was the son of William Herschel (1738–1822), the greatest astronomer of his time and also a first-rate mathematician. John Herschel joined with Babbage and a few others to try to bring the best of European mathematicians to England.

In 1813, Babbage and Herschel translated and published a key French work on calculus, and Babbage himself wrote several notable mathematical papers. Their efforts to revitalize British mathematics were soon successful, and Babbage found himself elected as a fellow of the Royal Society when he was 24 years old. The Royal Society was chartered, or sponsored, by the king in 1662 as a society composed of England's best scientists. Its members held regular meetings to keep each other informed of their work. They also published a journal to communicate scientific results to all of Europe. Membership in the Royal Society is a distinct honor, and it is still in existence today.

Using machines to compute

In Babbage's time, mathematical tables of all kinds were used in all sorts of practical activities. Insurance clerks and bankers as well as navigators, astronomers, and engineers used different types of tables to do their daily work. Babbage soon realized that not only did it take hundreds of mathematicians to compile these highly useful but very dull arithmetic tables, but that because of human error, they were not always perfectly accurate. Around 1820, he had an idea that he would pursue for the rest of his life. At an Analytical Society meeting, Babbage apparently looked at an error-filled table and stated that "all these mathematical tables might be calculated by machinery." Babbage soon set out to see if he could discover a cheaper and more accurate method of producing tables by what he called mechanical computation. In 1822, he built a small, hand-cranked model that could compile and print astronomical and logarithmic tables to an accuracy of six **decimal** places.

Government support

Babbage's machine so impressed the Royal Society that it gave its backing to his request of the British government for funding. How Babbage was able to succeed in this highly unusual request is not known, but as a person who had already almost single-handedly reformed British mathematics, he probably was listened to when he argued that the national government had an obligation to support science. He was given more than 17,000 British pounds to build a full-scale machine called a difference engine that would calculate navigational tables for the Royal Navy. He was supposed to do this in three years.

Progress was slow and very expensive, however, and Babbage was soon spending some of his own inheritance in order to keep going. One of the major practical problems he encountered was that his technical demands were so precise that very often new tools had to be designed and custom-crafted. By 1834, the difference engine was nowhere near completion and the government had withdrawn its support for the project, in part because of its ambitiousness and complexity. Babbage remarkably not only had a new, even bolder plan for a new machine, but he wanted the government to fund this one as well.

Analytical engine

Although Babbage had produced only small pieces of his difference engine, he was convinced that his new analytical engine, which would be powered by steam and whose operating instructions were to be stored on punched cards, would be a far more powerful tool. According to his design, it would do any kind of arithmetic and be able to solve problems involving different types of operations, such as one calling for **addition** followed by **division**. As conceived on paper by Babbage, this programmable, automatic machine is now considered to be the direct ancestor of the modern computer. The British government, however, was not about to fund Babbage's plans any further, and Babbage himself was rapidly using up his entire inheritance.

Babbage was still not about to give up however, and by 1848 he proposed a scaled-down version of the analytical engine (which he called difference engine #2). Funding was again an impossibility, and Babbage never built this machine either. By the time of his death in 1871, he still had not completed his machine.

Charles Babbage

Charles Babbage

A model of Charles Babbage's difference engine.

Babbage and his other accomplishments

Although Babbage's life was dominated by his obsession with mechanical computing, he still was able to compile a remarkable amount of highly different accomplishments. Early in his career, he made contributions to such fields as geology, anthropology, and astronomy. He studied glaciers, advised the government on a more efficient postal system, and invented the "cowcatcher," an angled, metal frame attached to the front of a railroad locomotive that knocks clear any debris that is on the tracks. Babbage also ran unsuccessfully for Parliament, devised a signalling code for lighthouses, and invented an ophthalmoscope (an instrument used to view the inside of the eye).

Babbage also helped establish several other science-related organizations in England. In 1820, he helped found the Royal Astronomical Society; in 1831, the British Association for the Advancement of Science; and in 1834, the Statistical Society of London. As with his work on mechanical computing, he showed himself to be a man with a passion for improving (and organizing) things. He also had a strong belief in using new tools and technologies to improve society.

In 1828, his mathematical reputation was high enough for Babbage to be elected the

The world's first computer program

The world's first computer programmer may have been the daughter of English poet Lord Byron (1788–1824). Augusta Ada Byron, the countess of Lovelace (1815–52), was a bright, well-educated, and socially connected young girl. At the age of 18, she went to a party hosted by English mathematician Charles Babbage, whose guests often included the likes of Charles Dickens (1812–70). Byron quickly took an interest in Babbage's steam-driven calculating machine and studied—and understood—his plans for an analytical engine. This machine was designed to take instructions and numerical data from punched cards and would make and analyze calculations.

In 1842, an article had been written in Italian about Babbage's invention and Byron was asked to translate it for publication in England. When she found that the article only described the mathematical concepts by which the engine would work, she decided to add a series of notes. These notes turned out to be not only the first clear explanation of the mechanics of Babbage's engine, but they also provided illustrations of how the machine might be instructed to perform particular tasks. In doing this, Ada Byron created the world's first computer program. Since she signed her long article only with the initials A. A. L., (for Augusta Ada Lovelace) few knew it was even her work. In 1980, the U.S. Department of Defense gave the name "Ada" to a programming language it commissioned.

Lucasian professor of mathematics at Cambridge University. (The Lucasian professorship is the most famous academic chair in the world. It was created and funded by Henry Lucas, a member of Parliament.) But Babbage did not want to leave his mechanical computing work and move there, so he never taught at the university and simply kept the position until 1839. In his later years, Babbage reportedly turned into a grouchy, bitter man who would pick a fight with anyone about anything. His silliest and saddest public fight was against organ grinders—street musicians who kept him awake with their music.

In his life's work however, the biggest problem Babbage encountered, which neither he nor anyone could overcome, was the simple fact that he was a man too far ahead of his time. Although his ideas may have been too advanced for most people to grasp, the

Charles Babbage

really impossible obstacle was that his technical demands were beyond the engineering ability of the time. A good example of this was the "mill," the heart of his analytical engine. This part was to consist of 1,000 columns of geared wheels. His simpler difference engine would have required a total of 25,000 precision-gauged brass and steel parts. Such demands for accurately made, precisely engineered parts were simply beyond the ability of the craftsmen that he could find. The solution was for Babbage to use electro-mechanical devices rather than mechanical ones, but the electric light bulb was not even invented until 1879. Despite his obvious failure to build a finished, working machine that would "crunch numbers," Babbage is considered to have foreshadowed every aspect of the modern computer.

For More Information

Abbott, David, ed. *The Biographical Dictionary of Scientists: Mathematicians.* New York: Peter Bedrick Books, 1986.

Asimov, Isaac. *Asimov's Biographical Encyclopedia of Science and Technology.* Garden City, NY: Doubleday & Company, 1982.

Biographical Dictionary of Mathematicians. New York: Charles Scribner's Sons, 1991.

Campbell, Kelley Martin, ed. *The Works of Charles Babbage.* New York: New York University Press, 1988.

Collier, Bruce. *Charles Babbage and the Engines of Perfection.* Oxford, England: Oxford University Press, 1998.

MacTutor History of Mathematics Archive. "Charles Babbage." http://www-groups.dcs.st-and.ac.uk/~history/Mathematicians/Babbage.html (accessed on March 4, 1999).

Moseley, Maboth. *Irascible Genius: The Life of Charles Babbage.* Chicago: Henry Regnery, 1964.

Young, Robyn V., ed. *Notable Mathematicians: From Ancient Times to the Present.* Detroit: Gale Research, 1998.

Born November 9, 1731
Baltimore County, Maryland

Died October 9, 1806
Baltimore County, Maryland

African American mathematician and astronomer

Benjamin Banneker

Recognized as the first American black to achieve distinction in science, Benjamin Banneker was a mostly self-taught mathematician. He is best known for a very popular series of almanacs he compiled in the 1790s and for his work in surveying the boundaries for the District of Columbia.

Descendant of slaves and servants

Born on a farm near Baltimore, Maryland, Benjamin Banneker (pronounced BAN-ni-ker) was fortunate to have a remarkable set of grandparents. His grandmother, Molly Welsh, was a white English-woman who had been sent to the American colonies to serve seven years as an indentured servant. This meant she was basically in bondage, or unable to leave her employer, and her situation was close to that of being a slave. When her seven years of service was over, she moved west and staked out land to build a farm (an unusual thing for a solitary woman to do). She then purchased two African males from a slave ship on the coast, gave them their freedom, and soon married one named Bannaka (or Banneky). Claiming to be the son of an African chieftain (leader of a group), he had considerable agri-

> *"Ah, why will men forget that they are brethren?"*

cultural knowledge and experience, which made the farm a success. Molly and her husband, Bannaka, had a daughter named Mary who was born free. Like her mother, she also purchased a slave, freed him, and then married him. He took the name Robert Banneker and, with his wife Mary, had a son named Benjamin.

Early life and education

Young Benjamin learned how to read and write from his grandmother, Molly. She also arranged for the 12-year-old to attend a Quaker school that had just been started up nearby by a man named Peter Heinrich. Heinrich allowed Banneker to join the school, an experience that would prove very influential, as the young boy took to many Quaker customs and even adopted their manner of dress. At school, he demonstrated unusual natural ability in mathematics and soon went beyond what his teacher knew. He remained there, however, only until he had grown enough to work all day on the tobacco farm.

Demonstrates technical abilities

Although his formal schooling had been cut short, Banneker's interest in applying mathematics to technical problems deepened. When he was 21, he was able to examine up-close something he had never seen before—a pocket watch. This fascinating piece of engineering was shown to Banneker during one of his trips to the East coast to sell tobacco. Since he was so fascinated by it, its owner, Josef Levi, gave the watch to Banneker, who then took it home and studied its workings. After taking it apart and putting it together several times, he decided to build a larger version himself. He then sketched the wheels and gears and calculated mathematically the proportions (see **Ratio, proportion, and percent**) that each should have to make it work properly.

This work in itself was a major accomplishment for a basically self-taught young man from the farm. But he actually crafted an accurate, working clock mostly out of wood. After carving each gear and piece by hand and fitting them all together, he produced a clock when he was 22 that kept **time** to the hour, minute, and second and even struck a gong on the hour. This clock alone made him famous, at least locally, and it kept accurate time for more than 40 years.

Meets Ellicott family and works at surveying

Banneker inherited his parents' farm when his father, Robert, died in 1759, and he would remain there for the rest of his life. In 1772, however, his life was to change when the prominent Ellicott family moved nearby in Baltimore County and began to build a mill along the Patapsco River. Banneker soon was attracted by their clever use of machinery to automate the mill, and he became especially friendly with young George Ellicott, who shared many of Banneker's scientific interests, especially in mathematics and astronomy. Banneker's technical talents enabled him to be helpful at the Ellicott's mill, and once George realized Banneker's interests in science, he lent him some of his books in astronomy and higher mathematics. Banneker also inherited more books and instruments when Andrew Ellicott, George's father, died. The inheritance enabled him to begin his serious mathematical calculations of the stars and their constellations. One of his achievements was to predict correctly that a solar eclipse would occur on April 14, 1789, contradicting the date set by two prominent astronomers and mathematicians.

In 1791, Banneker became involved in a historic surveying process that would lead to the building of a national capital for the new nation of the United States. The surveyor, George Ellicott's cousin, Andrew Ellicott (1754–1820), had been selected by French-born American architect Pierre-Charles L'Enfant (pronounced lawn-FAWN) to conduct a boundary survey for what would become the federal district in the new city of Washington. Ellicott was familiar with Banneker's ability, especially his recent work compiling an astronomical almanac, and realized that he could trust Banneker to accurately maintain and use his all-important astronomical clock. This precision instrument was kept in Ellicott's tent and was crucial to the project, since it was the constant by which all other measurements and instruments would be guided. Banneker accepted this position, which required him not only to do a considerable amount of field work but also demanded that he be up well into the night.

There is a legend surrounding Banneker's role in laying out Washington's boundaries, streets, and buildings. It says that when the hot-tempered architect L'Enfant was dismissed from the project, he took all his plans with him. Legend has it that Banneker was

Benjamin Banneker

**Benjamin
Banneker**

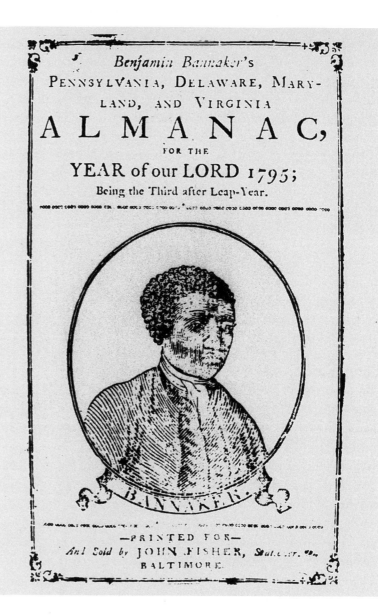

The cover of Benjamin Banneker's Almanac.

able to reproduce these plans entirely from memory in two days, thus saving the project and resulting in the Washington, D.C., that is known today. Historians now discount that story.

Banneker's almanac

No legend is needed, however, to add to the accomplishments of Banneker with regard to his famous *Almanac,* first published in 1792. Using borrowed books and instruments, Banneker learned astronomy and taught himself how to calculate an ephemeris (pronounced i-FEM-uh-rus)—a table predicting the daily positions of celestial bodies—and to make projections of lunar and solar eclipses. Almanacs were extremely popular in the eighteenth century, especially in the frontier and farming communities of the new United States. Almanacs contained ephemerides (pronounced i-FEM-uh-ruh-deez), which is plural for ephemeris. In revolutionary America, these ephemerides were basic to every household because they told farmers the exact hours for sunrise and sunset and included tide tables as well as times and dates for eclipses, holidays, phases of the moon, and other similar information.

In 1792, his work was published as *Benjamin Banneker's Pennsylvania, Delaware, Maryland and Virginia Almanack and Ephemeris, for the year of our Lord, 1792.* Published annually through 1797, his work became as common in mid-Atlantic households as the Bible.

Communications with Thomas Jefferson

Banneker had worked long and hard to produce all the calculations for his 1792 almanac. When it was ready in August 1791, he sent a manuscript copy to then–secretary of state Thomas Jefferson (1743–1826). Although a free man, Banneker felt deeply about the injustices done to blacks in America, nearly all of whom were slaves. Because he knew of Jefferson's key role in achieving American independence as well as his eloquent words concerning the rights of man, Banneker sent a copy of his almanac to Jefferson. He also wrote and included a 12-page letter, defending the intelligence of those of African descent.

Banneker urged Jefferson to fight against the prejudice that was "so prevalent in the world against those of my complexion . . . a race of beings, who have long labored under the abuse and censure of the world." Although Jefferson was himself a slaveholder, he wrote to Banneker that "nature has given to our black brethren talents equal to those of other colors of men." Banneker wisely printed Jefferson's letter in his 1793 almanac, and continued all his life to fight against slavery. Slavery would not be abolished until 1865, 59 years after Banneker's death.

Banneker never married, and there is a final legend about why he lived alone. Some say he fell in love with a slave named Anola when he was 28. When her master would not sell her to Banneker so he could free and marry her, he planned to run off with her and booked passage on a boat to England. When the plan fell through and Banneker was nearly killed, Anola was brokenhearted and killed herself by drowning. Banneker supposedly vowed never to marry so as to honor her memory and their love.

The mysterious burning of his house and laboratory on the same day as his funeral is no legend, however. Banneker is buried in Oella, Maryland. A museum in his honor operates in nearby Catonsville.

For More Information

Able, James A. "The Story of Benjamin Banneker." *Cricket*, February 1994, pp. 21–25.

"Bannekers Break Ground." *Jet*, September 30, 1996, p. 23.

Bedini, A. Silvio. *The Life of Benjamin Banneker*. New York: Scribner's, 1972.

"Benjamin Banneker to the Secretary of State." [Online] http://www.lib.virginia.edu/etext/readex/24073.html (accessed on March 4, 1999).

Elliott, Clark A. *Biographical Dictionary of American Science: The Seventeenth Through the Nineteenth Centuries*. Westport, CT: Greenwood Press, 1979.

Ferris, Jerri. *What Are You Figuring Now? A Story About Benjamin Banneker*. New York: Scholastic, 1988.

Haber, Louis. *Black Pioneers of Science and Invention*. New York: Harcourt, Brace & World, 1970.

Hudson, Wade, and Valerie Wilson Wesley. *Afro-Bets Book of Black Heroes From A to Z: An Introduction to Important Black Achievers for Young Readers*. East Orange, NJ: Just Us Books, 1997.

Maryland's African American Heritage. "Benjamin Banneker." [Online] http://tqd.advanced.org/3337/banneker.html (accessed on March 4, 1999).

Metcalf, Doris Hunter. *Portraits of Exceptional African American Scientists.* Carthage, IL: Good Apple, 1994.

Pinckney, Andrea Davis. *Dear Benjamin Banneker.* San Diego, CA: Harcourt Brace, 1994.

Potter, Joan, and Constance Claytor. *African Americans Who Were First: Illustrated with Photographs.* New York: Cobblehill Books, 1997.

Reimer, Luetta, and Wilbert Reimer. *Mathematicians Are People, Too: Stories from the Lives of Great Mathematicians.* Palo Alto, CA: Dale Seymour Publications, 1995.

Young, Robyn V., ed. *Notable Mathematicians: From Ancient Times to the Present.* Detroit: Gale Research, 1998.

Benjamin Banneker

Born April 24, 1919
Centralia, Illinois

African American statistician and educator

David Blackwell

Regarded as perhaps the greatest African American mathematician, David Blackwell has explored several different fields of mathematics while making major contributions in the application of game theory. A former fellow of the Institute for Advanced Study and the first black mathematician to be elected to the National Academy of Science, Blackwell is a natural teacher who loves to communicate the beauty of mathematics.

> *"Don't worry about the overall importance of the problem; work on it if it looks interesting. I think there's a sufficient correlation between interest and importance."*

Early life and education

David Harold Blackwell was born April 24, 1919, in Centralia, Illinois, the oldest of four children. His mother, Mabel Johnson, was a full-time homemaker. His father, Grover Blackwell, worked for the Illinois Central Railroad and managed the roundhouse, the facility where locomotives were turned around. Blackwell traces his mathematical ability to his paternal grandfather, who was a schoolteacher in Tennessee. He recalled that the first **algebra** book he ever saw was in his grandfather's library. As a youngster, he was always curious about games like checkers and wondered about such questions as whether or

David Blackwell

not the first player would always win. In high school the mathematics club advisor would challenge members with problems, and Blackwell was often able to think of solutions. Although southern Illinois was mostly segregated (the blacks separated from the whites) in the 1920s, Blackwell attended an integrated school and had no sense of being discriminated against. In a 1983 interview, he said, "My parents protected us from [discrimination] and I didn't encounter enough of it in schools to notice it."

During high school, Blackwell's interest in mathematics began to grow. As an exceptional student, he was able to graduate at the age of 16. In 1935 he entered the University of Illinois, intending to become an elementary school teacher after graduation. During his college career, however, he enjoyed his mathematics courses so much that he never took the education courses required for teacher certification. After his freshman year, Blackwell discovered that his parents had borrowed money to send him to college, so he decided to help them out by taking such jobs as washing dishes, waiting tables, and cleaning laboratory equipment. Despite working throughout his college years, Blackwell graduated in 1938 after only three years. He then received a two-year fellowship. He remained at the University of Illinois and entered its graduate school, raising his career goals in mathematics from elementary school teaching to high school teaching. He completed his master's degree in 1939 and continued on with his fellowship, receiving his Ph.D. in 1941.

Joins the Institute for Advanced Study and begins teaching career

After receiving his Ph.D. from the University of Illinois, Blackwell was awarded a Rosenwald Fellowship for a year of study at the Institute for Advanced Study (IAS) at Princeton. There, he became acquainted with Hungarian American mathematician **John von Neumann** (1903–57), whose work provided the basis for game theory. Game theory is the study of any game or situation involving strategy. It was the custom that members of the Institute be appointed honorary members of the faculty at Princeton. Years after Blackwell's appointment to IAS, he learned that certain individuals at Princeton had objected to his appointment because of his race. Only when the IAS director made unspecified threats did individuals at Princeton withdraw their objections.

After his year at IAS, Blackwell knew that he very much wanted to teach mathematics at the college level. So he wrote to 105 black colleges around the country. Although he was not aware of any racial discrimination directed at him, he simply assumed that his role would be to teach at a black college, so he did not even attempt to find a job at a non-black university. Eventually he accepted a position for the 1942–43 academic year at Southern University, a black institution in Baton Rouge, Louisiana. He then spent a year teaching at Clark College in Atlanta, Georgia, before joining in 1944 the faculty at Howard University, the most prestigious black institution of higher learning in the country. It was also in 1944 that Blackwell married Ann Madison, with whom he would have three sons and five daughters. By 1947, Blackwell had been promoted to full professor, and he served as head of the Howard mathematics department until 1954.

David Blackwell

Contributes to statistics and explores game theory

During his Howard years, Blackwell did some of his most original work. Intrigued and stimulated by a lecture he attended in 1946, he made his most significant contribution to modern **statistics** with a 1947 paper that established what has become known as the Rao-Blackwell theorem. This theorem uses the notion of "sufficiency"—which simplifies a statistical problem by summarizing data—to show how to estimate minimum variances or differences. In 1948, Blackwell began spending his summers working at the RAND Corporation headquarters in Santa Monica, California. There he further developed his application of game theory and eventually co-authored a book, *Theory of Games and Statistical Decisions,* published in 1950.

That same year, Blackwell accepted a professorship in statistics at the University of California at Berkeley and served as chairman of the Department of Statistics from 1956 to 1961. During the 1973–75 academic years, he directed the University of California Study Center for the United Kingdom and Ireland. He later delivered the prestigious Rouse Ball Lecture at the University of Cambridge. In 1981 Blackwell retired and became a professor emeritus at Berkeley.

The recipient of several honors, awards, and honorary degrees (from institutions such as Carnegie-Mellon, Yale, Harvard,

David Blackwell

Howard, and the National University of Lesotho in South Africa), he served as president of the Institute of Mathematical Statistics in 1955 and was awarded the John von Neumann prize in 1979. His work has been applied in many fields, and his statistical research has been as important to the field of accounting as his game theory ideas have contributed to the strategies of economics. Throughout his career, Blackwell has been primarily interested in achieving a real mathematical understanding of anything he was working on, and has always pursued problems that interested him.

For More Information

Albers, Donald J., and G. L. Alexanderson, eds. *Mathematical People: Profiles and Interviews.* Boston: Birkhauser, 1985.

Blackwell, David. *Theory of Games and Statistical Decisions.* Mineola, NY: Dover Publications, 1980.

Duren, Peter, ed. *A Century of Mathematics in America.* 3 vols. Providence, RI: American Mathematical Society, 1988–89.

McMurray, Emily J., ed. *Notable Twentieth-Century Scientists.* Detroit: Gale Research, 1995.

Young, Robyn V., ed. *Notable Mathematicians: From Ancient Times to the Present.* Detroit: Gale Research, 1998.

Born November 2, 1815
Lincoln, England

Died December 8, 1864
Ballintemple, Ireland

English algebraist and logician

George Boole

As the founder of the modern science of mathematical **logic**, George Boole was responsible for creating the branch of mathematics known as Boolean **algebra.** The original ideas of this self-taught genius were eventually taken up by others and came to have broad applications in the design of **computer** circuits and telephone switching, as well as in such fields as **probability** theory.

Humble origins

George Boole (pronunciation rhymes with POOL) was born in Lincoln, England, the son of a shoe-maker. Although his father had a high respect for learning and was himself interested in mathematics and the making of optical instruments, a serious decline in his business affected his son's future. Young Boole was able to attend only an elementary school and a commercial school briefly before he left to help earn money for the family. Despite this, he knew the importance of an education and was able to get help learning Latin. After that, he learned Greek, French, Italian, and German on his own. His talent was such that when a local paper printed his translation of a Latin poem, a scholar accused him of

> *"Boole's system of logic is but one of many proofs of genius and patience combined."*
>
> —*Indian-born English mathematician Augustus De Morgan*

plagiarism, saying that no 14-year-old could have done something so polished.

George Boole

As the young Boole continued to try to improve himself and to help his poverty-stricken family, he considered joining the church. Instead, he chose to make a living in the field of education. At the age of 16, he obtained a job as an assistant teacher in an elementary school. By the time he was 20 years old, he was ready to open his own school. All the while, Boole had been educating himself in order to be a better teacher. Since he considered most of the available textbooks to be useless, he consulted the classics. He read and mastered on his own such difficult works as *Principia Mathematica* by English mathematician **Isaac Newton** (1642–1727) and the writings of the French greats, Pierre-Simon Laplace (1749–1827) and **Joseph-Louis Lagrange** (1736–1813). At 19 years old, Boole had already earned a local reputation as an expert on Newton, and was even asked to give an address at a special event commemorating Newton as a Lincoln resident. When printed in 1835, this address was Boole's first scientific publication.

Establishes reputation and enters professional world

With his steady teaching and dedication of every spare moment to mathematics, Boole soon was contributing regularly to the newly founded *Cambridge Mathematical Journal.* In 1844 his originality was recognized by the Royal Society of London, England's most prestigious scientific society, which awarded him a gold medal in 1844 for his paper discussing how algebra and calculus could be combined. This honor enabled him to start a correspondence with some of the famous British mathematicians of his day, one of whom encouraged him to apply for a university position in 1849. Although Boole had no degree or even university education, he was given the Chair of Mathematics at the newly established Queens College in Cork, Ireland. He had been selected on the basis of his reputation, which was based solely on his research publications.

Founds mathematical logic

By the time Boole was given his professorship at Queen's College, he had already published what was recognized as a ground-breaking work on the subject of mathematical logic. In 1847, his pamphlet entitled *The Mathematical Analysis of Logic* offered the unique argument that logic (sound or valid reasoning) was more closely related to mathematics than it was to philosophy. By 1854, Boole was ready to fully explore this new idea, and in that year he published his pioneering work, *An Investigation of the Laws of Thought.* This landmark work founded what is called mathematical logic, or symbolic logic.

Boole's highly original work enabled him to use symbols rather than words to perform ordinary reasoning. His idea was that if one used symbols in place of a statement, then the relationship between two statements could be written as an algebraic equation. This revolutionary way of looking at mathematics argued that mathematics was much more than simply "the science of measurement and number," and that it was a much broader system that people could use to actually show their logical thinking. It was no mistake that Boole's book had the words "laws of thought" in its title, since it was his goal to both make reasoning easier and to make it more precise by discovering (and showing mathematically) the rules of logical reasoning.

Modern computer applications

As Boole's symbolic logic was first applied by mathematicians, it enabled them to use symbols in their proofs instead of words (whose meanings might be mistaken or confusing). Eventually, however, symbolic logic, which also used what is known as "binary" mathematics, found a much more practical use. Binary means that something is composed of only two elements or two parts. In Boole's logical system of algebra, things either shared a particular property or they did not. His algebra therefore had only two values, the number 0 and the number 1. Boole's system was able to reduce all human reasoning to yes-or-no situations or choices.

It was this two-digit binary code (0-1; yes-no; on-off; add-subtract) that the first computer scientists used to work out programs of logical commands. From the beginning, electronic computers were programmed with binary mathematics. Boole, born more than a century before the first computer, had reduced logic to algebra, combined it with the binary numbering system, and thus offered twentieth-century computer designers a way to instruct a machine to perform commands.

George Boole

George Boole

Success and tragic death

As the self-educated son of a shoemaker, Boole achieved considerable personal and professional success. After accepting the Chair of Mathematics and further adding to his considerable reputation as a highly original mathematician, he married Mary Everest, the niece of Sir George Everest (1790–1866), a professor of Greek at Queen's College and the man for whom the world's highest mountain is named. Boole and his wife had five daughters, one of whom became a mathematician. Boole also received honorary degrees from Oxford and Dublin and was elected a fellow of the Royal Society of London as well as a member of the Royal Irish Academy.

In 1864—in the prime of his career—Boole died suddenly, having just turned 49. An extremely conscientious instructor, he had walked two miles in drenching, cold rain, trying to get to class on time to deliver a lecture. After lecturing in his wet clothes, he soon contracted pneumonia and died.

For More Information

Boyer, Carl B., and Uta C. Merzbach. *A History of Mathematics.* New York: John Wiley & Sons, 1989.

Cortada, James W. *Historical Dictionary of Data Processing: Biographies.* New York: Greenwood Press, 1987.

Hollingdale, Stuart. *Makers of Mathematics.* London: Penguin Books, 1989.

MacTutor History of Mathematics Archive. "George Boole." http://www-groups.dcs.st-and.ac.uk/~history/Mathematicians/Boole.html (accessed on March 4, 1999).

Young, Robyn V., ed. *Notable Mathematicians: From Ancient Times to the Present.* Detroit: Gale Research, 1998.

Born March 3, 1845
St. Petersburg, Russia

Died January 6, 1918
Halle, Germany

German analyst and set theorist

Georg Cantor

As the founder and creator of set theory, Georg Cantor profoundly influenced twentieth-century mathematics and earned himself a well-deserved place of honor in the history of mathematics. During his lifetime, however, he encountered mostly resistance and opposition when he offered his radical ideas on sets and the notion of infinity. Despite his less-than-successful career and his difficult life, Cantor offered ideas that would lead to entirely new fields of mathematics.

> *"In mathematics, the art of proposing a question must be held of higher value than solving it."*

Early life and education

Although Georg Ferdinand Ludwig Philipp Cantor (pronounced CON-tor) was born in St. Petersburg, Russia, he was not Russian. In fact, nothing about him or his family was as it first appeared. His father, Georg Woldemar Cantor, was a successful Danish merchant who had settled in Russia. The elder Cantor was born Jewish but had converted to Protestantism. To make matters more confusing, the woman he married, Maria Böhm, was a Catholic. Georg was the oldest of three children, all of whom inherited a strong artistic streak from their mother, whose forebears included a very famous violinist. As was the practice of the day, the children were first educated at home before being sent to school.

Georg Cantor

At school, young Cantor showed considerable talent in mathematics at an early age, but his father encouraged him to be an engineer instead of a mathematician. The family moved to Frankfurt, Germany, when Cantor was 11 years old, and he was sent to schools in Wiesbaden and Darmstadt. By 1862 when he was ready to attend the university in Zurich, Switzerland, he had convinced his father to allow him to give up engineering for his first love, mathematics. After his father died suddenly the following year, Cantor transferred to the University of Berlin to study mathematics, physics, and philosophy. At Berlin, Cantor was fortunate to study with three of Germany's best mathematicians, Karl Weierstrass (1815–97), Leopold Kronecker (1823–91), and Ernst Kummer (1810–93). Cantor was a good student and in 1867, he received his Ph.D.

Begins teaching career

For two years, Cantor could not find a teaching position at a university and spent the time teaching mathematics at a girl's school. Finally, in 1869 he joined the faculty of Halle University. This was not one of the best universities in Germany, but Cantor felt he was at least teaching at the appropriate level. By 1872 he was an associate professor there and felt ready to marry. In 1874 he married Vally Guttmann, a friend of his sister's, with whom he was very much in love. His wife's sunny temperament was a contrast to Cantor's serious, often melancholy, side. Over the years, they would have five children, and an inheritance from his father partially made up for the poor pay he received teaching at Halle. Even after he became a full professor at Halle in 1879, ambitious Cantor wanted to move to a more prestigious, better-paying university.

Founds set theory

Since moving to Halle, Cantor had been thinking about a concept that nearly all mathematicians since the Greeks hated to consider—the notion of infinity. In 1874 he published a paper in which he showed that by using what he called set theory, it was possible to represent different levels or orders of infinity. Until Cantor, mathematicians considered the concept of infinity as describing something like limitless growth, and believed that logically one could never assign a quantity to it because it simply kept on going. In Cantor's "set" logic, however, the never-to-be-reached limit is viewed as a number itself, which Cantor called a "transfinite number." This number was the idea of infinity made actual or real, he proposed. Cantor went further, however, and suggested that an entire series of transfinite numbers represent different orders of infinity.

In this almost wild attack on everyone's common sense, Cantor had few followers. French mathematician Jules-Henri Poincaré (1854–1912) summed up the opinion of most when he said, "Later generations will regard [Cantor's idea of infinity] as a disease from which one has recovered." Despite such universal criticism, Cantor would not give in. To him, a set was simply a collection of similar things (in this case, numbers). Cantor argued that describing what the members or elements of a set have in common—as well as not in common with members of other sets—and how set elements relate to each other and to those of another set, would prove to be an important problem-solving technique.

Extreme opposition by former teacher

From the very beginning of Cantor's work on infinity, he encountered unforgiving opposition from his former teacher, Leopold Kronecker. As the editor of the journal to which Cantor submitted his first major paper in 1874, Kronecker deliberately delayed its publication. Once it was published, Kronecker made it his life's mission to stamp out what he considered to be Cantor's mathematical heresy (an opinion different from the prevailing opinion). Whether he was motivated by professional jealousy or was truly convinced intellectually that Cantor was wrong, Kronecker went much too far in his condemnation of Cantor and often used his more prestigious professional position to obstruct Cantor's ideas.

From a personal standpoint, Cantor was not up to the battle with Kronecker. As a person whose nature was to submit to authority, Cantor could not seem to defend himself properly. Further, as a lowly professor in a second-rate university, he had little firepower to shoot back at the well-established, Berlin-based Kronecker. Whenever Cantor applied for a post to Berlin—the city where all young and upwardly mobile mathematicians worked—he was turned down time after time, usually with Kronecker having something to do with it.

Georg Cantor

Georg Cantor

By 1884, Cantor had managed to get all his theories published, though they were essentially ignored. Realizing that he had indeed lost every battle and would probably lose the war to his stronger opponent, Cantor apparently lost all faith in himself and his work and experienced a complete nervous breakdown. Although Cantor would slowly improve and do other important work, he was never again the creative mathematician he had been. Even after Kronecker's death in 1891, Cantor often suffered severe bouts of depression and had to be hospitalized.

Despite this burden, Cantor planned and founded the German Mathematical Society in 1889. Always interested in bringing mathematicians together to further their work, he also was instrumental in establishing the first International Congress of Mathematicians held in Zurich, Switzerland, in 1897. Perhaps most important, he helped found a journal specifically for young researchers who could not get their work published in journals controlled by establishment mathematicians. Toward the end of his career, Cantor began to achieve some recognition. He was made an honorary member of the London Mathematical Society and was awarded a medal by the Royal Society of London. He died however in the psychiatric clinic of Halle University on January 6, 1918, never having taught anywhere else.

Legacy

Cantor's life story is tragic because only after his death was he proved not only to have been right but to have given mathematics a powerful new tool to open up entire new fields of research. Cantor's contribution was not so much as a problem-solver but more in the special way he had of asking questions that opened entirely new areas of mathematical research. He was a truly creative mathematician.

For More Information

Abbott, David, ed. *The Biographical Dictionary of Scientists: Mathematicians.* New York: Peter Bedrick Books, 1986.

Biographical Dictionary of Mathematicians. New York: Charles Scribner's Sons, 1991.

Dauben, Joseph Warren. *Georg Cantor: His Mathematics and Philosophy of the Infinite*. Princeton, NJ: Princeton University Press, 1990.

MacTutor History of Mathematics Archive. "Georg Ferdinand Ludwig Philipp Cantor." http://www-groups.dcs.st-and.ac.uk/~history/Mathematicians/Cantor.html (accessed on March 4, 1999).

Muir, Jane. *Of Men and Numbers: The Story of the Great Mathematicians*. New York: Dover Publications, 1996.

Young, Robyn V., ed. *Notable Mathematicians: From Ancient Times to the Present*. Detroit: Gale Research, 1998.

Georg Cantor

Born September 24, 1501
Pavia, Italy

Died September 21, 1576
Rome (now present-day Italy)

Italian algebraist and physician

Girolamo Cardano

Girolamo Cardano is one of the more fascinating characters not only in the history of mathematics but in the history of science in general. A brilliant physician and mathematician who wrote more than 400 books (nearly 150 of which were published), his major work, *Ars Magna,* presented what was certainly the most complete treatment of **algebra** in the middle of the sixteenth century. As the first great Latin treatise on algebra, it was considered one of the great mathematical books of its day. Cardano also applied mathematical methods to the study of physics and was the first to consider the laws of **probability** mathematically.

> *"[Cardano wrote] a little of everything, from . . . the construction of machines [to] the usefulness of natural sciences, [from] the evil influence of demons [to] the laws of mechanics."*
>
> —*From* Dictionary of Scientific Biography

Early life and education

Girolamo (sometimes called Geronimo) Cardano (pronounced car-DON-oh) was born in Pavia, an ancient city in northern Italy that is just south of Milan. (A variation of his last name was Cardan, the Latin spelling.) His father, Fazio Cardano, an educated man who made his living in the legal profession, had at one time been considered a gifted mathematician and also is known to have been a friend of

Girolamo Cardano

Leonardo da Vinci (1452–1519). Unfortunately for Fazio's son, Girolamo, he did not marry the boy's mother, Chiara Micheri, until several years after the child was born. This meant that Girolamo was illegitimate (born without his parents being married) and would be at a disadvantage in Renaissance society in certain situations. For example, Cardano was denied a license to practice medicine in Milan. The College of Physicians initially turned down his request on the grounds that he was illegitimate.

As a youngster, Cardano was weak and often sick. In his autobiography, he describes being born "half dead," and says he was revived "in a bath of warm wine." As he grew, he was often mistreated by his parents. His father never was able to make enough money to keep the family comfortable, and both he and his wife were hot-tempered and sometimes whipped the young boy.

Still, it was from his father that Cardano received his first lessons in reading and mathematics. At 19 years old, Cardano entered the local academy in Pavia but soon moved to the University of Padua. Cardano had decided to become a doctor, and Padua had a great medical tradition. In writing about his life, Cardano said that when a young friend of his died suddenly, he became acutely aware not only of how uncertain life could be but how quickly the young man was forgotten. Cardano decided then that the only way to not be forgotten was to become famous. Describing himself as an "opportunist," Cardano chose to study medicine because it provided the most opportunities for success. At Padua, Cardano excelled and also made a name for himself as a top debater. He graduated with a doctorate in medicine in 1526.

Begins career as a physician

Cardano wanted to practice medicine in a large, rich city like Milan. But when he was denied a license to practice, Cardano went to the much smaller town of Saccolongo, where he practiced without a license. There he met and married Lucia Bandarini in 1531, with whom he had three children. Cardano later wrote that these were the happiest days of his life. However, Cardano was a man of many interests, and one of these was gambling—a practice he had picked up while at school. Some say Cardano gambled nearly every day for the rest of his life, whether he needed to or not.

Finally, with the help of some influential noblemen, Cardano obtained a teaching position in mathematics in Milan. As he lectured in mathematics at the university, he resumed his study of a subject that he always loved and began putting together notes for what would become more than one book of mathematics. Since he was finally granted his medical license, Cardano practiced medicine at the same time. Soon, because of his success in treating several influential patients, he became one of the most sought-after doctors in Milan. By 1536, Cardano had a thriving medical practice and was able to give up teaching, although he still maintained his interest in mathematics. Eventually, he became one of Europe's best-known doctors. Rich men and even kings tried to lure him to their country to be their personal physician. Cardano later wrote that he turned down the kings of Denmark and France as well as the queen of Scotland.

Mathematical contributions

Cardano was not a man to ever waste a minute, so when he was not practicing medicine or gambling, he was writing about mathematics. Altogether, he wrote 21 books on mathematics, eight of which were published. His first book, *Practica arithmetice,* was published in 1539.

Also in 1539, Cardano learned that an Italian mathematician named Niccolò Tartaglia (c. 1499–1557) knew how to solve third-degree, or cubic, equations. At this time, although algebra was used heavily in the marketplace, it lacked the precision and finish of **geometry**. (See accompanying sidebar for more information on Tartaglia.) One thing that algebra could not do was solve equations of the third degree or those in which cubes, like x^3, appeared. These equations were much more complex than simple linear (first degree) or quadratic (second degree) equations. First degree equations (x^1) are called linear equations because any graph made of them always results in a straight line. Equations become more complicated when the unknown factor x is raised to a power of 2 (x^2, or x times itself). These second degree or quadratic equations show their complexity by graphing as a curve.

In the sixteenth century, mathematicians and scientists did not share knowledge the way they do today, and although Tartaglia did know the solution, he would not reveal it to Cardano. Finally, after much back-and-forth, Tartaglia agreed to tell because Car-

Niccolò Tartaglia

During the Renaissance (14th century–16th century), mathematicians were very much a part of the sometimes violent world in which they lived. Italian algebraist Niccolò Tartaglia was only a boy when the French invaded his town of Brescia, Italy. During the massacre that followed the attack, Tartaglia's father was killed. Tartaglia hid in a cathedral, but was severely wounded. Left for dead, the boy had been slashed by a sword and received severe cuts to his skull, jaw, and palate (roof of his mouth).

Tartaglia's mother found him in the church barely alive. Having no resources to help him but her "old wives" knowledge of medicine, she decided that since a dog licks its wounds and heals them, she would do that for her son. She licked his wounds for days, and although he finally recovered, the boy was left with a speech impediment that caused him to stutter. This earned him the nickname "tartaglia," meaning "stammerer." (Born with the name Fontana, the nickname stuck, and he eventually adopted Tartaglia as his name.) Despite his speech problems, Tartaglia made many contributions to mathematics used in ballistics and engineering. He also translated the works of Euclid of Alexandria (c. 325–c. 270 B.C.) and Archimedes of Syracuse (287–212 B.C.) into a modern language.

dano took an oath, swearing "by the sacred Gospel," and "as a true Christian" never to reveal the rule to anyone until Tartaglia had published it himself.

Cardano kept this promise for six years until he learned that the solution had been originally discovered by Italian mathematician Scipione dal Ferro (1465–1526) as early as 1515. Armed with this proof, Cardano considered himself released from his oath. When he published his major work on algebra called *Ars magna,* it contained the cubic solution. Although Cardano made sure that he gave full credit to dal Ferro and Tartaglia in his book, Tartaglia was outraged and began a long campaign accusing Cardano of perjury (lying under oath), among many other things. In spite of Tartaglia's actions, Cardano's book was very well received, not only because it contained Tartaglia's solution but because it presented many new ideas in algebra that would eventually become the basis for a theory of algebraic equations.

Unstable life and personal tragedies

In 1543, Cardano accepted the chair of medicine at the University of Pavia and should have lived comfortably the rest of his life. However, in addition to his own personal problems, such as his compulsive gambling and his obsession with omens (events viewed as good or bad luck for the future) and horoscopes, his family life became a nightmare. The death in 1546 of his wife at the age of 31 left him with three children to raise, and he did not do a very good job of it. When his oldest son, Giambattista, who Cardano thought showed signs of being a gifted physician, married a girl with a bad reputation who appeared to be after his money, Cardano sent them to live with his down-and-out relatives. Within two years, the woman was dead by poison and Giambattista was accused. Despite his father's influence and assistance with lawyers, the son confessed. Cardano is said never to have gotten over his son being convicted, tortured, and then beheaded in 1560.

Cardano eventually left Milan in 1562 for Pavia and later moved on to Bologna where he taught at the University of Bologna. In his autobiography, Cardano describes his years there as plagued by false accusers and even by plots to murder him. Despite his obviously paranoid state of mind, Cardano continued to publish books on many subjects at an amazing rate. Eighteen of his books were published after he had turned 70 years old.

His life took another bad turn in 1570 when he was accused by the church of committing an act of heresy (an opinion different from the prevailing opinion). It is not certain what he did, although most think he was imprisoned for having cast the horoscope of Jesus Christ (c. 6 B.C.–A.D. c. 30), therefore suggesting that events in his life were influenced by the stars. This was unacceptable to the Catholic Church, who considered Christ to be divine. After several months in prison, Cardano was released on the condition that he abandon teaching. After moving to Rome in 1571, he was able to obtain a lifetime pension from Pope Gregory XIII (1502–85) in 1573. He remained in that city, writing, studying, and still casting horoscopes until he died in 1576.

A final legend about Cardano says he had forecast the day of his death to be September 21, 1576, and that when he was still very much alive on that day, he committed suicide to make his prediction come true. Cardano led a turbulent, often peculiar life, but

Girolamo Cardano

despite his failings and faults, he left behind a body of mathematical work that made him a pioneer of algebra. He therefore succeeded in having his name remembered throughout the centuries.

For More Information

Biographical Dictionary of Mathematicians. New York: Charles Scribner's Sons, 1991.

MacTutor History of Mathematics Archive. "Girolamo Cardano." http://www-groups.dcs.st-and.ac.uk/~history/Mathematicians/Cardan.html (accessed on March 4, 1999).

Muir, Jane. *Of Men and Numbers: The Story of the Great Mathematicians.* New York: Dover Publications, 1996.

Pappas, Theoni. *Mathematical Scandals.* San Carlos, CA: Wide World Publishing/Tetra, 1997.

Siraisi, Nancy G. *The Clock and the Mirror: Girolamo Cardano and Renaissance Medicine.* Princeton, NJ: Princeton University Press, 1997.

Young, Robyn V., ed. *Notable Mathematicians: From Ancient Times to the Present.* Detroit: Gale Research, 1998.

Girolamo Cardano

Born August 21, 1789
Paris, France

Died May 23, 1857
Sceaux, France

French number theorist

Augustin-Louis Cauchy

Besides his major contributions to the mathematical aspects of both physics and astronomy, Augustin-Louis Cauchy published seven books and about eight hundred papers in mathematics. During his long career, he did so much pioneering work in so many mathematical fields that more concepts and theorems were named for him than for any other mathematician.

Early life and education

Augustin-Louis Cauchy's father, Louis-François Cauchy (pronounced KO-she), was a brilliant classics student who went on to be a lawyer and to serve the French king in many positions. He married Marie-Madeleine Desestre in 1787, with whom he had four sons and two daughters. Augustin-Louis was the oldest of the children. When the French Revolution broke out the year Cauchy was born, his father moved the entire family from Paris to the small village of Arceuil. As a former high government official who was closely associated with the monarchy, Cauchy's father felt he would become a target of the sometimes murderous radical elements of the Revolution known as "The Ter-

> *"Cauchy is mad and there is nothing that can be done about him, although, right now, he is the only one who knows how mathematics should be done."*
>
> —*Norwegian algebraist Niels Abel*

ror." Cauchy spent the first 11 years of his life in Arceuil, and although the family often had to do without many things, they were in the company of some of France's best scientists.

Augustin-Louis Cauchy

As a youngster, Cauchy's health was poor, and since the Revolution had shut down most of the schools, his father educated him in languages and religion at home. However, young Cauchy soon would benefit from the visits to his family's home made by such eminent scientists as Pierre-Simon Laplace (1749–1827) and Claude-Louis Berthollet (1748–1822). It is said that **Joseph-Louis Lagrange** (1736–1813) recognized the boy's brilliance and warned his father against exposing him to too much mathematics at too early an age. This was interesting advice from a man who was himself a professor of mathematics at the age of 16.

When things had settled down in Paris, Cauchy's father accepted a position with the new government and the family returned there in 1800. At the age of 13, Cauchy attended his first school, L'École Centrale du Pantheon, where he excelled in classical languages. After spending many months in preparation, he then entered L'École Polytechnique in 1805 where he first encountered mathematics. Two years later, he entered the famous L'École des Ponts et Chausses to study engineering. As an outstanding student, he was assigned to the Ourcq Canal project and by 1810 had received a high-ranking commission in Cherbourg as a military engineer.

Begins mathematical career

After working a short time on the Ourcq Canal, he moved to the Saint-Cloud bridge and then on to the harbor of Cherbourg. There, he worked long hours helping to ready the port facilities for the planned invasion of England by French emperor Napoléon Bonaparte (1769–1821). While still at Cherbourg and laboring under an extremely heavy workload, Cauchy managed to do some real mathematical research on his own in 1811. He continued work on mathematics the next year, and it was probably during this period that he decided to make it his career. In September 1812, he returned to Paris for health reasons. Modern speculation about his problem ranges from severe depression to simple overwork.

When his health improved in 1813, Cauchy chose not to return to Cherbourg and applied for an academic position, which he did not get. Although he lost out on several other positions, he continued to maintain a steady output of new mathematical papers. After finally landing a position as assistant professor at the L'École Polytechnique in 1815, he won the Grand Prize of the L'Académie Royale des Sciences the next year. This prize and the many solutions to previously unsolved problems that he was steadily publishing began to bring him a considerable reputation. Soon he was teaching at both Le College de France and the Sorbonne, and students would often come a considerable distance to attend his classes in Paris.

Augustin-Louis Cauchy

Publishes his work

In 1818, Cauchy married Aloise de Bure, whose family was in the book publishing business. The couple would have two daughters. Soon Cauchy was publishing his lectures and was able to produce three excellent textbooks that would stand the test of time. Some think that his three books on analysis and calculus published during this time are among the most important of his writings. Cauchy continued his amazing mathematical output, generating two manuscripts a week. The weekly bulletin, *Comptes Rendu,* finally had to place a limit on the number of pages a manuscript could have, mainly because of Cauchy. He also founded his own personal journal, *Exercises de mathematique,* in 1826.

Difficult as a person

Even as a young man, Cauchy had always been intensely religious, and he often presented his views too often or too strongly. When he was 21 and working at Cherbourg, he wrote to his mother that he was being called "proud, arrogant and self-infatuated" because of his religious views. That he would sometimes bring the issue of religion into his scientific work also did not make him popular, and he seldom enjoyed good relations with his fellow scientists. Finally, his extreme religious conservatism spilled over into politics, and as a loyal supporter of the monarchy he was an enemy of radicals, liberals, and revolutionaries.

Enters exile with his king

In 1830, the July Revolution occurred in France. When rioters gained control of Paris, the French king, Charles X (1757–1836), abdicated (left the throne) and fled to Switzerland. As a strong

**Augustin-Louis
Cauchy**

supporter of King Charles (who had made Cauchy a baron), Cauchy refused to swear an oath of loyalty to the new king, Louis-Philippe (1773–1850), and followed the exiled Charles, first to Switzerland, then to Italy. It is not known exactly why Cauchy felt compelled to flee France, but forever loyal, Cauchy eventually went to Prague, Czechoslovakia, where he became tutor to Charles's son from 1833 to 1838. During these years, Cauchy did little productive mathematical work.

When the situation in Paris improved, Cauchy returned in 1838 and resumed his activity at the L'Académie des Sciences. From then on, his mathematical productivity resumed, and over the remaining nineteen years of his life, he published approximately 500 manuscripts in fields as different as pure mathematics, astronomy, and mechanics. Cauchy died of a bronchial condition on May 23, 1857.

A man of puzzling contradictions

As a mathematician, Cauchy was obviously brilliant and an extremely hard worker. His volume of published work is nearly unsurpassed. As a person, however, success is not so obvious. He was a man of extremely strong religious views, and this attitude seems to have influenced his personality and his relationships. Some described him as a man who took a leading role in charities; others said he was a bigoted, selfish, and narrow-minded fanatic. Although the truth may be somewhere in between those two extremes, it is known that Cauchy's life lacked any real close human relationships and that despite his deep religious feelings, he allied himself with a king who was famous for his scandalous and immoral behavior.

Despite any personal failings he may have had, Cauchy's work survives him to this day. His greatness as a mathematician rested in his ability to focus directly on the fundamental aspects of a problem and then to leave it for others to elaborate upon, while he went on to yet another problem. Cauchy's greatest contribution to mathematics was his insistence on using only the most demanding and exact methods. This compulsion to be somewhat rigorous (which was the complete opposite of some of his more careless contemporaries), made Cauchy one of the first true modern mathematicians.

For More Information

Abbott, David, ed. *The Biographical Dictionary of Scientists: Mathematicians.* New York: Peter Bedrick Books, 1986.

Belhoste, Bruno. *Augustin-Louis Cauchy: A Biography.* New York: Springer Verlag, 1991.

Biographical Dictionary of Mathematicians. New York: Charles Scribner's Sons, 1991.

MacTutor History of Mathematics Archive. "Augustin-Louis Cauchy." http://www-groups.dcs.st-and.ac.uk/~history/Mathematicians/Cauchy.html (accessed on March 5, 1999).

Young, Robyn V., ed. *Notable Mathematicians: From Ancient Times to the Present.* Detroit: Gale Research, 1998.

Augustin-Louis
Cauchy

Born October 26, 1911
Chekiang province, China

Chinese American geometrist

Shiing-Shen Chern

Credited with bringing **geometry** back into the mainstream of mathematical research, Shiing-Shen Chern has had a long and highly productive career that is identical with the growth of differential geometry. Differential geometry is today considered a major subject in mathematics largely due to Chern's work. One of his mathematical discoveries, called "fiber bundle" geometry, has been used by physicists to form the basis of theories about the fundamental forces of the universe.

> *"Today, differential geometry is a major subject in mathematics and a large share of the credit for this transformation goes to Professor Chern."*
>
> —*Chinese physicist Chen-Ning Yang*

Early life and education

Shiing-Shen Chern (pronounced SHING-SHEN CHERN) was born October 26, 1911, in Kashing, China. Kashing is in the province of Chekiang on the east coast of central China. Chern's father was Lien Chang and his mother was Mei Han. As a bright youngster, Chern had the advantage of being able to study **algebra,** geometry, and trigonometry at a grade level that is the American equivalent of junior high. Much more advanced than most other students, Chern was accepted into Nankai University in Tientsin when he was only 15 years old. As a small university of about 300 students, Nankai had only three schools: literature, science, and business. Chern's obvious intellectual abilities directed him into the science school, where he soon discovered that he was clumsy at his laboratory work (which he did not really enjoy anyway).

Because of Chern's problems in the laboratory, his teachers steered him away from biology and chemistry and toward mathematics. Chern was lucky. He was able to study under a Harvard Ph.D. named Dr. Li-Fu Chiang, an excellent mathematics teacher. Chiang also taught modern mathematics, that is, the more advanced type of mathematics, which was rarely taught at the time in China. At Nankai under Chiang, Chern discovered geometry to be the subject that most attracted his mathematical interest. In 1930, Chern graduated from Nankai with three other classmates.

Wanting to continue learning, Chern took and passed the entrance exam and entered graduate school at Tsing Hua University in Peking in 1931. He was the only graduate student in mathematics to enter the university that year. He was hired as an assistant to Dan Sun, who had studied at the University of Chicago. Since Sun's research area was a relatively new field called projective differential geometry, Chern took up his teacher's specialty. Differential geometry applies calculus equations to points on a geometrical figure and creates a more general picture of that figure's geometrical characteristics. During his years at Tsing Hua, Chern began to write his own papers on this subject.

In 1934, Chern received a scholarship to study in the United States. But he really preferred to go to Germany and study under well-known geometer Wilhelm Blaschke (1885–1962). Having met Blaschke when he was visiting Peking in 1932, Chern knew he would like to work with him. After receiving permission to go to Germany instead of the United States, Chern moved in November 1934 to the University of Hamburg in Germany and worked under Blaschke for a year. In February 1936, Chern received his doctorate from Hamburg.

Chooses career in geometry

At this point in his life, Chern finally had to make a decision about what kind of mathematician he was going to be. Having narrowed his next step down to two options, he would have to

Elie-Joseph Cartan

A gifted teacher and original mathematician, French number theorist Elie-Joseph Cartan (1869–1951) began life as the son of a village blacksmith and rose to become recognized as one of the most important mathematical figures of the twentieth century.

Cartan was a modest, good-humored and easy-going man. He especially enjoyed his happy home life. His four children, all bright and talented, brought both happiness and tragedy into his life. His oldest son, Henri Paul, became a prominent mathematician, and his daughter, Hélène, became a successful teacher of mathematics who also published mathematical papers of her own. His younger sons, however, both died tragically. Jean, a composer, died of tuberculosis at age 25. Louis, a physicist, was arrested during World War II (1939–45) by the Germans, who were occupying his native France. Since Louis was a member of the French Resistance, he was imprisoned by the Nazis and executed in 1943.

Elie-Joseph Cartan lived to be 70 years old. He died in Paris on May 6, 1951, after a long illness.

choose between specializing in algebra or in geometry. With another year remaining on his scholarship, he could remain in Germany and work with Emil Artin (1898–1962), studying algebra and number theory. His other option was to go to Paris, France, to work with Elie-Joseph Cartan (1869–1951) on differential geometry. (See accompanying sidebar for more information on Cartan.) Chern was tempted by what he called the "organizational beauty" of Artin's algebra, but in the end, his love of geometry won out and he decided to go to Paris.

By choosing Cartan, Chern chose to study with the leading geometer in the world at that time. After awhile, Chern was able to meet regularly with Cartan. His time in Paris proved especially productive, as he learned much about Cartan's approach and techniques. By the summer of 1937, Chern was ready to return home to China, where he hoped to help improve mathematics at Tsing Hua University.

Shiing-Shen Chern

War alters plans

While traveling from Vancouver, British Columbia, Canada, to Shanghai, China, in August 1937, Chern learned that China and Japan were at war. His ship did not stop at Shanghai but instead went to Hong Kong. From there, Chern went directly to the city of Changsa, China, where both Tsing Hua and Nankai universities had been relocated. After teaching at Tsing Hua for two months, he followed the university as it relocated again to Kunming, China, to escape the advancing Japanese. In 1939, Chern married Shih-Ning Cheng, and the couple eventually had two children, Paul and May. Although he enjoyed teaching during his six years at the university, Chern found that the war had isolated him from most progress in mathematics.

Postwar career

As World War II (1939–45) started to turn against Japan, China began to reestablish contact with the rest of the world. In 1943, Chern received an invitation to study at the Institute for Advanced Study (IAS) in Princeton, New Jersey. His work had especially impressed mathematicians Oswald Veblen (1880–1960) and Hermann Weyl (1885–1955). They offered him the same welcome given to many other famous wartime refugees with special talents. Chern accepted the IAS invitation.

Chern remained at the Institute for two years and did much productive work as well as establish many long-lasting friendships. While at the Institute, he gained considerable fame by proving an important formula. He also became associate editor of the *Annals of Mathematics*. When the war ended in 1945, Chern returned to China and organized a Mathematics Institute in Nanking. He operated it like a graduate school until the fall of 1948 when the civil war between the Communists and the Nationalists broke out in China. As violence threatened his city, Chern once more was forced to leave. He returned to the Institute for Advanced Study by the end of 1948.

Remains in America

In 1949, Chern received an appointment as a full professor at the University of Chicago. He remained there until 1960 when he joined the University of California at Berkeley. He was active there until 1979 when he became an emeritus professor. At Berkeley, he was the director of the Mathematical Research Institute. During his long career, Chern made many significant mathematical discoveries, some of which are named after him. One of his most interesting geometrical discoveries was his "fiber bundles." Fiber bundles turned out to be exactly what physicists needed to try to relate the fundamental forces of the universe—gravity, electromagnetism, and weak and strong nuclear forces.

Until recently, Chern traveled regularly to China, giving lectures and meeting with fellow mathematicians. As an internationally recognized mathematician, he was elected to the National Academy of Science (U.S.) in 1961 and was made a foreign member of the Royal Society of London. Among his awards are the National Medal of Science in 1975 and Israel's Wolf Prize for 1983–84. In 1979, an entire symposium was held in his honor.

Today, Chern is most satisfied by the accomplishments of his many students. Distributed as they are throughout the world, two in particular are noteworthy. The 1957 Nobel prize winner in physics, Chen-Ning Yang (1922–), is a former student, as is the 1982 Fields medalist, Shing-Tung Yau (1949–). Today, much of the credit for the major role in mathematics played by differential geometry must go to Shiing-Shen Chern.

For More Information

Albers, Donald J., and G. L. Alexanderson, eds. *Mathematical People: Profiles and Interviews.* Boston: Birkhauser, 1985.

Henderson, Harry. *Modern Mathematicians.* New York: Facts on File, 1996.

MacTutor History of Mathematics Archive. "Shiing-Shen Chern." http://www-groups.dcs.st-and.ac.uk/~history/Mathematicians/Chern.html (accessed on April 14, 1999).

McGraw-Hill Modern Scientists and Engineers. New York: McGraw-Hill, 1980.

Shiing-Shen Chern

Circle

A circle is a closed curve whose every point is the same distance from its center. One of the most familiar shapes in **geometry**, a circle is also considered to be one of the most pleasing of all shapes, perhaps because it appears continuous and seems to have no beginning and no end. One major property of a circle is that every simple closed curve completely separates its interior from its exterior.

Background

Circles occur naturally in nature and can be found nearly everywhere. They also can be extremely practical shapes, often playing an important role in art, architecture, and industry. Early humans saw circles created when they tossed a pebble into a still body of water and watched as the ripples of concentric circles (circles with a common center) worked their way toward shore. People in more advanced societies saw circles in the growth rings of trees they had sawed down. Whoever invented the wheel understood the practical advantages of a circle, and later inventions like the clock and the compass worked on circular faces. The word circle comes from the Latin *circulus,* meaning "ring" or "hoop." Eventually, the Latin word came to refer to anything real or abstract that looked like a ring.

Area the amount of space a flat geometrical shape occupies; the region inside a given boundary

Chord a line segment that joins any two points on a circle and does not necessarily go through its center

Circumference the distance completely around the outside of a circle; its perimeter

Concentric two or more circles of different size that have the same point as their center; circles that are inside one another

Diameter a line segment that joins two points on a circle and passes through its center; the longest chord possible in a circle

Indigenous people who are original to a certain area or environment; native

Intersection two lines that have a common point and necessarily cross each other

Perimeter the distance around a polygon, obtained by adding the lengths of its sides; the perimeter or distance completely around a circle is called its circumference

Radius a line drawn from the center of a circle to some point on the circle's boundary or edge; it is half the length of the diameter

Ratio the relationship between two quantities, which is obtained by dividing two things; for instance, the ratio of 3 to 2 is written 3:2 or $\frac{3}{2}$

Secant any straight line that intersects a circle at two points or cuts through its outer edges

Tangent a straight line that intersects a circle at only one point or touches its outer edge at only one point

As one of the basic shapes of geometry, circles were studied by the Babylonians and Egyptians, who had their own rules for finding the **area** of a circle (how much space is contained within it). Although a circle would seem to be a shape with no separate parts, there are names for certain segments that indicate their differences.

Parts of a circle

The center of a circle is the fixed, middle point from which every other point on the circle is the same distance. Taken from the Greek *kentron*, meaning "sharp point" or "peg," the derivation of center is connected to the notion of driving a peg with a rope attached into the ground and then scratching a line in the ground with the end of the fully-extended rope while walking completely around the peg. The result is a circle.

The radius of a circle is a line drawn from the center to some point on the circle. This comes from an unknown Latin word meaning "staff" or "rod"; the radius looks somewhat like a rod that connects the inside of the circle to its outer edge.

A chord joins any two points on a circle and does not necessarily go through the center. When two points on a circle *do* go through the center, however, that chord is called the diameter. The diameter is the longest chord possible in the circle.

Any straight line that intersects a circle at two points or cuts through its outer edges is called a secant. "Secant" comes from the Latin verb *secare*, meaning "to cut." Finally, a straight line that intersects a circle (touches its outer edge) at only one point, is called a tangent. This word is derived from the Latin adjective *tangens*, meaning "touching."

The distance completely around an object or a shape is called the **perimeter**; applied to a circle, however, it is called the circumference. Taken from the combination of two Latin words, *circum*, meaning "around," and *ferre*, meaning "to bring or carry," the circumference of a circle is the part that is "brought around." Described another way, it is the total length of the simple closed curve called a circle. The ancient Greeks discovered by trial and error that the circumference of a circle divided by its diameter seemed to give the same answer regardless of how big or small the circle was. Experience would prove them correct.

Circle

Tree rings are an example of circles appearing naturally.

Another way of looking at the measurement of a circle is that the ratio (the relationship obtained by dividing two things) of the distance around a circle to the length of its diameter is 3.14 to 1. (See **Ratio, proportion, and percent.**) This ratio is the same for all circles and it came to be called "pi," or π. Thus, the formula for a circle's circumference *(C)* is $C = 3.14 \times$ diameter, or $C = \pi d$. Knowing the value of **pi** also allows for calculation of the area of a circle. Once the length of the circle's radius has been measured, the following formula can be used to determine the area *(A)*: $A = 3.14 \times$ radius squared, or $A = \pi r^2$.

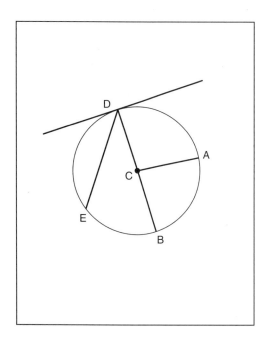

A diagram of a circle. Point C is the center; AC is the radius; BD is the diameter; AC, BD, and DE are all chords; and the straight line outside the circle is a tangent.

The concept of a circle seems to have a place in every culture regardless of **time.** Indigenous peoples do a circle dance, and the ancient Chinese used the circle to contain and unite "yin and yang," or all the opposing forces in the world. (In nature, yin represents darkness, cold, and wetness; yang represents light, warmth, and dryness.) Artists often use a closed curve to express a profound idea or feeling. Finally, logicians sometimes speak of a circular argument. In general, the circle can be a powerful, universal symbol for perfection, as well as for the idea of eternity, since the circle is continuous and seemingly has no beginning or end.

For More Information

Heddens, James W., and William R. Speer. *Today's Mathematics: Concepts and Classroom Methods.* Upper Saddle River, NJ: Merrill, 1997.

Ross, Catherine Sheldrick. *Circles: Fun Ideas for Getting A-Round in Math.* Reading, MA: Addison-Wesley, 1993.

Smoothey, Marion. *Let's Investigate Circles.* New York: Marshall Cavendish, 1993.

Wheeler, Ruric E. *Modern Mathematics.* Pacific Grove, CA: Brooks/Cole Publishing, 1995.

Computer

A computer is a machine that automatically performs calculations and processes data with both speed and precision. Today's
powerful digital computers can perform billions of calculations per
second and have opened up new branches of mathematics.

History and background

The word computer originally referred to a person who computes
or who puts numbers together using mathematical procedures. In
very ancient times, such people were highly valued. Once certain
societies became sufficiently skilled and knowledgeable about
mathematics, they sought mechanical aids to help them calculate
faster. The oldest mechanical computing device was probably the
abacus. The earliest versions involved lines drawn in the sand or
on a dustboard, and it later evolved into rows of bead-like counters
strung on wire, with each row representing a separate power of
ten. Although its true origins are not fully known, the abacus may
have been used by the Babylonians as early as 2400 B.C. Following
this, it was regularly used by the Greeks and Romans and eventually made its way to India. Around A.D. 1200, the abacus entered
China, probably brought there by Arab traders. In Europe, it was

Abacus a manual computing device consisting of a frame holding parallel rods or wires strung with movable, bead-like counters

Analog computer an early type of computer that converts numbers or quantities into another model or form, such as the column of mercury in a thermometer

Binary a numeral system used by modern computers that contains only two digits, 0 and 1; any number is represented by some sequence of the two

Digital computer a modern type of computer that processes information in the form of numbers or digits

Hardware the physical equipment or machinery of a computer; its processor, monitor, and other devices

Integrated circuit a tiny piece of material on which is imprinted a complex series of electronic components and their interconnections; a computer chip

Memory the part of a computer that stores and preserves information and programs for retrieval

Slide rule a device operated by hand that uses sliding logarithmic scales to reduce complex computations to addition and subtraction; replaced by the hand-held calculator

Software all of the programs, routines, and instructions that control a computer's hardware and direct its operation

Storage the memory system of a computer that keeps information for later retrieval

extensively used throughout the Renaissance (from the fourteenth century to the seventeenth century).

The first real calculating machines were developed in Europe during the seventeenth century. In 1614, Scottish mathematician **John Napier** (1550–1617) invented what were called "Napier's bones" or "Napier's rods." These were long sticks made of bone or ivory with a **multiplication** table on the face of each. When they were mounted in a box that looked like a chessboard with numbers in it squares, calculations could be done by turning the rods by hands. This was a forerunner of the slide rule, which was invented by English mathematician William Oughtred (1575–1660) in 1622. In 1642, 19-year-old French mathematician Blaise Pascal (1623–62) invented the first automatic calculator. Until this device existed, all previous machines required people to operate them. Pascal's machine only needed a person to enter the numbers and read the answer, for it performed **addition** and **subtraction** by means of a set of wheels linked together by gears. (See sidebar on Pascal in the **Probability** entry.) Thirty years later, German mathematician **Gottfried Leibniz** (1646–1716) built a mechanical multiplier that was a major improvement. Despite advances made in the next century, these and all other devices were slow and never entirely accurate.

With the work of English mathematician **Charles Babbage** (1791–1871), the focus finally switched from simple calculators to real computers. Babbage spent a lifetime working first on his "difference engine" and then on his more ambitious "analytical engine"—a machine that would contain all the basic elements of a modern computer. The analytical engine was designed to have storage, memory, a way of working between the two, and an input-output device. Unfortunately, Babbage was ahead of the technology of his time, since the only power available to him was steam. To make matters worse, no one could make the precision parts his machine needed. Babbage never did complete his computer.

By 1944, Babbage's dream was realized by a team at Harvard University led by American physicist Howard Aiken (1900–73), who built Mark I, the first digital computer. Today's computers are digital, and they differ in kind from early analog types. Analog computers converted numbers or quantities into some other model or analog, such as a column of mercury in a thermometer. Unlike modern digital

Computer

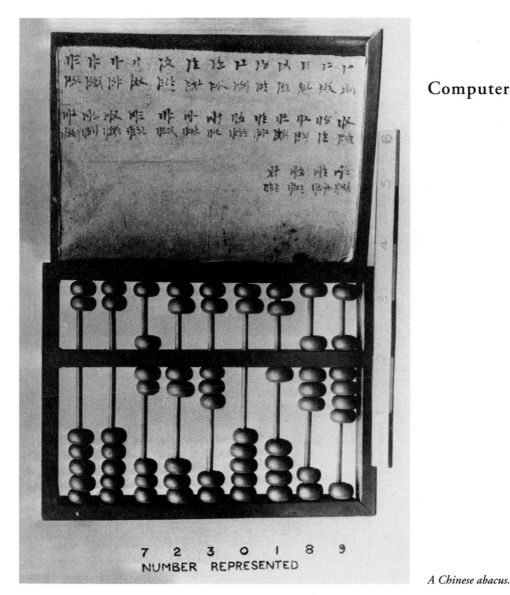

7 2 3 0 1 8 9
NUMBER REPRESENTED

A Chinese abacus.

computers that process information in the form of numbers and actually count them, analog computers had to translate a quantity into some other form. Analog computers had to do many things at once and soon gave way to the speedier and highly accurate digital computer which worked on a binary numeral system. The binary system uses only two digits—0 and 1—and any number is represented by some sequence of those two digits. Since 0 and 1 correspond to the "on" and "off" (or "open" and "closed") states of an electric current, digital computer design is both simplified and extremely fast.

The Mark I computer was a breakthrough but it was not completely electronic. As an electromechanical machine (a mechanical system controlled by electricity), it measured over 50 feet long and carried out instructions fed into it on punched paper tape. In 1946, the Electronic Numerical Integrator and Computer (ENIAC), the first fully electronic computer, was up and running. It was immediately replaced, however, by a computer designed by Hungarian American mathematician **John von Neumann** (1903–57), at Princeton's Institute for Advanced Study. Von Neumann's computer had an internally stored program that carried out all its functions. Stored programs made it possible for machines to carry out their programs at electronic speeds.

The programs used within computers are called "software," and the various parts of the actual machinery are called "hardware." After ENIAC and von Neumann's machines, the history of computers has steadily progressed toward smaller, faster, more powerful machines. The first major breakthrough was replacing the bulky, old vacuum tubes with transistors. Transistors are small, electronic devices containing a semiconductor that acts as an amplifier, detector, or switch. The transistors, in turn, were replaced by integrated circuits, or silicon computer chips. As a result of this miniaturization, computers became smaller as they became faster and more powerful. By the early 1980s, personal computers for home and office use became practical, and by the end of the millennium, computers had become an integral part of most major businesses worldwide.

For doing mathematics, computers offer the advantages of great speed, high capacity for calculation, and an ability to perform a task with endless repetition if necessary. Modern high-speed computers enable mathematicians to collect data and test their hypotheses (educated guesses) on examples that the computer produces. Using computers, today's mathematicians can fully explore a theory that would have been impossible to do any other way. Computers also allow mathematicians to visualize or actually see data as it is presented graphically and to manipulate it and even perform simulations. (Simulations are representations or imitations of an event, process, or system.) Finally, computers enable mathematicians to perform proofs (the step-by-step process of validating a theory) that would be too numerous or too time-consuming to perform by traditional means.

For More Information

Borman, Jami Lynne. *Computer Dictionary for Kids—and Their Parents.* Hauppauge, NY: Barron's Educational Series, 1995.

Shasha, Dennis E. *Out of Their Minds: The Lives and Discoveries of 15 Great Computer Scientists.* New York: Copernicus, 1998.

Spencer, Donald D. *Great Men and Women of Computing.* Ormond Beach, FL: Camelot, 1999.

Wright, David. *Computers.* New York: Marshall Cavendish, 1996.

Coordinate graphing

A coordinate graph is a drawing that shows the relation between certain sets of numbers. The graph also locates a point on a surface.

History and background

The basic idea behind what is today called coordinate **geometry** was devised by French mathematician **René Descartes** (1596–1650). Descartes reportedly came up with the concept while lying in bed watching a fly on the ceiling and thinking of a way to describe the fly's path. While this story may or may not be true, it has also been suggested that the geographic plan of most cities could have been what prompted the idea to Descartes. Historically, a city's main streets are laid out at right angles to each other and eventually form a criss-cross, or grid pattern, of intersecting lines. Locating a particular intersection would be accomplished by having a "set," or pair, of street names and going to the spot where the two meet or cross one another.

The concept of grid patterns is something most people are familiar with today. But in the seventeenth century when Descartes first

Coordinate graphing

WORDS TO KNOW

Axes the intersecting lines of a coordinate system; made up of the horizontal axis (x-axis) and the vertical axis (y-axis)

Equator the imaginary circle drawn around the center of the Earth's surface; a line equidistant from the North and South poles

Grid a pattern of regularly spaced horizontal and vertical lines forming squares, as on a map or chart

Intersect to cut across or through; to cross or overlap

Latitude the angular distance north or south of the Earth's equator; indicated by horizontal lines on a map

Longitude the angular distance east or west from the prime meridian at Greenwich, England; indicated by vertical lines on a map

Perpendicular when lines intersect and form a right angle

Set a collection or group of particular things

wrote about it as a mathematical tool, it was a major breakthrough in mathematics. Although French mathematician **Pierre de Fermat** (1601–65) discovered his own version of coordinate geometry before Descartes, he kept it to himself and did not publish any of his findings.

The word coordinate comes from the combination of two Latin words, *co,* meaning "together with," and *ordo,* meaning "straight row." Thus, a coordinate system can be said to put numbers in a row on a grid of horizontal and vertical lines.

Descartes was a philosopher as well as a mathematician. In 1637, he published his masterpiece entitled *Discours de la methode.* The complete title is translated as *A Discourse on the Method of Rightly Conducting Reason and Seeking Truth in the Sciences.* Although Descartes regarded this title as his greatest work, the most lasting and significant contribution was an appendix or long footnote of only 106 pages titled *La Géométrie.* This appendix contained his work on coordinate, or analytic, geometry.

Description and use

The key notion that Descartes realized while lying in bed that fateful day was that in order to describe the relationships between points on a plane, it was necessary to have a definite frame of reference on which to base everything. Out of this idea evolved what came to be called coordinate geometry, or analytic geometry.

Descartes's invention was essentially the linking of two fields—**algebra** and geometry—that were considered separate. He was able to demonstrate how geometric problems could be solved algebraically and how algebraic equations could be plotted geometrically. Descartes achieved this by creating a grid system using two sets of parallel lines, with each set perpendicular to the other. These lines are called coordinate axes. The point where they intersect (marked zero) is the starting point of the system. Using such a grid system, it was possible to give an "address" to every point on a plane.

The particular type of graph that resulted from Descartes's system came to be called a rectangular coordinate system. This system has pairs of numbers (each of which is called an ordered pair) that are usually written in parentheses. The order of the numbers (or components) is important since the first represents the "x-axis," which

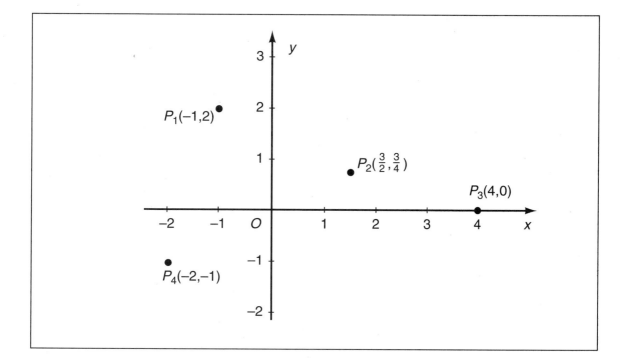

A coordinate graph shows the x-axis and the y-axis, as well as points representing four different pairs of numbers.

is always the horizontal line. The second number represents the "y-axis," which is always the vertical line. An ordered pair can thus be graphed using two number lines that intersect (at a point called zero) to form a right angle. The point on the graph is "plotted" or located on the spot that corresponds to the ordered pair. If that pair were (4,2), for instance, it would be plotted by going 4 units from zero to the right along the x-axis (horizontal), and then up 2 units parallel to the y-axis. The point where they meet, or intersect, is then labeled A. Plotting another ordered pair in the same manner results in a point labeled B, and so on. These points can be connected to form a line graph.

The use of coordinate graphing allows numerical quantities to be shown in picture form, making them clearer and more understandable. Graphs are used to illustrate all kinds of data, offering a consistent format that is familiar and easy to read. This type of system is used every time a traveler must identify a city on a map. In fact, one of the more useful applications is the use of lines of latitude and longitude that form a coordinate graphing system over the entire Earth. The parallel lines of latitude fan out from the equator (the zero point) and intersect the parallel lines of longitude running vertically from the North Pole to the South Pole. Coordinate graphing thus allows every point on the Earth's surface to be identified and located. In everyday life, hardly a day goes by that a reader's eyes are not drawn to a graph in a newspaper or magazine displaying some sort of quantified information. In many ways, it shows the validity of the old saying, "A picture is worth a thousand words."

For More Information

Boyer, Carl B., and Uta C. Merzbach. *A History of Mathematics.* New York: John Wiley & Sons, 1989.

Rogers, James T. *The Pantheon Story of Mathematics for Young People.* New York: Pantheon Books, 1966.

West, Beverly Henderson, et al. *The Prentice-Hall Encyclopedia of Mathematics.* Englewood Cliffs, NJ: Prentice-Hall, 1982.

Wheeler, Ruric E., and Ed R. Wheeler. *Modern Mathematics for Elementary School Teachers.* Pacific Grove, CA: Brooks/Cole Publishing, 1995.

Currency

Currency refers to the actual money, usually coin and paper, being used in a country. Historically, currency referred to anything that was accepted by people as a medium of exchange. Today, each different country has its own basic unit of money called its currency.

Background and history

Currency, or money, has been described as a social convention (a man-made thing upon whose purpose everyone generally agrees). Before there was such a thing as currency, primitive people had to barter to get something they wanted but did not have. Bartering simply means trading one set of goods or services for another set of goods or services. The invention of currency separated the buying from the selling. This meant that if a person had something he wanted to sell, he did not have to find someone with something he wanted in exchange for it. Rather, he only had to find someone who wanted it and who had money or local currency. With this currency, a person in turn could purchase something else from someone (or perhaps save his currency to increase his wealth).

Currency

Since currency is a social convention, the medium of currency or what form it takes is entirely arbitrary. Today, most countries generally use paper and metal coins, but earlier peoples and cultures used such objects as beads, shells, stones, and even whale's teeth.

The standardized and certified system of currency used today is thought to have originated in Lydia (a Greek state in Asia Minor in what is now western Turkey) around the seventh century B.C. In Lydia, a system of metal blocks or coins developed. These objects bore a primitive punchmark indicating that the king certified that each was of the same value. This principle of a government guaranteeing its currency is still in use today. The Greek *drachma* and the Roman *denarius* were both made of silver and were for a time the standard coin of trade in the civilized world.

Like coinage, paper money is also a social convention. The first money made from paper was used in China during the seventh century A.D. Five hundred years later, Italian adventurer Marco Polo (1254–1324) described his first encounter with Chinese currency, which was paper instead of coins. European currency remained mostly coinage until the beginning of the banking system in the seventeenth century when bank notes were issued. (Bank notes are paper issued as money by government-authorized banks.) In 1690, Massachusetts was the first colony to produce paper currency called bills of credit. With the revolution against England in 1775, the Continental Congress issued so many notes called continentals that the expression "not worth a continental" became another way of saying something was close to worthless.

After the Revolutionary War, the new United States set up a new monetary system in 1792, making the dollar its basic unit of currency. As a former colony of England, the United States had used the British monetary system, which had proved to be increasingly difficult. The British system was based on the pound sterling, worth about 20 shillings; each shilling was worth 12 pence. Around 1690, British kings started issuing gold coins bearing their likenesses. Called sovereigns, the gold coins were worth about a pound. This coin co-existed with the guinea, worth about one pound plus one shilling.

To prevent further confusion and difficulty with converting, U.S. secretary of state Thomas Jefferson (1743–1826) proposed a strictly **decimal** system of currency—still used today—along with a decimal (metric) system of **weight**s and measures. While the United States did not accept the weights and measures system, the new monetary system was adopted. Currency was issued in denominations of multiples of ten as the standard unit. The new system proved to be extremely simple and was readily accepted.

The concept of writing and using money amounts in decimal form is basic to this currency system. Therefore, a penny is $\frac{1}{100}$ of a dollar and is written as .01; a nickel is $\frac{5}{100}$, or $\frac{1}{20}$ of a dollar (.05); a dime is $\frac{10}{100}$, or $\frac{1}{10}$ of a dollar (.10); a quarter is $\frac{25}{100}$, or $\frac{1}{4}$ of a dollar (.25); and a half-dollar is $\frac{50}{100}$, or $\frac{1}{2}$ of a dollar (.50).

The euro

On January 1, 2002, ten years after the Maastricht Treaty committed 11 European nations to a common currency, the "euro" will replace the French franc, the Italian lira, the German mark, and eight other different European currencies. On that date, the national currencies of France, Italy, Germany, Austria, Belgium, Finland, Ireland, Luxembourg, the Netherlands, Portugal, and Spain will disappear for good. All those countries will have the same monetary system based on the euro. Of the 15 countries in the European Union, Great Britain, Denmark, and Sweden have not yet decided to join the switch to the euro, and Greece wanted to switch but was prevented until its economy stabilizes.

Each of the eight euro coins will have a common European side (tails) and a different national side (heads). The paper money—consisting of seven bill denominations—will be identical for all.

On January 1, 1999, the euro became legal tender throughout Europe, beginning a three-year transition to the date when the final switchover to the euro takes place. Although the euro will eliminate the regular currency conversions that occur on a daily basis throughout Europe, it will still be necessary to convert U.S. dollars to euros as well as euros to U.S. dollars. There will be approximately 1.1 U.S. dollars to the euro.

Currency conversion

Despite the fact that nearly all of Europe has adopted a single currency called the euro, there is still a need for what is called currency conversion. (See accompanying sidebar for more information on the euro.) This process is the changing of one country's currency into the currency equivalent of another country. To do this conversion, a formula or equation is used that is keyed to what is called the exchange rate. This rate fluctuates daily, but to convert from a foreign currency to U.S. dollars, divide the foreign currency amount by the rate of exchange. Therefore, if a hotel room in Mexico costs 200 pesos, and the exchange rate for pesos is 5.88, 200 is divided by 5.88; the room will cost $34.01 in American money.

For More Information

Cribb, Joe. *Money.* New York: Alfred A. Knopf, 1990.

Early cultures often used such objects as stones as currency. Pictured here are ancient stone rings from the Solomon Islands.

Parker, Nancy Winslow. *Money, Money, Money: The Meaning of the Art and Symbols on United States Paper Currency.* New York: HarperCollins Children's Books, 1995.

Resnick, Abraham. *Money.* San Diego: Lucent Books, 1995.

Wade, William W. *From Barter to Banking: The Story of Money.* New York: Crowell-Collier Press, 1967.

Weatherford, J. McIver. *The History of Money: From Sandstone to Cyberspace.* New York: Crown Publishers, 1997.

Decimals

Decimals, like **fractions,** are used to represent part of a whole. They are described as another way of writing a fraction whose denominator is some power of ten. The decimal system is also a positional or place-value system in that the value of any numeral depends on the place it occupies in reference to the decimal point.

Background

The Hindus in India devised the written symbols for numerals used today (called Arabic numerals). (See sidebar on Arabic numerals in the **al-Khwārizmī** entry.) It is believed that they used these numerals with a 10-based or "decimal" way of counting. The word decimal comes from the Latin word *decem,* meaning "ten." While 4000-year-old Babylonian clay tablets show that the Babylonians used a decimal system similar to today's method, it was instead a "sexagesimal" system (based on the number 60) rather than a decimal system (based on the powers of ten). Thus, instead of "1½" or "1.5," the Babylonians would write "1 30" and use a space to indicate where a decimal point goes now. No one knows exactly when the Hindus created their decimal system, but as early as 250 B.C. a number system using base-ten was written in Brah-

Decimals

WORDS TO KNOW

Computation the act or method of carrying out a mathematical process

Denominator in a fraction, the numeral written below the bar or line; it tells how many parts the whole has

Equivalent something that is essentially equal to something else

Fractional divided into smaller parts or pieces of a whole

Numerator in a fraction, the numeral written above the bar or line; it tells how many parts are being considered

Place value (positional notation) the system in which the position or place of a symbol or digit in a numeral determines its value; for example, in the number .123, the 1 occupies the tenths place, the 2 is in the hundredths place, and the 3 is in the thousandths place

Sexagesimal a numeration system using 60 as a base; used by the Babylonians

mi, a script used in the Sanskrit language. When the Hindus combined this with their already-established numeral system (including zero) and their use of positional notation or place-value, they created a sophisticated and very useful system of mathematics.

With the Arab invasion and conquest of parts of India during the 700s, Arab mathematicians were exposed to and eventually adopted much of this system. Around 825, Arab algebraist and astronomer al-Khwārizmī (c. 780–c. 850) wrote a popular book in which he recommended the decimal system to merchants and mathematicians everywhere. By around the year 1000, the system had spread via the Middle East to Spain where it would later be taken up by European merchants. It was readily accepted by the counting-house experts in large Italian and German shipping firms. They had been exposed to decimals and knew how much quicker and easier they could do their accounts as opposed to using the old system of Roman numerals. In 1202, in his influential publication *Liber abaci,* or *Book on Counting,* Italian mathematician **Leonardo Pisano Fibonacci** (c. 1170–c. 1240) tried to persuade scientists and scholars of the merits of the decimal system. However, the decimal system did not receive widespread use in Europe until the sixteenth century.

Around 1500, German mathematician Christoff Rudolf (1499–1545) produced a book that attempted to explain the decimal system. But it was not until Dutch mathematician **Simon Stevin** (1548–1620) wrote his *De Thiende (The Art of Tenths)* that the decimal system received its first systematic treatment. Stevin persuasively argued that decimal fractions could be added, subtracted, multiplied, and divided as easily as **whole numbers** and that their use made all kinds of computation much easier. After Stevin, it was left to Scottish mathematician **John Napier** (1550–1617) to make the decimal point popular. Stevin's system of notation was very clumsy, and although Napier did not invent the decimal point, it was he who offered instruction on using a dot or a comma to separate the decimal fraction from the whole number. After the French Revolution, the French adopted a metric system of **weights** and measures that was based on the decimal system.

Description and use

The idea of place-value is basic to understanding decimals. Just as with whole numbers, the place each digit occupies gives it a certain value. Knowing that in a three-digit number like 384 the 4 means units of ones (4), the 8 means units of tens (80), and the 3 means units of hundreds (300) also helps a person to grasp the decimal system. In this system, all places to the right of the decimal point represent fractional parts of 1. Therefore, one place away indicates tenths (0.5 = five-tenths), two places indicates hundreds (0.05 = five-hundredths), three places indicates thousands (0.005 = five-thousandths), and so on. The coinage system used in the United States is a familiar example of the decimal system since money amounts are used and written in decimals. A penny is $\frac{1}{100}$ of a dollar and is written .01. A dime is one tenth of a dollar and is .10. Since the ten-based coinage system is used, American youngsters can handle the coin system as soon as they learn arithmetic.

Fractions can easily be converted into decimals, and decimals can easily be converted into fractions. Decimals, however, are much easier with which to work. The decimal equivalent of a fraction is the denominator divided into the numerator. Thus, for the fraction $\frac{3}{4}$, 4 is divided into 3 and .75 is obtained. This method is also the way a baseball player's batting average is calculated (by dividing the number of at-bats (denominator) into the number of hits (numerator). If a hitter goes 3 for 4, then he or she is batting .750. That means the hitter has gotten a hit 75 percent of the time he or she was at bat.

With the availability of inexpensive electronic calculators that solve fractional problems by using decimals, fractions have been used less than ever. The adoption of the metric system (which is ten-based) by U.S. scientists has also done much for the further rise of decimals. Overall, the convenience and easy use of decimals have made them widely popular not only in science but in industry and commerce as well, all of which increasingly depend on calculators and **computers.**

For More Information
Barnett, Carne, et al. *Fractions, Decimals, Ratios, and Percents: Hard to Teach and Hard to Learn?* Portsmouth, NH: Heinemann, 1994.

Bryant-Mole, Karen. *Fractions and Decimals.* Santa Clara, CA: EDC Publications, 1995.

Decimals

Decimals

Miller, Charles D., et al. *Mathematical Ideas.* Reading, MA: Addison-Wesley, 1997.

Patriarca, Linda A., et al. *Decimals: A Place Value Approach.* Orangeburg, NY: Dale Seymour Publications, 1998.

West, Beverly Henderson, et al. *The Prentice-Hall Encyclopedia of Mathematics.* Englewood Cliffs, NJ: Prentice-Hall, 1982.

Born March 31, 1596
La Haye (now Descartes), Touraine, France

Died February 11, 1650
Stockholm, Sweden

French algebraist, geometer, and philosopher

René Descartes

René Descartes was a philosopher whose single method for discovering truth was to apply science—by which he meant mathematics—to all aspects of life and nature. He deeply believed that the **logic** and proofs of mathematics offered the certainty that all other sciences lacked, and that mathematics was both the connecting link between and the key to understanding all the sciences. His invention of analytic **geometry** would revolutionize mathematics by combining **algebra** and geometry to the betterment of both.

> *"I think, therefore I am."*

Early life and education

René du Perron Descartes (pronounced day-CART) was born in La Haye, France, southwest of Paris. His father and mother, Joachim Descartes and Jeanne Brochard, were well-to-do landowners. His father's profession was law. Descartes's mother's family came from the military, and he would eventually inherit enough property from her to stay financially independent. His mother died shortly after giving birth to René, her third child, who was so sickly that he also was not expected to survive. Although he did live, he remained a weak, unhealthy child who was coddled both at home and at school.

René Descartes

As a quiet, studious, and thoughtful child—his father called him "my little philosopher"—Descartes was sent to a new school called La Flèche that was run by Jesuit priests, and he prospered there. The bright boy was a favorite and was allowed to remain in bed as long as he liked and to read anything he desired. This habit of staying in bed and actually working there would remain with him throughout his life.

At La Flèche he received what was then a modern education, and his favorite subject was mathematics. However, after studying at La Flèche for eight years, he believed that the only thing he was sure of was his own ignorance. By the age of 18 then, he had formed an extremely low opinion of the entire state of knowledge available to mankind. He was further concerned that mathematics—the only branch of knowledge he considered to be worthwhile because of its certainty—had not been used to form the basis of more areas of learning. Despite these opinions, he went to the University of Poitiers for two more years to study law.

In 1616, Descartes received his law degree, but decided to abandon formal education altogether and to travel and experience things, or in his own words, to study "the great book of the world." Since he was by now financially independent, he decided to become what can only be described as a "gentleman soldier." A gentleman soldier was a person of wealth who joined an army not for combat but for the benefits of rank, prestige, and travel.

Just past his twenty-second birthday, Descartes joined the army of Maurice of Nassau (1567–1625), the prince of Orange, who was beginning another campaign against Spanish forces who were trying to recapture their lost colonies in Holland. There, Descartes did little but wander and study, but he did meet a mathematician, Isaac Beeckman (1588–1637), who recognized his originality and talent in mathematics and who inspired him to devote his creative energy to the field he loved. It was just after meeting Beeckman that Descartes would discover a way of studying geometry that would eventually lead him to what was to become analytic geometry.

"Which way of life shall I follow?"

Bored with Holland, Descartes left to join the forces of the duke of Bavaria, "without knowing precisely against what enemy they were to march." While his army was settled peacefully in its winter quarters, Descartes did little but eat, sleep, and study. But one night in November 1619, he had three dreams that he claimed gave real direction to his life. One of those dreams was about a book containing the Latin words *Quid vitae sectabor iter?* meaning "Which way of life shall I follow?" Descartes interpreted this and his other vivid dreams to mean that he been wandering in search of truth, and that now he would follow the true path to knowledge.

Thus armed with a passionate mission—the search for truth—and never one to lack confidence or ever doubt himself, Descartes decided to go about his mission in two ways. First, he would always work alone, and second, he would start from scratch and begin his new studies by systematically calling into doubt everything he had learned or been taught. It was at this moment in his life that he uttered his famous words, "I think, therefore I am." By this he meant that the only thing he could be sure of at the beginning of this process was that he existed.

Moves to Holland and begins his masterpiece

After resigning from the military, Descartes spent some years living in France and traveling throughout Europe visiting other scientists. In 1628 he decided to live in Holland since he felt that it was more tolerant to new or radical ideas than other parts of Europe. He felt he was proved correct a few years later when Italian mathematician **Galileo** (1564–1642) was persecuted by the Catholic Church in Rome, Italy, primarily for his scientific ideas.

Throughout most of his life, Descartes usually preferred to live alone. He never married and had few close friends. During his years in Holland when he became well-known, he changed his residence at least 24 times in order to maintain his necessary privacy. Despite keeping his address a secret from all but his closest friends, people eventually learned his address and sought him out (which always resulted in him choosing to move again).

It was in Holland that Descartes did most of his writing, and since he sought after truth of all kinds, he wrote on nearly every scientific subject. He studied and wrote on physics, astronomy, meteorology, optics, embryology, anatomy, physiology, psychology, geology,

and even medicine and nutrition. Finally, his masterpiece was published in 1637 with the title *Discours de la methode*. The complete title is translated as *A Discourse on the Method of Rightly Conducting Reason and Seeking Truth in the Sciences*. Although he regarded this as his greatest work, the most lasting part and that which would be his most significant original contribution was an appendix or long footnote of 106 pages entitled *La Géométrie*. It was this appendix that contained his analytic geometry.

Birth of analytic geometry

What came to be known as analytic geometry was Descartes's joining of two fields—algebra and geometry—that everyone thought were entirely separate. Also called coordinate geometry, this new method would prove useful in **coordinate graphing** and in the making of maps, among other things. By using a vertical line and a horizontal line and marking zero where they intersect, it was possible to represent every point on a line by two numbers. Descartes also showed that this would work for curves as well as for straight lines. He thus showed how geometric problems could be solved algebraically, and how algebraic equations could be illustrated geometrically. Although French mathematician **Pierre de Fermat** (1601–65) arrived at analytic geometry independently and well before Descartes, de Fermat did not publish his research or findings.

Today, anyone who uses graph paper, reads a street map, or studies latitude and longitude (north-south and east-west measurements in relation to the equator) applies analytic geometry. Descartes also was the first to use certain letters in an equation to label constants (which he took from the beginning of the alphabet) and variables or unknowns (from the end of the alphabet). Despite a lifetime of philosophizing and writing in many different fields, his mathematics alone have stood the test of time.

Dies in Sweden

By 1649, Descartes had achieved a reputation throughout Europe as one of the continent's greatest philosophers and scientists. That year, however, he was persuaded by the young queen of Sweden into joining the Swedish court as her personal tutor and the organizer of a Swedish academy of science. The 23-year-old Queen Christina (1626–89) had been writing to Descartes for three years,

René Descartes

Opposite page:
A nineteenth-century engraving shows René Descartes pointing out a landmark on a map to Sweden's Queen Christina.

René Descartes

trying to get him to join her growing group of scholars at Stockholm. As soon as Descartes accepted, she sent a ship that picked him up and took him in the middle of winter to Sweden—a country he called "the land of rocks and bears." The demanding and eccentric queen soon had the frail philosopher, who worked best in a warm bed, getting up and trudging through the deep cold three times a week for a philosophy lesson at five o'clock in the morning. Unable to continue this extreme pace for very long, Descartes died on February 11, 1650, ten days after contracting pneumonia.

Descartes came to view all of nature as understandable by purely mechanical explanations. This applied even to human beings who, he said, did not have a spiritual or non-material side that made them unique. As a result, Descartes tended to shut out any emotion in his life. He was never especially close to his siblings and preferred the solitary life. Although he could definitely be described as anti-social, he is known to have had a daughter, Francine, whom he loved very much. The child's mother was Descartes's serving girl, Helene. Sadly, the five-year-old child died in 1640, probably of scarlet fever. History knows her name only because Descartes happened to write of her in the flyleaf of one of his books. He never did record the full name of the girl's mother.

For More Information

Asimov, Isaac. *Asimov's Biographical Encyclopedia of Science and Technology.* Garden City, NY: Doubleday & Company, 1982.

Cottingham, John, ed. *The Cambridge Companion to Descartes.* Cambridge, England: Cambridge University Press, 1992.

Gaukroger, Stephen. *Descartes: An Intellectual Biography.* Oxford, England: Oxford University Press, 1995.

MacTutor History of Mathematics Archive. "René Descartes." http://www-groups.dcs.st-and.ac.uk/~history/Mathematicians/Descartes.html (accessed on March 5, 1999).

Muir, Jane. *Of Men and Numbers: The Story of the Great Mathematicians.* New York: Dover Publications, 1996.

Pappas, Theoni. *Mathematical Scandals.* San Carlos, CA: Wide World Publishing/Tetra, 1997.

Strathern, Paul. *Descartes in 90 Minutes.* Chicago: Ivan R. Dee, Inc., 1996.

Young, Robyn V., ed. *Notable Mathematicians: From Ancient Times to the Present.* Detroit: Gale Research, 1998.

René Descartes

Division

Division is the process of finding how many times one number is contained in another. One of the four basic arithmetic operations (**addition, subtraction, multiplication**, and division), division also has been described as a way of separating a group of things into equal parts. Division has the same sort of opposite relationship to multiplication that subtraction has to addition, and therefore can be said to "undo" what multiplication does.

Description and use

Since division is probably the most complicated of the four fundamental arithmetic operations, it is best to understand how to add, subtract, and multiply before attempting to learn how to divide. It is safe to assume that division was discovered by early man probably about the same time as the idea that multiplication took hold (which itself was after addition and subtraction). It is simple to see that the problem 4 divided by 2 can be thought of as finding the number which when multiplied by 2 will give 4.

As with multiplication, division is a binary operation, meaning that numbers are divided two at a time. The number being divided is called the dividend; the number by which it is divided is called the divisor; and the answer, or result, is called the quotient. (In the problem, "14 divided by 2 equals 7," 14 is the dividend, 2 is the divisor, and 7 is the quotient.) Unlike multiplication, however, division is neither commutative or associative. This means that the order of the numbers cannot be changed (which *can* occur in addition or multiplication, according to the commutative property) or, with three numbers, grouped in any way (which *can* occur in addition or multiplication, according to the associative property).

Sometimes the division of numbers does not come out even and the number left over is called the remainder. This number is always less than the divisor (for example, 23 divided by 4 equals 5, with 3 as the remainder). Long division refers to the method of dividing numbers in which the problem is mostly written out. It is contrasted to short division, in which most of the work is done mentally.

Division is taught two ways. The simplest and oldest version is called the subtraction model, or scaffolding. This method finds how many 4's are contained in the number 20 by repeatedly subtracting 4 from 20 ($20 - 4 = 16$; $16 - 4 = 12$; $12 - 4 = 8$; $8 - 4 = 4$; $4 - 4 = 0$) and shows that it takes 5 steps. No one actually performs this operation now since it takes too long (although calculators do it very quickly), but it is a helpful method when beginning to learn the concept of division. The subtraction model of division is probably the oldest and is the one used by the abacus as well as by modern electronic calculators.

After the repeated subtraction method came the "galley" method of division. Probably of Hindu origin, the galley method was a favorite until the seventeenth century when the present division system came to be. Called the galley method because the completed calculation was horizontal and resembled the shape of a ship or boat (the galley), this method was popularized by the Arabs. It looks strange today because the divisor was written on the bottom and the subtractions were placed on top. The easier and shorter way of doing simple division can be described as the missing factor method. Once the multiplication table is known, a person can think of the problem 20 divided by 4 as also being $4 \times ? = 20$. This missing factor, or missing addend (a number added to another number), model is the best example of just how closely division and multiplication are related.

The present method of doing division with the divisor on the left of a bracket evolved from a method called a *danda*. Danda comes from the Hindu word for "giving," since this method "gives" a remainder from the dividend after a partial product has been subtracted. After 1491 when the danda method first appeared in a printed book, it began to appear more and more, and by the seventeenth century it had replaced the galley method.

"The Pulverizer"

In mathematics, "the pulverizer" is not a wrestler but rather a rule that uses division to "crunch" numbers and find the greatest common divisor of two numbers. This method was popularized by Hindu mathematician Aryabhata the Elder (c. 476–550).

Born in the royal city of Patna in India, Aryabhata wrote what became recognized as the first major work on Hindu mathematics. This work not only summarized the knowledge of his predecessors but laid the foundation for future mathematical developments in both the East and the West. In India, his book held the same stature as that of Euclid's in ancient Greece.

Division is also identified closely with fractions. Besides being used to represent the parts of a whole, fractions are also used to express division. Although the fraction ¾ means three out of four equal parts, it also means 3 divided by 4. In fractional terms then, the numerator (3) is the dividend, and the denominator (4) is the divisor. Division is also the way a large fraction is reduced to a smaller one, or even to its lowest terms. Thus, the fraction ⁸⁄₁₆ becomes ⁴⁄₈ when divided by 2, and then ²⁄₄, and eventually ½ when continually divided by 2.

Division symbol

The first printed book to contain today's division symbol (÷) was a 1659 introduction to **algebra** written by Swiss mathematician Johann Heinrich Rahn (1622–76). This symbol was adopted and popularized by English mathematician John Wallis (1616–1703) and was used in both Great Britain and the United States, although not immediately on the European continent where just the colon (:) was used. Some math books used in America during the eighteenth century indicated division by using ")("—a pair of reversed parentheses. These symbols may have been a brief version of the traditional bracket-like way of dividing. Very often, nineteenth century Americans—and people in other countries even today—would write the problem "6 divided by 3 equals 2" as "3)6(2."

English mathematician John Wallis helped popularize the division symbol.

Types and uses

As one of the basic operations of arithmetic, division is used by nearly everyone in almost all everyday situations. One of the most common uses is when one divides something into groups of equal size. This is called "division by measurement" when the size of a group is known, but not how many groups. For example, when starting out with 32 baseballs, how many groups are there when 4 balls are placed in each group? The answer is 32 divided by 4, or 8 groups. When the question is reversed—how many baseballs (of a total of 32) must be put in each group to total 8 equal groups—the answer is 4 balls each (32 divided by 8). This is called "division as partition" when one wants to learn the number of parts.

Whether trying to divide a pizza equally, checking on multiplication, or cutting a recipe in half, division is a fundamental tool of mathematics that has proven as indispensable to the sciences as it is to everyday life.

For More Information

Eichhorn, Connie, and Mary Garland. *Whole Numbers: Multiplication and Division.* Upper Saddle River, NJ: Globe Fearon, 1996.

Groza, Vivian Shaw. *A Survey of Mathematics: Elementary Concepts and Their Historical Development.* New York: Holt, Rinehart and Winston, 1968.

Heddens, James W., and William R. Speer. *Today's Mathematics: Concepts and Classroom Methods.* Upper Saddle River, NJ: Merrill, 1997.

Julius, Edward H. *Arithmetricks: 50 Easy Ways to Add, Subtract, Multiply, and Divide Without a Calculator.* New York: John Wiley and Sons, 1995.

Rogers, James T. *The Pantheon Story of Mathematics for Young People.* New York: Pantheon Books, 1966.

West, Beverly Henderson, et al. *The Prentice-Hall Encyclopedia of Mathematics.* Englewood Cliffs, NJ: Prentice-Hall, 1982.

Born March 14, 1879
Ulm, Württemberg, Germany

Died April 18, 1955
Princeton, New Jersey

German American physicist and mathematician

Albert Einstein

Ranked on a par with **Isaac Newton** (1642–1727) as a revolutionizer of physics, Albert Einstein is responsible for changing how we think about space, **time,** and matter. He also introduced a new concept of what constitutes a mathematical law of the universe. His relativity theory suggested that there was an entirely new way of looking at the universe; when proved correct, it became the first real change in physics since the days of Newton. Einstein's mathematics was essential to his breakthroughs in physics.

> *"The most beautiful thing we can experience is the mysterious. It is the source of all true art and science."*

Early life and education

Albert Einstein (pronounced INE-stine) was born March 14, 1879, in Ulm, a city in southern Germany. His father, Hermann Einstein, and mother, Pauline Koch, had long-time roots in that part of Germany. Einstein and his family moved to nearby Munich, Germany, in 1880 when his father's business, a small electrical plant, did badly. A year later, Einstein's sister, Maja, was born.

As a child, Einstein was anything but advanced—he did not even speak until he was three years old. When he did speak, he had so

Albert Einstein

much trouble that his parents thought that he might be intellectually impaired. When he was five, Einstein was sent to a Catholic elementary school, although his family was Jewish. At age 10, he was enrolled in the Luitpold Gymnasium in Munich. By the time he was 15, he experienced some difficulties there that resulted in his leaving the school for a time. One of Einstein's biographers wrote that Einstein so hated his school environment that he pretended he was about to have a nervous breakdown and therefore received a medical excuse to stay away. A different biographer noted that Einstein was expelled from school as a disruptive influence.

It is understandable why Einstein wanted out of his schooling situation. His family had moved to Milan, Italy—his father's business having failed again—and left Einstein in Munich to stay in school. Before rejoining his family in Italy, Einstein was able to convince his mathematics teacher to certify that he was prepared to begin college despite the fact that he had not received his high school diploma. Einstein was interested only in mathematics, and he did especially poorly in Latin and Greek. When he left, one of his teachers told him he would never amount to much. By the time Einstein rejoined his family in Italy at the age of 15, he was so disgusted with German ways that he persuaded his father to apply for a revocation of his son's German citizenship. This was not typical behavior for anyone, especially a teenager, but his father agreed and the authorities granted his request two years later. One effect of him renouncing his German citizenship was that he could return to Germany without being arrested as a draft dodger. From 1896 until he became a Swiss citizen in 1902, Einstein was basically a man without a country.

For most of his first year in Italy, Einstein spent his time traveling, relaxing, and teaching himself calculus and higher mathematics. In 1895, he failed the entrance exam for a Swiss technical school where he planned to major in electrical engineering. He then enrolled at a high school in Aarau, Switzerland, that he liked very much, and made rapid progress. Able to enter the technical school in 1896, he soon grew to hate it as much as he did the high school in Munich. He skipped many classes, refused to study for certain exams, and instead read a great deal of mathematics and theoretical physics on his own. He finally was able to pass his exams with the help of a friend's excellent lecture notes, and graduated with a teaching degree in 1900.

Unable to find a permanent job, Einstein supported himself as a tutor until a friend arranged for him to apply for a job in the Swiss Patent Office in the city of Bern. He accepted the job in February of 1902, became a Swiss citizen, and began what would prove to be the most productive years of his life.

Writes five landmark papers

Since his new job put very few demands on his time, Einstein decided to use it productively and began also to work for his doctorate at the University of Zurich. The level of his work and the range of his thought was such that in a single year, 1905, Einstein produced five different papers, all of which were published that same year in the *German Yearbook of Physics.*

The first of these papers had to do with the phenomenon known as "Brownian motion." Brownian motion was first discovered in 1827 by Scottish botanist Robert Brown, who noticed that when viewed under a microscope, grains of pollen suspended in water moved about irregularly. In his paper, Einstein showed that the pollen grains were being bombarded by water molecules. He also worked out the mathematical equations that predicted the distance traveled by the particles and their relative speed as well. His ideas were soon proved experimentally by others. The really important contribution, however, was the information his equations provided science about the nature of atoms and molecules.

His second paper was concerned with another scientific puzzle called the "photoelectric effect." First observed in 1888 by German physicist Heinrich Hertz (1857–94), the photoelectric effect involves the release of electrons from a metal that occurs when light is shined on the metal. Scientists were puzzled because the number of electrons released was not determined by the intensity of the light but rather by its frequency, or wavelength. Einstein determined for the first time that light travels in tiny, discrete bundles, or "quanta," of energy, named after the quantum theory proposed by German physicist Max Planck (1858–1947) in 1900. Einstein's explanation was later proved correct by the experiments of others. His work not only laid the foundation for several other fields of inquiry but won him the 1921 Nobel Prize in physics.

Einstein is best known for his third paper of 1905, in which he introduced the special theory of relativity. In this remarkable "thought experiment," Einstein turned traditional science upside down and showed that nearly everything people thought about space and time was wrong. Einstein assumed that everything in the universe was changeable except one thing—the speed of light.

Einstein was able to show that motion is relative to whomever is observing it. A person flying inside a jetliner flying at 600 miles per hour doesn't feel that he is going that fast because he is going with it. A person on the ground looking at the jet fly by has an entirely different sense of its speed. Einstein argued that because measurements of time and mass depended on whether or not one was in motion and how fast one was going, time would actually move slower for a person going near the speed of light. It meant, too, that the mass of an object would increase. A baseball thrown at 99 percent of the speed of light would weigh as much as a bowling ball!

Einstein's ability to create mathematical expressions for such a highly complex situation enabled him to accomplish what no one before him had even tried. His final two papers of 1905 extended and refined his work on relativity and led to his famous $E=mc^2$ formula: energy equals mass times the speed of light squared.

Role of his wife

Not long after Einstein began working at the Patent Office, he married Mileva Maric, a fellow physics student at college, on January 6, 1903, despite strong objections from his parents. She was of Serbian and Greek Orthodox heritage and her parents lived in Hungary. The couple eventually had two sons, Hans Albert and Edward. Apparently they also had a daughter, Liserl, born at Mirac's parents' home in Hungary in 1902, before they were married, but the child was given up for adoption and no trace of her remains.

In recent years, there has been some controversy concerning the role of Einstein's wife in his work. In 1990, the case was made that Maric actually did a significant portion of the mathematical calculations involved in much of Einstein's important early work. There are letters to her in which Einstein refers to "our papers" and "our work on relative motion." Also, although he and Maric were divorced in 1919, Einstein gave her the money he received from his Nobel Prize. However, Einstein never publicly acknowledged that his wife ever made any contributions to his work. Soon after his divorce, he married his widowed cousin Elsa Einstein. She and Einstein had no children together.

Gains recognition and refines relativity

Einstein submitted his final paper of 1905 as his doctoral dissertation. The University of Zurich awarded him his Ph.D. the same year. Despite his brilliant series of 1905 papers—any one of which would have assured his place in the history of science—fame did not come to Einstein immediately. After spending a year as a "privatdozent," or unsalaried instructor, at the University of Bern in Switzerland, he accepted a poorly paying teaching position at the University of Zurich in 1909. As time passed and recognition of Einstein's 1905

accomplishments began to grow, prospects began to improve. In 1913, a position was created for him at the Kaiser Wilhelm Institute for Physics in Berlin, Germany, and Einstein became director of scientific research. He held this position from 1914 to 1933.

By 1916 Einstein was ready with his final version of relativity, which he now called the general theory rather than the special theory. He had used the word "special" to suggest that the theory was true under certain special circumstances. With additional work, he was ready to say that it was true in a much broader way. The mathematics behind this work was complex and difficult. When the recognized expert on Einstein's work, English astronomer and physicist Arthur Stanley Eddington (1882–1944), was told that there were only three people in the world who understood Einstein's theory, he is reported to have replied, "Who's the third?"

By 1924, all three phenomena that Einstein had predicted with his general theory of relativity were proved experimentally by others. First, the planet Mercury did move a bit closer to the Sun than Newton's theory of gravitation had predicted. Second, light from a star did bend as it passed close to a massive body like the Sun. Third, the wavelength of light did lengthen as it passed close to the Sun. In 1919, when the first two results were demonstrated by the Royal Society, Einstein became world famous. The public placed him on a par with Isaac Newton. He became a hero to ordinary people who barely grasped his theories.

Leaves Germany and joins the Institute for Advanced Study

In early 1933, the situation in Germany had become difficult for Einstein, who was both a Jew and a pacifist (someone who prefers using peaceful means to resolve conflicts). The Nazi party made it clear that his relativity theories were in conflict with their views. So when the Institute for Advanced Study in Princeton, New Jersey, offered him a position, he accepted. He remained at the Institute for the rest of his life. As war broke out in Europe, Einstein was instrumental in convincing U.S. president Franklin D. Roosevelt (1882–1945) that an atomic bomb could be built. A letter to Roosevelt from Einstein and others led to the creation of the Manhattan Project, which consisted of scientists who successfully developed the world's first atomic bomb. Einstein did not participate in

Opposite page:
A young Albert Einstein stands in his Berlin studio in the early 1920s.

Literary mathematics

In 1935, Albert Einstein spoke of the connection between mathematics and literature, saying "Pure mathematics is, in its way, the poetry of logical ideas." The fact is, several well-known writers have in some way been concerned with mathematics.

One of the earliest and most famous of these was English poet Geoffrey Chaucer (c. 1340–1400), who wrote a book to teach his son how to use an astrolabe. Medieval astronomers used this ancient instrument to measure the altitude of the sun, stars, and planets. Users needed to have a knowledge of geometry and ratios. In his *Poetry and Tales,* American poet and story writer Edgar Allen Poe (1809–49) discusses algebra and geometry in at least two of his stories. In three of his popular novels, French writer Jules Verne (1828–1905) mentions geometric communication with terrestrials and the mathematics necessary for space voyages. And American writer Edna St. Vincent Millay (1892–1950) wrote a poem on the beauty of mathematics entitled, "Euclid Alone Has Looked on Beauty Bare."

that project although he became a U.S. citizen in 1940. After the war, he lent his support to the causes of nuclear disarmament (removal of nuclear arms), world government, and the movement to create a Jewish state in the Middle East.

A list of his honors and awards is far too numerous to state. At the time of his death on April 18, 1955, he was certainly the world's best known and most widely admired scientist. The name Einstein had become synonymous with genius.

For More Information

Cwiklik, Robert. *Albert Einstein and the Theory of Relativity.* New York: Barron's Educational Series, 1987.

Daintith, John, et al. *Biographical Encyclopedia of Scientists.* London: Institute of Physics Publishing, 1994.

Gleick, James. *"Albert Einstein." Time,* March 29, 1999, pp. 75–78.

Goldberg, Jake. *Albert Einstein.* New York: Franklin Watts, 1996.

Goldenstern, Joyce. *Albert Einstein: Physicist and Genius.* Springfield, NJ: Enslow Publishers, 1995.

Hammontree, Marie. *Albert Einstein: Young Thinker.* New York: Aladdin, 1986.

Ireland, Karin. *Albert Einstein.* Englewood Cliffs, NJ: Silver Burdett Press, 1989.

MacTutor History of Mathematics Archive. "Albert Einstein." http://www-groups.dcs.st-and.ac.uk/~history/Mathematicians/Einstein.html (accessed on April 14, 1999).

McPherson, Stephanie Sammartino. *Ordinary Genius: The Story of Albert Einstein.* Minneapolis: Carolrhoda Books, 1995.

Young, Robyn V., ed. *Notable Mathematicians: From Ancient Times to the Present.* Detroit: Gale Research, 1998.

Born March 26, 1913
Budapest, Hungary

Died September 20, 1996
Warsaw, Hungary

Hungarian computer scientist and number theorist

Paul Erdös

Considered one of the great mathematicians of the twentieth century, the legendary and highly eccentric Paul Erdös has been described as "the prince of problem solvers and the absolute monarch of problem posers." Having written more than 1,500 papers, Erdös was a true genius whose gift was to pose problems that pointed the way to productive new areas of mathematical research. He also has been credited with laying the foundation of computer science by establishing the field known as discrete mathematics.

> *"My brain is open."*

Early life and education

Paul Erdös (pronounced AIR-dosh) was born in Budapest, Hungary, just before World War I (1914–18) broke out. Both his parents were high school mathematics teachers. His father, Lajos, was captured during the war by the Russian army and spent six years as a prisoner in Siberia. His mother, Anna, became extremely protective of young Paul after his two older sisters died of scarlet fever, just days before Paul was born. Anna so pampered her only surviving child that he never really learned to do the everyday things that most adults take for granted. Some say he never even buttered his own bread until he was 21.

Paul Erdös

A true child prodigy (an extremely smart individual), Erdös could multiply three-digit numbers in his head at the age of three. In a 1979 interview, Erdös recalls his first awareness of negative numbers: "It was fairly obvious that I could calculate very well when I was four. At that age I told my mother that if you take away 250 from 100, you have 150 below 0." Erdös was first schooled at home by his parents and a governess (a person who helps teach children at home). He finally went to school, but his mother abruptly took him out when his father became a prisoner of war. She taught Erdös herself after that.

Erdös entered the University of Budapest at the age of 17, and by the time he was 20, he had already discovered a proof for Chebyshev's theorem. This theorem says that for each **integer** greater than one, there is always ay least one **prime number** between it and its double. By the time Erdös was 21, he had already received a Ph.D. in mathematics from the University of Budapest. That same year (1934), he left Hungary to complete a postdoctoral fellowship in Manchester, England. As Erdös was Jewish, Hungary and most of Europe was a dangerous place for him. So he went to the United States in 1938. This proved to be a wise decision, as four of his relatives would be murdered during the Nazi reign of terror that was to come.

Begins unique traveling lifestyle

Erdös once told a journalist, "I have a basic character that I always wanted to be different from other people. It's very, very much ingrained. From an early age I automatically resisted pressure to be like others." Erdös would eventually resist "being like others" so well that he would invent a truly unique lifestyle that included no permanent home and no formal job. Further, he would study mathematics as often as 19 hours a day, 7 days a week. He never married or even dated another person. His working style has been described as "one life-long, continuous lecture tour."

To concentrate absolutely on his one and only love, mathematics, Erdös arranged (or ignored) the details of everyday life so that he did not have to bother with the things that occupy so much of everyone else's time. Money, property, clothing, and even social and personal relationships either did not exist for him or existed only so he could do the one thing he loved—mathematical research and problem-solving.

Described by his biographer, Paul Hoffman, as "probably the most eccentric mathematician in the world," Erdös spent the bulk of his adult life literally living out of a suitcase. Except for some years in the 1950s when he was not allowed to enter the United States (because some U.S. congressmen believed he might have Communist sympathies), his life was a continuous series of going from one meeting or seminar to another. (During those years, Erdös lived mostly in Israel.) A typical visit with a mathematical colleague meant that Erdös would arrive confident of his welcome. He would expect his host to lodge him, feed him, do his laundry or anything else he needed, and arrange for him to get to his next destination. Incredibly, there were always plenty of hosts who were willing to put up with him. This was a man who slept only three to five hours a night and who might wake his hosts in the middle of the night by banging pans to say that he was getting wet because a window in his room was open!

Collaborative professional style

More than probably any mathematician, Erdös sought out other mathematicians with whom he would work (and share the credit), usually resulting in a co-authored paper. Often he would look for younger mathematicians and encourage them to work on problems that he had not solved. He created an awards system as an incentive and would pay as much as $3,000 for a solution. Erdös often sought out problems that appeared simple, but in fact were not. He was especially fascinated by problems involving number relationships. He also established prizes in Hungary and Israel to recognize outstanding young mathematicians. Erdös himself won several awards and prizes, one of which, the Wolf Prize in Mathematics, gave him $50,000. He also received a small salary from the Hungarian Academy of Sciences and was usually paid by the universities he visited. With minimal expenses of his own, Erdös was able to endow scholarships and give money awards.

Because of his constant travel, Erdös met and collaborated with so many individuals that his friends invented the term "Erdös number" to describe their close connections to him, as well as to show how much they thought of him. The system worked this

Paul Erdös

Paul Erdös

way. If someone co-authored a paper with Erdös, they had an Erdös number of one. If someone worked with someone else who had worked with Erdös, that person had an Erdös number of two, and so on. According to his obituary in *The New York Times,* 458 persons had an Erdös number of one; an additional 4,500 could claim an Erdös number of two. Given that he published more than 1,500 papers in his lifetime, these large numbers are not surprising.

Genuine eccentric

As a truly unique individual whose genuine strangeness made him so likeable, Erdös understandably left many stories behind when he died. In fact, the circumstances of his death at 83 years of age were oddly close to the way he wanted to die. He once said, "I want to be giving a lecture, finishing up an important proof on the blackboard, when someone in the audience shouts out, 'What about the general case?' I'll turn to the audience and smile. 'I leave that to the next generation,' I'll say, and then I'll keel over." Erdös nearly got his wish, dying of a heart attack at a mathematics conference in Warsaw, Poland. Although he was not in the middle of a lecture, he had indeed solved a problem—his last—the day before.

Paul Erdös was a man described both as one of this century's great mathematicians and as one of the world's worst houseguests. He was a person who was hopeless with material things yet valued people and was always kind to them. Naturally hyperactive, he also drank a great deal of espresso (very strong coffee) and even took amphetamines (drugs that stimulate the nervous system). When friends worried about the pace of his life and asked him to normalize it a bit, he would say, "There is plenty of time to rest in the grave."

For More Information

Albers, Donald J., and G. L. Alexanderson, eds. *Mathematical People: Profiles and Interviews.* Boston: Birkhauser Boston, 1985.

Hoffman, Paul. "Man of Numbers." *Discover,* July 1998, p. 118–23.

Hoffman, Paul. *The Man Who Loved Only Numbers: The Story of Paul Erdös and the Search for Mathematical Truth.* New York: Hyperion, 1998.

Hoffman, Paul. *Paul Erdös.* http://www.paulerdos.com (accessed on March 5, 1999).

Lemonick, Michael D. "Paul Erdös: The Oddball's Oddball." *Time,* March 29, 1999, p. 134.

Mackenzie, Dana. "Homage to an Itinerant Master." *Science,* February 7, 1997, p. 759.

MacTutor History of Mathematics Archive. "Paul Erdös." http://www-groups.dcs.st-and.ac.uk/~history/Mathematicians/Erdos.html (accessed on March 5, 1999).

Schechter, Bruce. *My Brain Is Open: The Mathematical Journeys of Paul Erdös.* New York: Simon & Schuster, 1998.

Young, Robyn V., ed. *Notable Mathematicians: From Ancient Times to the Present.* Detroit: Gale Research, 1998.

Paul Erdös

Born c. 325 B.C.
Egypt (presumably)

Died c. 270 B.C.
Alexandria, Egypt (presumably)

Greek geometer and logician

Euclid of Alexandria

Regarded as the founder of **geometry,** Euclid is by far the most influential mathematician of all time. Until the twentieth century, his name alone was a synonym for geometry. ("Did you read your Euclid?" the teacher would ask). Although not an original mathematician, his greatest contribution was to collect in one book, known as the *Elements,* all the important parts of the best work done by the Greek mathematicians who preceded him. This masterful work became both a model for the logical method as well as the standard text on geometry for well over 2,000 years.

> *"There is no royal road to geometry."*

Few facts of his life

Very little is known about the man who would become so influential to mathematics. Only two things are certain. Euclid (pronounced YOO-clud) taught in Alexandria, Egypt, after Plato (c. 428–348 B.C.) but before **Archimedes of Syracuse** (287–212 B.C.). Some believe that Euclid may have been a student at Plato's Academy (which continued long after Plato's death). As to Euclid's place of birth, no one knows for sure. Early Arab writers said he was a Greek born in Tyre (on the southern coast of what is now

Lebanon), but he may have been Egyptian. His arrival in Alexandria came about ten years after that city's founding by Alexander the Great (356–323 B.C.) in 332 B.C. By then Alexander was dead, but his city was ruled by Ptolemy I (c. 367–282 B.C.).

King Ptolemy began what might be described as a research institute that was called the Museum. The Museum was established as a great center of learning, and besides employing a staff of professional teachers, it housed the world's largest library. At one point, some 500,000 volumes were reportedly collected there. Euclid was among the first of the scholars to be associated with the Museum, and he established his own school of mathematics there.

Those who mention Euclid in their writings always describe him as a wise, patient, and kind teacher and as a good-natured, modest man who was completely devoted to the study of mathematics. Some insight into his personality is gained by two quotes attributed to him. When asked by King Ptolemy himself, who was observing a geometry class that Euclid was teaching, whether there was a shorter way to master the subject, Euclid replied with his famous quotation, "There is no royal road to geometry." Another time when a student asked, "What will I get by learning these difficult things?" Euclid ordered that he be given a Greek coin, "for he must make a profit from what he learns." In such ways, Euclid made the points that in mathematics, short-cuts (even for kings) cannot replace study and practice, and students should appreciate the subject for its own sake.

As with the place of his birth, it is not known where Euclid died, although it is assumed he remained in Alexandria. The date he died is guessed to be around 270 B.C.

Euclid's *Elements*

Next to the Bible, Euclid's *Elements* is probably the most reproduced book in the Western world. Since the invention of mechanical printing around 1455, more than 1,000 editions have appeared. Before that, of course, it had an earlier life of over 1,500 years in manuscript (handwritten) form. Throughout, it has never stopped being used or being influential, and most of the elementary geometry taught today is based on it.

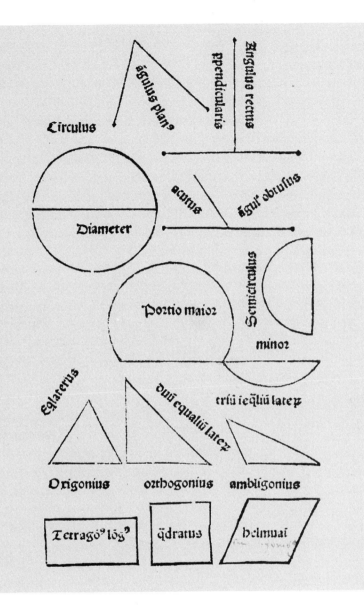

Euclid of Alexandria

Geometric diagrams from a page in Euclid's Elements.

In writing the *Elements,* Euclid wisely selected the most important mathematical axioms (statements that are assumed true without proof) created by the Greek masters who had gone before him. By skillfully weaving them all together, he was able to unify 300 years of Greek mathematical thought. His work was much more than simply putting pieces together, however; the book's success is entirely due to how he presented and handled the work of others. Not only did he carefully choose which axioms to include but he arranged the theorems himself and offered his own proofs and demonstrations in a clear, skillful, and highly logical manner.

It is ironic that nowhere in the *Elements,* probably the most influential textbook in history and one that molded all geometrical thinking, did Euclid ever use the word "geometry." Perhaps Euclid deliberately avoided using the word because in his time it meant "earth measurement," and his book dealt with much more than that. Centuries later, the word "Géométrie" appeared on the printed page. In the first printed version published in Venice (now part of Italy) in 1482, the Latin title page reads "elementorum Euclidis" (the elements or basics of Euclid), which accounts for why it came to be popularly known as the *Elements.*

Besides the specific mathematics contained in its 13 books, the *Elements* is famed for shaping the way people in the West thought about and actually solved problems. The logical method that Euclid laid down involved several orderly steps. First, one states axioms; then, one demonstrates by a clear line of reasoning that something else must follow or flow from those given truths or axioms. This creates a pattern of thinking that moves from the given A, then to B, and finally to C. This kind of reasoning is called synthetic, or deductive, when it proceeds from the known to the unknown in logical steps. Not only did these careful steps suit the teaching of mathematics perfectly but this method became the standard procedure for scientific investigation centuries later. As a method of logical thinking, it was used by the young Abraham Lincoln (1809–65), who later wrote that studying Euclid improved his mind and increased his "powers of **logic** and language."

The *Elements* is divided into 13 books or chapters, only the first six of which deal with plane geometry. The last seven books deal mainly with the more complicated number theory, irrational numbers, and solid geometry. (See also **Rational and irrational numbers.**) In those first six books of elementary geometry, Euclid proceeds in a most systematic and sometimes extremely dull manner to logically describe and establish the most basic and simple truths that everyone can agree on about lines, points, **circles,** and simple shapes.

Euclid based his thinking on only ten basic axioms that are very simple and obvious. Some of these are well-known and still quoted today, such as, "The whole is greater than the part" or "All right angles are equal to each other." While overly simple and obvious, in geometry the axioms represent the rules of the game from which all geometry follows. What Euclid eventually produced were simple theorems or conclusions that could be demonstrated and proved. Once proved, these simpler theorems would, in turn, lead to more elaborate theorems. Like a sound, well-constructed building, Euclid's geometry contained parts that were all related and tied to one another.

Importance of *Elements*

Euclid's contribution to geometry was more than just the creation of a useful mathematical tool to study the shapes and sizes of figures. It also went beyond him showing both the beauty and usefulness of geometry. Most important of all was its demonstration of what can

Eratosthenes measures the Earth

One of the more unappreciated but really spectacular feats demonstrating the uses of geometry was achieved by Greek mathematician and astronomer Eratosthenes. While he was librarian of the university at Alexandria, Eratosthenes (pronounced air-uh-TOS-thuh-neez) correctly calculated the circumference of the Earth (the distance completely around the globe). His estimate of around 25,000 miles is within one percent of today's estimate.

The method Eratosthenes used was ingenious, yet simple. The measurements he made during the summer solstice (the sun's highest point in the sky) showed that when the sun was directly overhead where he stood in Alexandria, it was at the same time seven degrees from its high point at the city of Syrene in southern Egypt. To him, this meant that the Earth's surface must be curved rather than flat. He then realized that it would be possible to calculate the size of the Earth (or find its circumference or perimeter) by using the known distance between these two actual places. His calculations were naturally based on the assumption that the Earth is a sphere, or round (and thus has a total of 360 degrees).

Nearly two thousand years later, when Christopher Columbus (1451–1506) was planning his voyage east, Eratosthenes' estimate of 25,000 miles was considered far too large, and it was dismissed by nearly everyone. It is almost certain that Columbus would have never left Spain had he known how vast a sea he had to cross before reaching any land.

be achieved by human beings who use their natural powers of reasoning to think logically and systematically.

Euclid built an entire, and at times very complex, mathematical system from only ten simple principles or axioms. From his example, people in the West learned that some very powerful and profound ideas can be discovered by properly using the power of reason. Euclid not only inspired people but he showed them a step-by-step method of how to reason properly, as well as how to tell when something was not reasonable. In many ways then, Euclid is not only the father of geometry, but he is also the teacher, through his geometry, of the science of logic.

Euclid of Alexandria

Although a few works of Euclid's besides the *Elements* do exist, other very significant works in which he went far beyond it are lost. Such scientific greats as **Galileo** (1564–1642) and **Isaac Newton** (1642–1727) are known to have been inspired and influenced by Euclid. It was Eratosthenes (c. 276–c. 194 B.C.), however, a friend of Archimedes, who studied at Alexandria after Euclid, who first demonstrated to the world the usefulness of geometry. As a geographer as well as a mathematician, Eratosthenes used Euclid's theorems to devise a practical method of measuring the circumference of the Earth. He not only was extremely accurate but also demonstrated (around 240 B.C.) that the Earth was round. Such is the power of Euclid's geometry. (See accompanying sidebar for more information on Eratosthenes.)

For More Information

Abbott, David, ed. *The Biographical Dictionary of Scientists: Mathematicians.* New York: Peter Bedrick Books, 1986.

Burton, David M. *Burton's History of Mathematics.* Dubuque, IA: Wm. C. Brown Publishers, 1995.

MacTutor History of Mathematics Archive. "Euclid of Alexandria." http://www-groups.dcs.st-and.ac.uk/~history/Mathematicians/Euclid.html (accessed on April 15, 1999).

Simmons, George F. *Calculus Gems: Brief Lives and Memorable Mathematics.* New York: McGraw-Hill, 1992.

Young, Robyn V., ed. *Notable Mathematicians: From Ancient Times to the Present.* Detroit: Gale Research, 1998.

Born April 15, 1707
Basel, Switzerland

Died September 18, 1783
St. Petersburg, Russia

Swiss geometer, physicist, and number theorist

Leonhard Euler

Recognized as the most prolific mathematician of all time, Leonhard Euler wrote so many papers and books that he may even be one of the most prolific writers on any serious subject. He made significant contributions to several mathematical fields and expanded the scope of nearly every branch of mathematics. He was also a brilliant teacher and had a deep influence on the teaching of mathematics.

> *"I can do just what I wish [in my research]. . . . [King Frederick of Germany] calls me his professor, and I think I am the happiest man in the world."*

Early life and education

Leonhard Euler (pronounced OY-lur) was born in Basel, Switzerland, to Paul Euler and Marguerite Brucker and was the first of their six children. His father was a Protestant minister, as was his mother's father. (Euler's parents expected him to study religion and make it his profession.) Euler spent his childhood in the nearby village of Riehen, where his father was in charge of a parish in 1708. The family was not well-off and lived for some time in a two-room house. Although Euler had a photographic memory and was so advanced that he received his master's degree at the age of 16, few stories tell of his being a child prodigy (someone with an exceptionally high level of intelli-

The Bernoulli family

The remarkable Bernoulli family of Switzerland produced eight noted mathematicians over a span of three generations during the seventeenth and eighteenth centuries. Originating in Antwerp, Belgium, the family left there because of religious persecution and settled first in Frankfurt, Germany, and finally in Basel, Switzerland.

Jakob Bernoulli (1654–1705) was the first mathematician of the clan, despite his father's opposition. Jakob is best known for his work on probability. His brother, Johann (1667–1748; shown at left), also went against his father's wishes and became a mathematician; he pioneered the development of calculus.

The brothers were very competitive and were often involved in many disagreements. Johann's son, Daniel (1700–82), was an extremely talented mathematician and was actually tossed out of his father's house for winning a competition that his father had expected to win. There were two more Johanns, another Jakob, and two more Nikolauses—all mathematicians. To make matters more confusing, some family members used French versions of their first names (so, sometimes, Jakob was Jacques and Johann was Jean). Their surname remained unchanged however, and today there are at least six mathematical theorems, equations, or functions named after a Bernoulli.

gence). Evidence of his very early intellectual ability is seen in his studying and understanding a particularly difficult book on **algebra** that dated back to the sixteenth century.

Euler first attended school in Basel where his grandmother lived. However, mathematics was not taught there, so he was tutored privately by a university student. Although Euler's father was a minister, he appreciated mathematics more than most since he himself had studied mathematics under the great Swiss mathematician, Jakob Bernoulli (1654–1705). (See accompanying sidebar for more information on the Bernoulli family.)

Not quite fourteen, Euler was accepted by the University of Basel where he studied philosophy and law. At that time, the university had an excellent reputation in Europe because of the leadership of Johann Bernoulli (1667–1748), Jakob's brother. While Euler was there, he made it a point to meet Johann. Bernoulli advised him to study mathematics on his own and volunteered to help him on Saturday afternoons. Following this advice, he studied mathematics as well as his formal courses and received his bachelor's degree in 1722. A year later he received his master's degree in philosophy and joined the university's department of theology, according to his father's wishes. This compromise did not last long. Euler knew that he loved mathematics too much to simply put it aside and become a minister.

Career mathematician

Euler soon found, however, that actually working in the field of mathematics was entirely different than studying it for the love of the subject. He learned that there were only a few teaching positions at the University of Basel. He soon discovered that for mathematicians beginning their careers in Switzerland, jobs were very scarce. Despite this, Euler wished to leave theology and did not want to succeed his father as a pastor in the village of Riehen.

Daniel Bernoulli, one member of the great mathematical Bernoulli family.

Fortunately, Euler again received help from Johann Bernoulli, who had earlier recognized Euler's considerable mathematical talent and was able to convince Euler's father that the young man's future was not with the church. Although his father agreed, the 17-year-old Euler could not find a position in mathematics. Finally, when he was 19 years old, Euler heard from two other members of the Bernoulli family, Daniel (1700–82) and Nicholas (1687–1759), who had gone to Russia to work for the newly organized St. Petersburg Academy of Sciences. They had been able to persuade the Russian authorities to offer Euler a position teaching physiology (the study of the functions of cells, tissues, and organs of living things). Although he had no medical background, Euler began to study immediately, with plans to somehow apply mathematics and whatever mechanics he knew to this new field. On April 5, 1727, Euler left Basel for Russia and would never return to Switzerland again.

St. Petersburg Academy life and career

Although he had been hired to teach in a medical field, Euler nonetheless was able to assume a position in mathematics that he

Leonhard Euler

held for three years. He immediately began producing top-quality mathematical papers, and in 1731 he became professor of physics at the Academy of Sciences. When Daniel Bernoulli decided to return to Basel in 1733, Euler was only 26 years old, yet he was able to take over Bernoulli's job, which was considered the top mathematical position in St. Petersburg.

Euler found his work stimulating, since he was surrounded by groups of eminent scientists with whom he could discuss and exchange ideas. A man of broad culture who knew several languages, Euler could speak about numerous scientific subjects with the many distinguished colleagues around. He also met and married Katharina Gsell, the daughter of Swiss artist Georg Gsell, who taught at St. Petersburg. Together they had 13 children, but only 5 reached maturity. In Russia, too, Euler lost the sight of his right eye. There are conflicting stories as to how this happened, but both involve his work. One version says that he strained his already infected eye by working too long and hard. Another version says that he injured his eye by staring at the sun too long trying to solve a problem in astronomy.

Euler remained in St. Petersburg until 1741, when he left Russia and took his family to Berlin, Germany. In his 14 years in Russia, he published so much original mathematics of such high quality that he was known internationally. He also made solid contributions and even brilliant discoveries in such fields as the theory of numbers, mechanics, and analysis.

Finally, as a member of the Academy, Euler was called to work on many practical problems for the Russian government. He thus created a test for determining the accuracy of scales, developed a system of **weights** and measures, and supervised the government's department of geography.

Moves to Berlin

By 1740, the political situation in Russia had become unsettling. After the death of Peter the Great (1672–1725) and, later, his wife, Catherine I (1684–1727), the country was torn by disputes as to who should succeed to the throne. Euler decided to accept the offer of Germany's new leader, Frederick the Great (1712–86), who invited him to come to Germany and reorganize its Academy of Sciences. Euler and his family arrived in Berlin on July 25,

1741, and remained there for the next 25 years.

Then only in his thirties when he moved to Germany, Euler's seemingly inexhaustible energy allowed him to continue to write scores of mathematical papers, work for two academies at the same time (he still kept his ties to Russia), publish a book that became a classic of popular science, and carry out the many difficult projects assigned him by the king. He not only had an immense influence on scientific life in Germany but on many practical aspects of life as well. For example, he supervised the Academy's observatory and botanical gardens, advised the government on state lotteries, consulted on problems of insurance and widow's pensions, and corrected problems with canal projects, hydraulic systems, and even artillery. He was held in such high regard that when Russian troops occupied Berlin in 1760 during the Seven Years' War, Euler's house was given special protection by them. It was also during this time that Euler was able to lay down what is considered the foundations of mathematical physics.

Euler the workaholic

No one wrote and published more mathematics than Leonhard Euler. At the time of his death, he reportedly left enough papers behind to keep the printing presses busy for another thirty-five years.

Nothing seemed to slow Euler down—not living the bulk of his life in two different countries nor even going blind. In fact, his productivity increased after he lost his sight. Possessed of a phenomenal memory, Euler was able to repeat Homer's *Aeneid* from start to finish. He could even recall the first and last lines of every page of the particular edition he read!

French physicist François Arago (1786–1853) paid him the ultimate compliment: "Euler calculated without any apparent effort, just as men breathe, or as eagles sustain themselves in the air."

Returns to Russia

Although he worked in Berlin for a very long time, Euler never really got along with Frederick. When Catherine the Great (1729–96) came to the throne of Russia in 1762, she invited Euler to return to St. Petersburg (offering him a large estate and one of her personal cooks). In July 1766, Euler arrived in Russia and became director of the Academy of Sciences in St. Petersburg.

Soon after returning to Russia, Euler lost the sight in his remaining good eye because of cataracts and became totally blind by 1771. Despite blindness, the death of his wife, and a fire that destroyed nearly all his personal property, Euler made his time in

Leonhard Euler

Russia the most productive of his life. Nearly half of the 886 books and manuscripts that he produced were written during this second stay in Russia. One of his major contributions was his research into the motion and positions of the Moon. He also published several texts on calculus that became instant classics. Always a superior teacher, one of his best qualities was his willingness to explain in great detail exactly how he arrived at his discoveries.

A simple, generous, and kind man who was especially fond of children, Euler died of a stroke on September 18, 1783, while playing with his grandson.

For More Information

Biographical Dictionary of Mathematicians. New York: Charles Scribner's Sons, 1991.

MacTutor History of Mathematics Archive. "Leonhard Euler." http://www-groups.dcs.st-and.ac.uk/~history/Mathematicians/Euler.html (accessed on April 15, 1999).

Reimer, Luetta, and Wilbert Reimer. *Mathematicians Are People, Too: Stories From the Lives of Great Mathematicians.* Palo Alto, CA: Dale Seymour Publications, 1995.

Simmons, George F. *Calculus Gems: Brief Lives and Memorable Mathematics.* New York: McGraw-Hill, 1992.

Young, Robyn V., ed. *Notable Mathematicians: From Ancient Times to the Present.* Detroit: Gale Research, 1998.

Exponent

An exponent is a type of mathematical abbreviation in which a number placed to the upper right of another number (called the base) indicates the number of times the base will be multiplied by itself. This process is also called exponential notation.

Background

By the time of the great Greek mathematician **Archimedes of Syracuse** (287–212 B.C.), he and probably others understood that mathematicians needed a symbol or some shortened way to refer to the power of a number. Repeated **multiplication** of the same number was being done all the time. Just as the **addition** procedure of $4 + 4 + 4 + 4 + 4$ required the invention of a shorter and easier way to do the same thing (4×5), so too did the frequent use of $4 \times 4 \times 4 \times 4$ suggest that there was an easier way to express this repeated procedure.

Archimedes used the word "myriad" to stand for the number 10,000 (ten to the fourth power), and also used "myriad of myriads" to stand for 100,000,000 (ten to the fourth power times ten to the fourth power). Over the centuries, mathematicians suggested a variety of different symbols to indicate that a number was being multiplied by itself a certain number of times. Some of these were letters, Roman numerals, circled numbers, and even little pictures.

It was not until the seventeenth century that the modern system of writing exponents was suggested. In 1637, French mathematician and philosopher **René Descartes** (1596–1650) published his great work, entitled *Discours de la methode*. Included in this book was a 106-page section entitled *La Géométrie*, which contained, among other things, a notation system for expressing exponents. The word exponent comes from two Latin words, *ex*, meaning "away," or "out," and the verb *ponere*, meaning "to put." Combined, the word suggests exposing something or "putting it out" to be seen or noticed. When one number is put out to the right and above another number, it is therefore being "raised" to a power.

Description and use

Certain terms are used in exponential notation. The small number above and to the right of another number is called an exponent. The number being multiplied by itself (however many times) is called the base. Therefore, a number containing an exponent is called an exponential number. For example, 6^4 means simply 6 multiplied by itself 4 times ($6 \times 6 \times 6 \times 6 = 1{,}296$). This repeated multiplication of a number is called "raising a number to a certain power." Therefore, six to the fourth power is six times itself four times or "six to the fourth." For numbers that are to be multiplied by themselves twice or three times, however, the old Greek custom of saying something is "squared" or "cubed" is used. So, 6^2 is "six squared" and 6^3 is "six cubed."

The usefulness of exponents is found in their ability to convert multiplication into simple addition. This is not only an easier operation but it is time-saving as well. For example, multiplying 16 and 256 gives a product of 4,096. However, 16 is the same as 4×4, and 256 is the same as $4 \times 4 \times 4 \times 4$. Using exponential numbers, 16 is 4^2 and 256 is 4^4. Adding the exponents 2 and 4 equals 6, meaning the answer is 4^6, or 4,096. Therefore, the exponent of the answer is the sum of the exponents of the two numbers being multiplied. The reverse of this process works also for **division**, in which the exponents are subtracted. Exponents can be broadened if fractional and **decimal** exponents are used.

Exponent

The number of one-celled organisms that keeps a whale alive for a few hours is 400 trillion. Using exponents allows this number to be written as 4×10^{14}.

Exponent

Besides simplifying the work required in certain mathematical operations, exponents have proved useful to science. In many scientific disciplines, massively large and extremely small numbers are frequently used. For example, the number of one-celled organisms that will keep a whale alive for a few hours is 400,000,000,000,000 (400 trillion), and the shortest wavelength of visible light is .0000004 (4 ten-millionths) meters. Writing such numbers is much simpler if "scientific notation" is used. This involves decimal numerals written as the product of a power of 10 and a decimal numeral between 1 and 10. Thus, 400,000,000,000,000 is written as 4×10^{14}. A very small number like .0000004 is written as 4×10^{-7}.

Exponent

A related scientific concept is that of exponential increase or decrease. In biology, many populations of living creatures grow at an exponential rate. In economics, money in a savings account with compound interest grows exponentially. In chemistry, certain radioactive substances experience exponential decay in which they disintegrate at an ever increasing rate. In all of these cases, when a situation grows or decreases exponentially, it means that it changes by what is called an "order of magnitude." Thus the difference between 10^2 ($10 \times 10 = 100$) and 10^3 ($10 \times 10 \times 10 = 1,000$) is by far much larger than what it might first appear. Using exponents in these and other fields allows for the easy recording and calculation of extremely large and small changes and differences.

For More Information

Bergamini, David. *Mathematics.* Alexandria, VA: Time-Life Books, 1980.

Kline, Morris. *Mathematics for the Nonmathematician.* New York: Dover Publications, 1985.

Rogers, James T. *The Pantheon Story of Mathematics for Young People.* New York: Pantheon Books, 1966.

West, Beverly H., et al. *The Prentice-Hall Encyclopedia of Mathematics.* Englewood Cliffs, NJ: Prentice-Hall, 1982.

Born August 1601
Beaumont-de-Lomagne, France

Died January 12, 1665
Castres, France

French number theorist

Pierre de Fermat

Pierre de Fermat contributed to so many branches of mathematics that he was perhaps the greatest mathematician of the seventeenth century. He is credited not only as the founder of the modern theory of numbers but as the developer of the principles of analytic **geometry** as well. Together with French mathematician and physicist Blaise Pascal, he also developed the theory of **probability**. (See sidebar on Pascal in **Probability** entry.) Formally trained in law, Fermat eventually became a judge and King's Counsellor, but he demonstrated such extraordinary mathematical intuition and ability that he is called the "prince of amateurs."

> *"And perhaps, posterity will thank me for having shown it that the ancients did not know everything."*

Early life and education

Although there is some disagreement as to the year of his birth, most feel that the evidence for August 1601 is strong. Pierre de Fermat (pronounced FAIR-mah) was one of four children born in Beaumont-de-Lomagne, France, which is near Toulouse in southern France above the border with Spain. His father, Dominique, was a prosperous leather merchant, and his mother, Claire de Long, came from a family connected to the legal profession. Most likely, the young Pierre was

Pierre de Fermat

sent to a Franciscan monastery in Beaumont, where he received a typically classical education. Details of his higher education are also uncertain, but most researchers feel that he attended the University of Toulouse, possibly as early as 1621. Fermat received a bachelor's degree in civil law from the University of Orleans in 1631. That same year, he returned to Toulouse, married his fourth cousin, Louise de Long, with whom he later had five children, and began to practice law.

Legal career, mathematical hobby

Beginning his career as a lawyer for the local parliament, Fermat rose steadily while working for the government. After being named a judge in the criminal court in 1638, he was promoted to the high position of King's Counsellor in 1648. He would hold this position until he died. Throughout his life, Fermat enjoyed financial security, which likely was a factor in his ability to take time from his busy legal chores to indulge in his first love, mathematics.

Since Fermat was trained as a classical scholar and was fluent in Latin and Greek as well as in other languages, he took up one of the favorite pastimes of scholars of his time: the "restoration" of the lost works of ancient times. In the seventeenth century, classical scholars would try to restore the missing parts or entire works of Greek texts that had survived and were available to them. Fermat chose to extend the mathematical works of two Greek mathematicians, Pappus of Alexandria (c. A.D. 290–350) and Apollonius of Perga (c. 262–c. 190 B.C.). He did not, however, attempt this without a background in mathematics. When Fermat attended school in the 1620s and before he went off to study law, he learned about the works of French mathematician François Viète (1540–1603). Having met some of Viète's former students who were editing and publishing their master's works, Fermat became familiar with the new ideas for using symbols in **algebra,** and began a lifelong preoccupation with mathematics.

Prince of amateurs

Although Fermat was known as a mathematical genius, his life and habits do not fit the typical pattern of someone so blessed. First, he did not show any evidence of outstanding mathematical ability as a youngster nor did he start studying mathematics at a young age. Second, although he truly loved mathematics, he did not let it possess him and take over all aspects of his life. As a busy lawyer, he did not allow himself to work with any kind of passionate intensity when it came to mathematics. This is seen in his refusal to offer time-consuming, highly detailed proofs. He simply could not spare the time to go on and on. Third, Fermat did not seek fame by publishing his work. In fact, he communicated only by letter with other European colleagues and published just one thing in his life, which he did anonymously. Further, Fermat never traveled far from Toulouse, so the people with whom he conducted a lifelong correspondence never met him. All of these factors led to his being called the "prince of amateurs."

Fermat has been described by some as very shy and excessively modest. However, he had a demanding legal career at a high level of government and must certainly have been used to the professional life. Others say that he never allowed his mathematical writings to be published because he always considered it his hobby. He wanted to keep it that way since it allowed him pleasurable time away from the constant disputes that involved him as a lawyer and a judge. Still others say that he did not want to take the time to pay attention to every detail of his mathematics the way he would have to if he were to publish. He also seemed to enjoy stating a theorem without needing to offer any proof or without having to give a systematic account of how he reached his conclusions. Once he established a connection by mail with a few of the best mathematicians in France, he was perfectly satisfied to send his papers to them and not even keep copies for himself. One of these, French mathematician Marin Mersenne (1588–1648), served as a one-man link between Fermat and the scientific community. Fermat gained an international reputation mainly through Mersenne.

Mathematical contributions—analytic geometry

Along with French mathematician and philosopher **René Descartes** (1596–1650), Fermat is considered one of the two "fathers" of analytic geometry. Each man approached the subject differently, causing a long and bitter dispute over who was really first in his invention or discovery. Fermat eventually was shown to have invented his version as early as 1629, well before Descartes (although Descartes is usually recognized as the founder).

Pierre de Fermat

Pierre de Fermat

Analytic geometry can be described as the application of algebra to the study of geometry. When considering both, Fermat thought algebra to be a useful tool but found that its many rules and formulas often made it confusing. Geometry, he thought, while it showed much about the practical world, was often too abstract. Since neither was the perfect system, he thought that if he borrowed the best notions of algebra and the best approaches of geometry and somehow combined them, maybe the strengths of each would cancel out the weaknesses. He was correct. Analytic geometry—a branch of applied mathematics described as the geometry of graphs, or as geometry with numbers in it—has proved highly useful.

Mathematical contributions—theory of numbers

Fermat's most important work was in the development of modern number theory. This part of mathematics was his favorite pastime, and he loved searching for patterns and relationships among **whole numbers.** Many scholars feel that it was in this area of mathematics that Fermat's intuitive genius—in which he proceeded as much by "feel" or hunch as by intelligence and reasoning—was most brilliant. Number theory examines apparently simple and straightforward concepts, such as the way numbers relate to each other, but it is easy to miss its difficult and almost profound aspects. Fermat seldom missed the profound aspects and contributed many theorems (general statements that are proved or believed to be true) to number theory. One of these—known as "Fermat's last theorem"—for which he did not provide a proof, remained unproved until 1993 when **Andrew J. Wiles** (1953–) offered the first acceptable proof.

Other contributions

Fermat is also considered one of the founders, along with Blaise Pascal, of probability theory. When Pascal wrote to Fermat with some questions about gambling and games of chance, a correspondence began that led to their joint development of a mathematical theory of probability. Because of their work, later mathematicians have been able to establish laws that can be applied to situations of pure chance. The concepts they developed are felt in many aspects of modern life, from insurance and quality control to genetics and quantum mechanics. Fermat also contributed to the field of optics, authoring a law on how light travels. In many ways, Fermat came to some important conclusions about calculus before its inventors, **Isaac Newton** (1642–1727) and **Gottfried Leibniz** (1646–1716), were even born.

In 1651, Fermat survived a case of the plague, but from then on suffered from bad health. Although he stopped all his mathematical work and correspondence in 1662, he continued his legal work until days before he died in 1665. Because of his refusal to publish and his relatively casual involvement with mathematics, Fermat's influence during his lifetime was not as great as it should have been. Fortunately, his letters were saved by others, and his mathematical legacy and reputation were eventually appreciated.

Pierre de Fermat

For More Information

Abbott, David, ed. *The Biographical Dictionary of Scientists: Mathematicians.* New York: Peter Bedrick Books, 1986.

Aczel, Amir D. *Fermat's Last Theorem: Unlocking the Secret of an Ancient Mathematical Problem.* New York: Four Walls Eight Windows, 1996.

Eves, Howard. *An Introduction to the History of Mathematics.* Philadelphia: Saunders College Publishing, 1990.

MacTutor History of Mathematics Archive. "Pierre de Fermat." http://www-groups.dcs.st-and.ac.uk/~history/Mathematicians/ Fermat.html (accessed on April 15, 1999).

Mahoney, Michael Sean. *The Mathematical Career of Pierre de Fermat 1601–1665.* Princeton, NJ: Princeton University Press, 1994.

Ribenboim, Paulo. *Fermat's Last Theorem for Amateurs.* New York: Springer-Verlag, 1999.

Simmons, George F. *Calculus Gems: Brief Lives and Memorable Mathematics.* New York: McGraw-Hill, 1992.

Singh, Simon. *Fermat's Enigma: The Epic Quest to Solve the World's Greatest Mathematical Problem.* New York: Walker & Co., 1997.

Young, Robyn V., ed. *Notable Mathematicians: From Ancient Times to the Present.* Detroit: Gale Research, 1998.

Born c. 1170
Pisa (present-day Italy)

Died c. 1240
Pisa (present-day Italy)

Italian number theorist

Leonardo Pisano Fibonacci

A skilled and highly original mathematician, Leonardo Pisano Fibonacci is considered to be mainly responsible for the introduction and popularization in the West of what is today called Arabic numerals. As the most important mathematician of the Middle Ages, his published works on **geometry** and **algebra** also led to the revival of an interest in mathematics in the West.

> *"When I had been introduced to the art of the Indians' nine symbols through remarkable teaching, knowledge of the art soon pleased me above all else and I came to understand it. . . ."*

Benefits from extensive travels

In the last quarter of the twelfth century when Leonardo Fibonacci (pronounced fee-boh-NOT-chee) was born, few Europeans knew much about mathematics and certainly none wrote books on the subject. Fibonacci was born in the northern Italian city of Pisa, now famous for its leaning tower. Back then, Pisa was an important commercial city and had a population of about 10,000. Its merchants traded throughout the Mediterranean and maintained warehouses and even colonies on several coasts. Fibonacci's father, Guglielmo Bonacci, was a merchant and a government representative for the independent city-state of Pisa. Many think that

Leonardo Pisano Fibonacci

Fibonacci's last name came from a shortened version of the Italian phrase for "son of Bonacci," which is *filio Bonacci*. He is also known as Leonardo Pisano or Leonardo of Pisa.

When Fibonacci was 12 years old, his father was made the head of Pisa's trading colony in Bugia (now Bougie) on the north coast of Africa (now Algeria). He took his son with him to this crossroads of cultures, and there Fibonacci began his education in business. His father wanted him educated in the art of calculating, since he expected his son to join him as a merchant, and arranged for him to be tutored by a local schoolmaster in Bugia. This teacher, who remains completely unknown, provided the boy with a practical yet well-rounded education.

Besides getting a basic grounding in mathematics, Fibonacci also came to appreciate the wonders of science. In addition to his formal education, Fibonacci was able to broaden his knowledge by traveling extensively as he grew older. He spent time in Sicily, Greece, France, Syria, and Egypt. Wherever he went, he made sure he met local scholars and always tried to understand the system of arithmetic used by the merchants of those areas.

Mathematical writings

Around the year 1200, Fibonacci returned to his native Pisa and began a successful career in mathematics that eventually saw him become chief astrologer to the Holy Roman emperor Frederick II (1194–1250). Soon after his return home he published his first book called *Liber abaci*. Translated as *A Book on Counting*, or *Book of the Calculator*, the book's title is often wrongly thought to be *Book of the Abacus*. Written in four parts, each discussing **multiplication, addition, subtraction,** and **division,** the work mentions **fractions,** problem-solving, and geometry, and also discusses elementary algebra. Most important, however, is the book's strong recommendation that the Hindu-Arab, or Indo-Arabic, system of numbers be adopted in the West. Altogether, this book plus four other separate works of Fibonacci's have been preserved, and his collected works were finally published about 600 years after his death.

Introduces Arabic numerals to the West

Because of his Middle Eastern schooling and his considerable experience traveling, Fibonacci was convinced that the numbering system used by the Arabs—the actual way they wrote their numbers and then used them to do calculations—was far superior to the traditional Western or European method of Roman numerals. Because he was so familiar with both mathematical systems, he knew that the system using the numerals 0 through 9 was more practical and easier than using either Roman numerals (I, V, IX, etc.) or an abacus. Roman numerals, he argued, were adequate for adding and subtracting, but they were highly impractical for multiplication or division. Although the abacus, with its sliding beads or counters, worked well and quickly, it was still very clumsy. There was no way to check the result except to do the figuring all over again. Furthermore, if a different answer was obtained the second time, it was necessary to do calculations a third time or have someone else do the problem in order to know which was the right answer.

Fibonacci therefore began his book with the straightforward sentence: "These are the nine figures of the Indians: 9, 8, 7, 6, 5, 4, 3, 2, 1. With these nine figures, and with this sign 0 . . . any number may be written, as will be demonstrated. . . ." Fibonacci recognized that this system originated long ago in India with the Hindus and had eventually made its way to the Middle East to be adopted by the Arabs. Those number symbols formed the basis of today's symbols. However, when first suggested by Fibonacci and for some time after, they met considerable resistance. In 1299, the city of Florence actually ordered merchants to use only Roman numerals (or write the numbers out with words) and banned the use of the new Arabic numerals. (See sidebar on Arabic numerals in the **al-Khwārizmī** entry.)

People were not immediately comfortable with the new, unfamiliar symbols that seem so ordinary today. It was easy to misunderstand a number or to deliberately change one (a 0 can easily be turned into a 6 or a 9). Also, since the entire concept of the zero symbol was so revolutionary—"why have a symbol for something that means nothing at all?"—it would take a long time for the superiority of the new system to be realized and accepted.

Fibonacci revised his book and republished it in 1228. Its influence then slowly began to be felt in everyday life. The book provided a better explanation of the advantages of the Arabic numbering system, including the concept of zero. The book also stressed

Leonardo Pisano Fibonacci

Leonardo Pisano Fibonacci

the importance of the concept of "place," the position of a number in the new system (for instance, 34 is a different quantity from 43, although they both employ a 3 and a 4). Fibonacci's work also proposed the idea that a bar, or solid line, could be used to express a fraction (a value less than one unit). His other books dealt with algebra, trigonometry, and other more complicated forms of mathematics. But it was his *Liber abaci* that became the mathematical masterwork of the Middle Ages. It remained the standard text for at least two centuries after his death.

Career and influence

In his time, Fibonacci was also recognized as being highly knowledgeable about the works of classical mathematicians like **Euclid of Alexandria** (c. 325–c. 270 B.C.). Fibonacci had a wide reputation that eventually reached Emperor Frederick II, who invited Fibonacci to take part in a mathematical tournament. Fibonacci accepted the invitation to compete against several other mathematicians, each of whom received three questions or problems composed by the emperor's staff. Fibonacci answered them all correctly and from then on may have been connected with the royal court in some way.

Although the complete acceptance of Arab numerals in the West did not come about until possibly as late as the mid-1550s, Fibonacci is recognized as being responsible not only for their acceptance but also for the revival of mathematics itself in the West. If a date is sought for the awakening of Western mathematics from its sleep during the Middle or Dark Ages, it surely must be during the life of Leonardo Fibonacci.

For More Information

Abbott, David, ed. *The Biographical Dictionary of Scientists: Mathematicians*. New York: Peter Bedrick Books, 1986.

Burton, David M. *Burton's History of Mathematics: An Introduction*. Dubuque, IA: Wm. C. Brown Publishers, 1995.

MacTutor History of Mathematics Archive. "Leonardo Pisa Fibonacci." http://www-groups.dcs.st-and.ac.uk/~history/Mathematicians/Fibonacci.html (accessed on April 16, 1999).

Reimer, Luetta, and Wilbert Reimer. *Mathematicians Are People, Too: Stories from the Lives of Great Mathematicians.* Palo Alto, CA: Dale Seymour Publications, 1995.

Young, Robyn V., ed. *Notable Mathematicians: From Ancient Times to the Present.* Detroit: Gale Research, 1998.

Leonardo Pisano Fibonacci

Born March 21, 1768
Auxerre, Bourgogne, France

Died May 16, 1830
Paris, France

French mathematical physicist

Joseph Fourier

While studying the problem of heat conduction (the manner in which heat flows through an object from one point to another), Joseph Fourier was able to describe this transfer in purely mathematical terms. In doing so, he developed powerful new mathematical tools and influenced the field of mathematical physics.

> *"Yesterday was my 21st birthday; at that age Newton and Pascal had already acquired many claims to immortality."*

Early life and education

Jean-Baptiste-Joseph Fourier (pronounced foor-YAY) was born in 1768 in Auxerre, Bourgogne, France. His father, Joseph, was a tailor. After the death of his first wife, he married a woman named Edmée, with whom he had twelve children. Jean-Baptiste-Joseph, who went by Joseph, was the ninth child. His mother died when he was nine years old and his father died the following year. The orphaned Fourier was placed in a local military school by the town's archbishop. While there, he discovered a strong interest and liking for mathematics. By the age of 14, he completed his own study of the six-volume *Cours de mathematique,* written by French mathematician Etienne Bézout (1730–83). A year later, Fourier received first prize for his study of a work by French mathematical physicist Charles Bossut (1730–1814).

Joseph Fourier

Although Fourier wanted to join the military in 1787, he was turned down. He decided instead to train for the priesthood. He entered the Benedictine seminary of St. Benoît-sur-Loire but retained his strong interest in mathematics. By the time he was 21, Fourier had decided not to take his religious vows and had left the seminary and visited Paris. The following year he returned to Auxerre and accepted a teaching position at his old military school.

French Revolution

With the outbreak of the French Revolution in 1789, all of France was in turmoil. By January 1793, the French king, Louis XVI (1754–93), had been tried and executed and what became known as The Terror would soon begin. Fourier was inspired by the ideals of liberty and freedom and became involved in revolutionary (seeking extreme change) politics by joining the local Revolutionary Committee. He soon was greatly disturbed by the violence of The Terror. Although he was unable to resign, Fourier did attempt to play a moderate role by defending some of the innocent victims of the radicals. This led to his arrest in 1794, during which he himself came very close to losing his head to the guillotine.

When political changes resulted in Fourier's release, he attended the École Normale as a student (in 1795) and had the good fortune to be taught by one of the best mathematicians in France, **Joseph-Louis Lagrange** (1736–1813). That same year, Fourier was arrested by the new regime and charged with being a radical member of the Revolution. When his colleagues and professors all came to his support, he was again released. By late 1795, he returned to his school (now renamed École Polytechnique) as an assistant lecturer. In 1797 he succeeded Lagrange and took up the chair of analysis and mechanics.

Works for Napoléon

When French mathematician Gaspard Monge (1746–1818) was assigned in 1798 to serve as scientific advisor to French general Napoléon Bonaparte (1769–1821) during his expedition to Egypt, Monge selected Fourier to come along. Fourier had studied under

Monge at the École Normale. During this combination military-scientific campaign, Fourier conducted a variety of diplomatic activities and oversaw archaeological and scientific explorations and discoveries in Egypt. When Napoléon returned to France in 1799 and assumed absolute power, Fourier remained in Egypt.

In 1801, Fourier returned to France and was appointed by Napoléon to a top government position in the southern part of the country. Although Fourier wanted to return to teaching at the École Polytechnique, he could not leave Napoléon. While in his headquarters in the city of Grenoble, Fourier not only oversaw the draining of swamps and the construction of a highway but managed to do a considerable amount of mathematical research as well.

Mathematical treatment of the theory of heat

Fourier became interested and soon fascinated by the properties of heat when he was first introduced to the great warmth of Egypt's deserts. During his three years there, he tried to solve problems related to how heat flows from one point to another through a particular object. After he left Egypt, he remained concerned with the notion of heat and continued his research in Grenoble. The problem Fourier decided to take on was a very complex one since the flow of heat through an object is influenced by many variables. These variables include the temperature difference between two points, the conductivity of the material, and even the shape of the object.

In a highly original manner, Fourier approached this problem mathematically and discovered what has become known as Fourier's theorem. This theorem states that any periodic oscillation (a variation that eventually repeats itself in an exact way, that is, in a pattern) can be broken down into a series, which can then be added back together to restore the original oscillation. Fourier thus showed that something very complex can be broken down into a series of simpler mathematical equations.

After beginning his work on heat around 1804, Fourier finished a paper entitled, "On the Propagation of Heat in Solid Bodies," in 1807. Fourier's paper received considerable and justifiable criticism, so he did not publish it then but rather went back to work. In 1811, he received a prize for his reworked paper, but it was not

Joseph Fourier

until 1822 that he published his completed theory in his most famous book, entitled *Théorie analytique de la chaleur (Analytic Theory of Heat).*

Joseph Fourier

Fourier's theorem has proved especially useful in the study of any wave phenomena such as that of sound and light. The mathematical treatment of such wave-like forms has come to be called harmonic analysis.

Obsessed with heat

When Napoléon finally fell from power in 1815, Fourier was in Paris and basically had to start his mathematical career all over again. By 1817, however, he was accepted as a member of the reconstituted Académie des Sciences. In 1822, when his important book was published, he was elected to the powerful position of academy secretary. In 1827, he was elected to the Académie Français and later became a foreign member of the Royal Society of London.

Fourier's fascination with heat may have played a part in his own death. He was so taken with the powers of heat that he believed it was a key element to good health. He supposedly carried this idea to an extreme not only by keeping his living quarters almost unbearably hot but also by always bundling himself in several layers of warm clothing. Some speculate that he may have contracted an exotic illness in Egypt (possibly myxedema, which is an underfunctioning thyroid gland) that could have made him very sensitive to the cold. Fourier died ten days after falling down his own stairs. It is thought that his obsession with staying warm may have aggravated his heart condition, causing a heart attack and, therefore, his fatal fall down the stairs.

For More Information

Asimov, Isaac. *Asimov's Biographical Encyclopedia of Science and Technology.* Garden City, NY: Doubleday & Company, 1982.

Biographical Dictionary of Scientists. New York: Charles Scribner's Sons, 1991.

MacTutor History of Mathematics Archive. "Jean Baptiste Joseph Fourier." http://www-groups.dcs.st-and.ac.uk/~history/Mathematicians/Fourier.html (accessed on April 16, 1999).

Transnational College of LEX, and Alan Gleason, translator. *Who Is Fourier? A Mathematical Adventure.* Boston: Blackwell Science, 1995.

Young, Robyn V., ed. *Notable Mathematicians: From Ancient Times to the Present.* Detroit: Gale Research, 1998.

Joseph Fourier

Fraction

A fraction is a numeral representing some part of a whole. Written as two numerals separated by a bar or a line, such as *a/b*, a fraction generally stands for the number of equal parts into which something has been divided (with *b* standing for the whole and *a* indicating how many parts of the whole are represented). The fraction ⅖ indicates that there are 2 parts of something that has 5 equal parts. Also, a fraction symbol can be used to suggest a **ratio** (see **Ratio, proportion, and percent**) of some kind or a comparison of two quantities.

Background

The word "fraction" comes from the Latin *fractus,* which is the past tense of *frangere,* meaning "to break." Other related words like fragile, diffraction, fragment, and fractal come from this Latin root. The word fraction, therefore, literally means a piece broken off of something. For primitive humans, only natural or counting numbers were needed, since their society was not very complex and their use of mathematics was quite simple. As life and societies became more complicated, however, early civilizations came to

Denominator in a fraction, the numeral written below the bar or line; it tells how many parts the whole has

Equivalent fraction fractions that are of equal value; for example $\frac{5}{10}$ is the same as $\frac{1}{2}$

Improper fraction a fraction in which the numerator is equal to or greater than the denominator; the value of the fraction is always equal to or larger than 1; for example, $\frac{9}{8}$ is an improper fraction

Like fractions fractions with the same denominator; for example, $\frac{2}{7}$ and $\frac{4}{7}$ are like fractions

Minute a measure of time equal to $\frac{1}{60}$th of an hour

Mixed number a number consisting of an integer and a proper fraction; for example, $1\frac{3}{4}$ is a mixed number

Numerator in a fraction, the numeral written above the bar or line; it tells how many parts are being considered

Proper fraction a fraction in which the numerator is less than the denominator; for example, $\frac{2}{3}$ is a proper fraction

Ratio the relationship between two quantities, which is obtained by dividing two things; for instance, the ratio of 3 to 2 is written 3:2 or $\frac{3}{2}$

Second a measure of time equal to $\frac{1}{60}$th of a minute

Terms the numerator and denominator of a fraction

need and use fractions, but their knowledge was incomplete and they found fractions very difficult to work with.

Over 4,000 years ago, both the Babylonians and the Egyptians used fractions, with Babylonian astronomers basing their system on a whole divided into 60 parts. Their fraction for $1\frac{1}{2}$ was written as "1 30" (meaning $1\frac{30}{60}$), and was actually more like today's **decimal** fractions, with the Babylonians' space after 1 representing today's decimal point. This was a useful system for telling **time** and for measuring angles in minutes and seconds. Egyptian mathematicians used only what are called unit fractions, meaning that all their fractions had a numerator (or top number) of 1. Their unit fractions also were written with a dot or a sideways oval over the denominator. This symbol always stood for 1. This exclusive use of unit fractions made it necessary to show other fractions as sums of parts (so $\frac{2}{5}$ would not be written with a 2 above a 5 but rather as $\frac{1}{5} + \frac{1}{5}$).

The later Greeks did not like fractions nor did they like to break things up into parts. Greek mathematicians were very philosophical and believed that the number 1 had a kind of mystical quality, and that its special unity should not be divided. When they did use fractions however, they thought of them more as ratios and did the opposite of today's system by putting the numerator on the bottom and the denominator on top. They did not separate the two numbers by a line or bar, so today's $\frac{2}{5}$ looked like $^5_2$.

The Romans were more practical people and found fractions useful to their monetary system as well as for weighing and measuring. Often they would use a base of 12 to express fractions, with their pound having 12 ounces and their foot having 12 inches. Hindu mathematicians learned their fractions from the Greeks, and when the Arabs conquered part of India, they adopted the Hindu system of writing one numeral over another. To this method the Arabs added a fraction bar to separate numerals. As Arab knowledge eventually spread into Spain and then to Europe during the late 1400s, fractions eventually became part of the calculations of everyday life.

Description and use

A fraction or fractional number is written as two numerals separated by a line ($\frac{1}{5}$), and is commonly understood as representing something that has been divided into a certain number of parts. The numeral above the line or bar is called the numerator, and it tells how many parts are being considered. (In the fraction $\frac{1}{5}$, 1 is the numerator). The denominator is the numeral written below the line, and it tells how many parts the whole has. The numerator and denominator are called the terms of a fraction.

Different fractions have different names. When two fractions have different numerators but still indicate the same part of a whole ($\frac{2}{3}$ is the same as $\frac{4}{6}$), they are called equivalent fractions. The smaller equivalent fraction of a large fraction can be found by dividing both the numerator and denominator by the same **whole number** (other than 1). This process is called "reducing a fraction." Therefore, $\frac{4}{6}$ becomes $\frac{2}{3}$ when divided by 2. When no other number besides 1 can go into the numerator and denominator evenly, then the fraction is simplified or reduced to its lowest terms. An example is $\frac{16}{36} \div 2 = \frac{8}{18}; \frac{8}{18} \div 2 = \frac{4}{9}$.

There are other types of fractions as well. Like fractions have the same denominator ($\frac{1}{6}, \frac{5}{6}$). A proper fraction is when the numerator is less than the denominator ($\frac{1}{2}$). The opposite is called an improper fraction and always expresses a quantity larger than 1 ($\frac{5}{4}$). An improper fraction can also be changed into a mixed number—a whole number follwed by a proper fraction. (For instance, $1\frac{1}{4}$ is the same as $\frac{5}{4}$.) A mixed number can be converted into an improper fraction by multiplying the whole number and the denominator, and adding that result to the numerator; that number becomes the numerator and the original denominator remains the denominator. (For example, to change $1\frac{4}{5}$ to an improper fraction: $1 \times 5 = 5; 5 + 4 = 9; \frac{9}{5}$ is the improper fraction.)

The four basic arithmetic operations (**addition, subtraction, multiplication,** and **division**) can be used with fractions, as long as certain rules are followed. Addition and subtraction of like fractions is achieved by adding (or subtracting) their numerators and placing their sum (or difference) above their common denominator ($\frac{1}{4} + \frac{2}{4} = \frac{3}{4}; \frac{3}{4} - \frac{1}{4} = \frac{2}{4}$). To add fractions that are not like fractions, they must first be converted to like fractions. Like fractions are not necessary for multiplying fractions since the product of the two numerators is simply placed over the product of the two denominators ($\frac{2}{5} \times \frac{1}{4} = \frac{2}{20} = \frac{1}{10}$). With division of two fractions however, it must be remembered that the second fraction (the divisor)

Cooking with fractions

Many problems that were once done with fractions are now done with calculators that use decimal fractions. One place where traditional fractions still rule, however, is in the kitchen. Since virtually every American cookbook has recipes that measure ingredients in cups, teaspoons, and tablespoons, there is hardly a kitchen that does not have a stock of fractional cups and spoons in a nearby drawer.

A typical cluster of cups usually contains 1 whole cup, and a ¾, ½, ¼, and ⅓ cup. The spoon clusters are usually divided into 1 whole tablespoon, 1 whole teaspoon, and ¾, ½, ¼, and ⅛ teaspoon. These different measuring containers not only allow the cook to follow a recipe exactly, but they are also essential when the cook or baker needs to halve or double a recipe. It is at this point that a practical knowledge of fractions becomes really useful.

is turned upside down and that multiplication is then used. Thus, dividing ½ by ⅔ would be done by multiplying ½ by 3/2 (½ × 3/2 = ¾).

Fractions can also be written as decimal fractions, which are fractions whose denominator is some power of ten. Today's electronic calculators express fractions in this form, making the traditional fraction form less common. However, it remains an important and accepted way of expressing the parts of a whole (especially in the kitchen) as well as the ideas of division and ratio.

For More Information

Barnett, Carne, et al. *Fractions, Decimals, Ratios, and Percents: Hard to Teach and Hard to Learn?* Portsmouth, NH: Heinemann, 1994.

Bryant-Mole, Karen. *Fractions and Decimals.* Santa Clara, CA: EDC Publications, 1995.

Cummings, Alyece B. *Painless Fractions.* Hauppauge, NY: Barron's Educational Series, 1998.

Green, Gordon W., Jr. *Helping Your Child to Learn Math.* New York: Citadel Press, 1995.

Stienecker, David L. *Fractions.* Tarrytown, NY: Benchmark Books, 1995.

West, Beverly Henderson, et al. *The Prentice-Hall Encyclopedia of Mathematics.* Englewood Cliffs, NJ: Prentice-Hall, 1982.

Born February 15, 1564
Pisa (present-day Italy)

Died January 8, 1642
Arcetri, Italy

Italian mathematician, astronomer, and physicist

Galileo

Galileo is best remembered for his work on the telescope and for his clash with the Church over its doctrine that the Earth, rather than the Sun, was the center of the universe. He was also influential in establishing the importance of experimental evidence to the scientific method. As a mathematician, he was the first to use mathematics to understand physics systematically.

Galileo Galilei (pronounced gol-uh-LAY-lee gol-uh-LAY-oh) was born in Pisa, which is in Tuscany, the northern region of Italy. Known today only by the single name of Galileo, he was named in keeping with a Tuscan tradition of giving the oldest son a first name that was a slight variation of the last name—thus, Galileo Galilei. His father, Vincenzio Galilei, a musician and musical theorist, was descended from a formerly wealthy family from Florence, Italy. He married Giulia Ammannati in 1562, with whom he had seven children.

Galileo began his studies at home with a tutor, but when his family resettled in Florence around 1575, the young Galileo was sent

> *"I do not think it is necessary to believe that the same God who has given us our senses, reason, and intelligence wished us to abandon their use, giving us by some other means the information that we could gain through them."*

Galileo is best known for his improvements on the telescope.

to a school at the Benedictine monastery of Santa Maria at Vallombrosa. In 1578, Galileo decided, against his father's wishes, to become a novice in that religious order (which meant he would prepare to become a monk). His father took him out of school and brought him back to Florence. Since he was unable to obtain a scholarship for his son to attend the University of Pisa, his father returned him to school at the monastery. There Galileo remained until 1581, when he was enrolled at the University of Pisa as a medical student. His father tried very hard to keep him from studying mathematics, believing that his son would earn a much better living as a doctor than as a mathematician.

At the university, Galileo was not very interested in studying medicine. He alternated between being a student who didn't try very hard and being one who gave his teachers a hard time with his challenging questions. Because he was much more interested in mathematics than medicine, he arranged to study outside the university with Ostillio Ricci, a friend of his father's, who was also the mathematician to the grand duke of Tuscany. Although his father opposed this move at first, Galileo progressed very rapidly under Ricci. Galileo finally left the university and his future medical career at the age of 21. Back home in Florence, he continued to study mathematics, particularly the works of **Euclid of Alexandria** (c. 325–c. 270 B.C.) and **Archimedes of Syracuse** (287–212 B.C.).

Begins work in mathematics

From 1585 to 1589, Galileo taught mathematics privately in Florence and publicly in Siena and published a small booklet describing a balance he had invented. This invention brought him to the attention of the scholarly world at the age of 22, but Galileo had actually made his first real discovery as a teenager. While at the University of Pisa in 1581, he found himself watching a chandelier being swung by the wind. He thought that the time it took to swing back and forth was the same whether it swung through a large arc or a small one. He later experimented with two pendulums and discovered that he was correct. This principle would eventually be used by Dutch astronomer and mathematician **Christiaan Huygens** (1629–95) to build the first pendulum clock (grandfather clock). By 1588, Galileo had visited Rome and lectured in mathematics before the Florentine Academy.

In 1589, Galileo was given the chair of mathematics at the University of Pisa, having been turned down the year before by the University of Bologna. Two years later, his father died, which left Galileo, the oldest son, with heavy financial and family responsibilities. Unhappy with the low pay at Pisa and having upset some of the faculty with his criticism and disrespect, Galileo left Pisa when his three-year contract was over and moved to the chair of mathematics at the University of Padua in 1592. As a major center for some of the best scholars of Europe, Padua was a more open and free university than Pisa. Galileo thrived there.

In 1597, Galileo improved and was able to sell a mathematical instrument called the proportional compass. Galileo changed what had been a simple device with limited uses into a highly useful, sophisticated calculating instrument. He added scales to the proportional compass and hired a skilled craftsman to build it. He also

Galileo

A reproduction of Galileo's telescope.

wrote a book describing its use to engineers and military men. During his first decade at Padua, Galileo had three children (two daughters and a son) with Marina Gamba, whom he did not marry.

Challenges old physics

At Padua, Galileo used his knowledge of mathematics to study the behavior of falling bodies. He challenged such long-held beliefs as the incorrect notions that light objects fell more slowly than heavy ones and that some type of force had to be constantly applied to an object to keep it moving. In this area of physics, called mechanics, he discovered mathematically that two forces can act on a body at the same time, and that the body will always move in a parabolic curve. (For example, a ball shot from a cannon is pushed forward by the force of the explosion and downward by the force of gravity.)

Galileo proved to be a master at analyzing dynamic problems mathematically. In his day, however, **algebra** had not yet been applied to **geometry,** and the proofs he offered were all reached by using the geometric methods of the Greeks. Galileo also studied the strength of materials and basically founded the branch of physics now known as materials science. He used mathematics to show that if a structure (or even a person) increased in all its dimensions equally, it would grow weaker. For example, a deer that grew to the size of an elephant yet kept its original proportions (see **Ratio, proportion, and percent**) would not be able to stand.

Improves the telescope

During a visit to Venice in July 1609, Galileo learned of the invention in Holland of a magnifying tube that used lenses—a telescope. Although he never actually saw one of these new instruments, he built his own version in a month, kept improving its magnification, and by the end of the year had achieved a magnification of about 30 times—just about the practical limit for his kind of telescope. Turning his telescope to the skies, Galileo saw for the first time the surface of the moon with its mountains and discovered new, fixed stars as well as four satellites of Jupiter.

The sudden fame from Galileo's astronomical discoveries enabled him to return to his beloved Florence in 1610 as mathematician and philosopher to the grand duke of Tuscany. He remained the chief mathematician of the University of Padua but had no obligation to teach. Galileo journeyed to Rome the next year and was made a member of the Lincean Academy, the first truly scientific academy, founded in 1603.

Conflict with the Church

Having begun the age of telescopic astronomy, Galileo continued to explore the skies. As he did so, he became more convinced that the old, accepted version of an Earth-centered universe was incorrect. Famous Polish astromer Nicolaus Copernicus (1473–1543) was an earlier proponent of the same theory, but had been chastised for it.

Pietro Antonio Cataldi

On February 11, 1626, Italian mathematician and astronomer Pietro Antonio Cataldi (1548–1626) died in Bologna, Italy. Cataldi lived during the same era as his fellow countryman Galileo. He was an influential teacher and author of thirty mathematical works on such subjects as arithmetic, perfect numbers, and algebra.

After Cataldi's death, his will revealed that he desired to have his home be used to found a new school for mathematics and the sciences. For reasons unknown, his wish was never fulfilled. Years before, Cataldi had expressed his willingness to help others by arranging for copies of his arithmetic book, *Practica arithmetica,* to be given free by Franciscan monks to underprivileged children and some religious organizations. It is not known how either group reacted to this gift of a book that probably few could understand!

Galileo

For the next two decades, Galileo was in and out of trouble with traditional astronomers and Church authorities. With the publication in 1632 of his *Dialogue Concerning the Two Chief World Systems,* he apparently went too far. In 1633, an old, sick Galileo was brought before the Roman Inquisition (the arm of the Church empowered to deal with people whose thoughts differed from those of the Church) by Pope Urban VIII (1568–1644). Galileo was given a trial, sentenced to life imprisonment, and forced to take back his teachings. When he agreed to all these conditions, his sentence was reduced to permanent house arrest under surveillance.

The aged Galileo was allowed to return to his villa at Arcetri, in the hills above Florence, to be near his oldest daughter. Although she died soon after and the old man seemed to lose all interest in work, he eventually roused himself and produced one more great book, *Discourses and Mathematical Demonstrations Concerning the Two New Sciences.* He was forbidden to write and publish, but Galileo had the manuscript smuggled out of Italy, and it was published in 1638 in Holland. In this major work, mathematics played a key role. The book contained the basics of the mathematical treatment of motion and laid the foundation for modern physics. It also demonstrated that many problems of physics can be analyzed mathematically. The basis of Galileo's science was this very modern attitude toward mathematics.

Galileo lived four years after his book was published but was by then totally blind. Despite this setback, he had the companionship of several pupils as well as his son, Vincenzio. To the end, Pope Urban VIII denied his request to attend church at Easter or to see his doctors in Florence. It would take nearly 350 years for the Church to finally admit that it had wronged him.

For More Information

Asimov, Isaac. *Asimov's Biographical Encyclopedia of Science and Technology.* Garden City, NY: Doubleday, 1982.

Fisher, Leonard Everett. *Galileo.* New York: Atheneum, 1992.

Gillispie, Charles C., ed. *Dictionary of Scientific Biography.* New York: Charles Scribner's Sons, 1990.

Hightower, Paul W. *Galileo: Astronomer and Physicist.* Springfield, NJ: Enslow, 1997.

MacTutor History of Mathematics Archive. "Galileo Galilei." http://www-groups.dcs.st-and.ac.uk/~history/Mathematicians/Galileo.html (accessed on April 16, 1999).

Redondi, Pietro. *Galileo Heretic.* Princeton, NJ: Princeton University Press, 1987.

Young, Robyn V., ed. *Notable Mathematicians: From Ancient Times to the Present.* Detroit: Gale Research, 1998.

Galileo

Born October 25, 1811
Bourg-la-Reine, France

Died May 31, 1832
Paris, France

French algebraist and group theorist

Évariste Galois

Although he died before he turned 21 and his life's work did not total 100 pages—most of it unpublished—Évariste Galois contributed to several branches of mathematics and was able to play an important role in the birth of modern **algebra.** Nearly 15 years after his death, his work was first published; almost 40 years after he died, it was presented in a full and clear manner. Despite his tragically short and unlucky life, Galois performed highly original work that makes him recognized today as the founder of what is known as modern group theory.

> *"The most worthwhile scientific books are those in which the author clearly indicates what he does not know; for an author most hurts his readers by concealing difficulties."*

Early life and education

Évariste Galois (pronounced ay-vuh-REEST gal-WAH) was born in the French village of Bourg-la-Reine, outside Paris, on October 25, 1811, the second of three children. His father, Nicolas-Gabriel, was the well educated director of a boarding school and was also the village mayor. His mother, Adelaide-Marie Demante, was also well educated and came from a family of lawyers. Neither had any special talent or love for mathematics. His father was a cheerful man who enjoyed making rhymes, but his mother was much more serious and also very religious. She was young Galois's only teacher until he was 12, and she taught him religion and the classics.

Évariste Galois

In 1823, Galois was sent to a boarding school whose severe discipline policy was administered by domineering teachers. Although Galois got his first taste of mathematics there, he did not do well in school because he was considered defiant and a know-it-all. In fact, once Galois discovered mathematics, he wanted to study nothing else. He went so quickly through the school textbooks that he soon sought out and mastered the mature works of the top mathematicians in France, such as Adrien-Marie Legendre (1752–1833) and **Joseph-Louis Lagrange** (1736–1813).

Galois's mathematics teacher recognized the young boy's special talent for and unusual drive to learn the subject he loved, and he encouraged Galois to learn mathematics in a systematic fashion. But Galois was too impatient. Realizing that he was easily able to understand the most advanced mathematics, he became overly cocky and never learned how to express his ideas and solutions clearly. All his life he would be plagued by his inability to communicate mathematically with those who were slower than he was. Often he would solve a complicated problem mentally and show no written evidence of how he arrived at his conclusion.

Success and disappointments

Galois's career in mathematics began on a successful note: He was able to get his first mathematical paper published at the age of 17. Encouraged by this success, he reworked his paper (which now contained some fundamental discoveries) and submitted it as two papers in May 1829 to the Academy of Sciences (while he was still only 17). At this point, everything that could go wrong for the young mathematical genius did go wrong, and a series of unlucky events seemed to conspire against him. Respected Academy member **Augustin-Louis Cauchy** (1789–1857), who was to judge his papers, never did so. Some historians explain this behavior by the highly respected Cauchy by saying that he simply forgot or that he lost both papers. Others say that he advised Galois to revise his papers or to combine them and submit them the following year for the Academy's grand prize.

Spiral of failures and mistakes

With Cauchy's failure to judge Galois's papers came a series of misfortunes that are sometimes hard to believe but that would affect the young Galois deeply. First, his beloved father suddenly committed suicide in July 1829. As the village mayor, his father had had liberal ideas that enraged a young priest. The priest publicly circulated rumors to destroy his reputation. After his father's suicide, the villagers were so angry with the priest that the father's funeral ended in a riot.

The following month, Galois made a serious mistake by taking an important admissions exam a year before he had to and without any preparation, since he felt he knew more than his examiners. This may have been true, but when he then refused to explain his answers according to the standards expected by the school, he was rejected. This was a major disappointment to Galois, who very much wanted to attend the École Polytechnique, a top school that trained the best mathematicians and engineers. A second chance at the test proved even more disastrous, as Galois became so angry with one of his oral examiners that he threw an eraser at him.

By November 1829, Galois was forced to attend a school that trained only future teachers of secondary school. Despite this, in February 1830, he reworked his 1829 paper and submitted a new version to the Academy in hopes of winning its grand prize in mathematics. In a further amazing misadventure, Galois had the bad fortune to submit it to French mathematician **Joseph Fourier** (1768–1830), who promptly died before judging it, and the manuscript was lost. If Galois needed more proof that teachers, institutions, and all of official society were conspiring against him, he certainly had it.

Fatal involvement in radical politics

When the July 1830 revolution in France forced King Charles X (1757–1836) to abdicate (leave the throne), Galois became very involved in politics and joined an outlawed radical group. He was arrested twice in 1831 and was sentenced to six months in jail the second time. Following his release from prison during April 1832, he was somehow talked into a duel. The exact nature of the circumstances that led up to the duel are not clear, but some historians say he was taunted into a fight over a woman he knew. Others, howev-

Évariste Galois

Évariste Galois

er, state that he was provoked by police who were acting under orders. Whatever the reason for the challenge, Galois accepted it, and instead of readying himself for the fight of his life the next morning, he spent the entire night desperately trying to write down all of his mathematical ideas and discoveries. He entrusted them to a friend, saying that, "Eventually there will be, I hope, some people who will find it profitable to sort out this mess."

The duel took place in the morning of May 30, 1832, and Galois was shot in the lower abdomen. He laid for hours where he fell and was finally taken to a hospital where he died the next morning. Before he died, he tried to console his younger brother, saying, "Do not cry. I need all my courage to die at twenty." As with his father's funeral, there were riots.

Mathematical contributions

Galois's mathematical work was never fully appreciated by any of his contemporaries. It was not until 1846 that fragments were published by French mathematician Joseph Liouville (1809–82). Galois was shown to have produced highly original works on algebra—one of the most important functions of which is to solve equations. Galois was able to discover which equations could be solved using algebra and which could not. Once these essential elements of Galois's work became known, his ideas were eventually accepted and became an integral part of mathematics. By the twentieth century, the mathematical technique that Galois invented came to be known as "group theory" and turned out to be highly useful in working out quantum mechanics (one of the theories of physics that describes how the universe works).

For More Information

Abbott, David, ed. *The Biographical Dictionary of Scientists: Mathematicians.* New York: Peter Bedrick Books, 1986.

MacTutor History of Mathematics Archive. "Evariste Galois." http://www-groups.dcs.st-and.ac.uk/~history/Mathematicians/Galois.html (accessed on April 19, 1999).

Pappas, Theoni. *Mathematical Scandals.* San Carlos, CA: Wide World Publishing/Tetra, 1997.

Reimer, Luetta, and Wilbert Reimer. *Mathematicians Are People, Too: Stories from the Lives of Great Mathematicians.* Palo Alto, CA: Dale Seymour Publications, 1995.

Young, Robyn V., ed. *Notable Mathematicians: From Ancient Times to the Present.* Detroit: Gale Research, 1998.

Évariste Galois

Born April 30, 1777
Brunswick, Duchy of Brunswick (present-day Germany)

Died February 23, 1855
Göttingen, Hannover (present-day Germany)

German mathematician and astronomer

Carl Friedrich Gauss

Considered along with **Archimedes of Syracuse** (287–212 B.C.) and **Isaac Newton** (1642–1727) to be one of the three great mathematicians of all time, Carl Friedrich Gauss was a highly original thinker who made major discoveries in many different mathematical fields. He also made contributions to physics and astronomy. His almost superhuman ability to perform at the highest levels in any branch of mathematics he attempted led him to be called "The Prince of Mathematics" by his contemporaries.

Early life as a prodigy

Johann Carl Friedrich Gauss (pronunciation rhymes with HOUSE) was born in the town of Brunswick, in the duchy (territory ruled by dukes or duchesses) of Brunswick (in modern-day Germany), into a very humble, uneducated family. His father, Gebhard, was a gardener and laborer whose first wife had died after bearing him one child. His second wife, Dorothea Benze, was Johann's mother, and although she worked as a maid and could barely read, she was said to be intelligent. Later in life, Gauss would describe his father as "domineering, uncouth, and

> *"It is not knowledge, but the act of learning, not possession but the act of getting there, which grants the greatest enjoyment. When I have clarified and exhausted a subject, then I turn away from it, in order to go into darkness again."*

unrefined." His mother had a cheerful disposition and died at the age of 97.

Carl Friedrich Gauss

Gauss always said he learned to count before he could talk, and as a toddler he showed signs of being very special. Child geniuses were not always welcome in peasant Germany however, since they were considered to be God's favorites and therefore more likely to die young.

Gauss's father began to fully realize the boy's unique abilities one day when his three-year-old son watched him add up the payroll for his bricklaying crew and then pointed out that he had made a mistake, which he had. A more astounding episode took place when the eight-year-old Gauss was in school doing an assignment. When the teacher asked the class to add up all the numbers from 1 to 100, Gauss almost instantly scribbled 5,050 on his slate, declaring in German, "Ligget se!" or "There it lies!" Somehow, Gauss had already figured out that each pair of numbers—1 and 100, 2 and 99, 3 and 98, 4 and 97, and so on up to 50 and 51—added up to 101, and that the total of the 50 pairs must therefore be 50 times 101. Such an accomplishment was probably not too great a task for Gauss who, as a very small child, begged his father to teach him the alphabet and then went off and taught himself to read.

Education

By the time Gauss was 11, his teachers were fully aware of his immense talent. They persuaded his father that he should attend the Gymnasium (high school) and be trained for a profession rather than for the spinning trade as his father had planned. They also talked him into letting Gauss study after school instead of sending him to work to help support the family. As news of Gauss's intelligence spread beyond the village and reached the duke of Brunswick, he was brought to the castle to meet the duke. Gauss's computing ability so impressed the duke that he agreed to pay all Gauss's expenses and gave him a regular allowance. This support, which was similar to a grant from the government today, continued until the duke's death.

In 1792, Gauss entered the Brunswick Collegium Carolinum. Here, he would spend three years and greatly extend his mathematical abilities by studying the works of Newton, **Leonhard Euler** (1707–83), and **Joseph-Louis Lagrange** (1736–1813). Gauss left Brunswick in 1795 to study at the Göttingen University located in the next state of Hannover. Gauss supposedly chose Göttingen because of its superior library. At Göttingen, Gauss made a dramatic discovery that convinced him to be a mathematician rather than a philologist (one who studies language). In 1796 he was able to construct an equilateral **polygon** of 17 sides using only a straightedge (ruler) and a compass. This was a geometrical construction that everyone thought was impossible because not even the Greeks had been able to achieve it. This experience made Gauss realize that he truly loved mathematics. Gauss eventually received a doctorate in 1799 from the University of Helmstedt.

Carl Friedrich Gauss

Years of creativity

The years from 1796 to 1800 were so creative for Gauss that they are in some ways similar to Newton's shorter burst of creativity more than a century before. Both men entertained so many potentially rich ideas during these relatively short periods that they were able to spend the rest of their lives elaborating, extending, or proving them. In 1801, some of this extraordinary creativity was made public when Gauss allowed his *Disquisitiones arithmeticae (Arithmetical Investigations)* to be published. This work is generally considered to be his greatest accomplishment in mathematics. It formulated important new laws, introduced special theorems, offered several new proofs, and even suggested certain mathematical questions and concepts that are still considered today.

Transition to astronomer

Despite his great love for mathematics, Gauss spent considerable time during his early, creative years doing research in astronomy. In 1801, the same year that he published his great mathematical work, he also announced that he had calculated the orbit of a newly discovered asteroid (small bodies in space that orbit the Sun) named Ceres. This achievement made him internationally famous. Everyone realized how difficult it must have been to calculate the tiny asteroid's position with only a minimum of information available to him. His creation of a quick method for calculating its position and then predicting where it would next appear,

Carl Friedrich Gauss stands in the observatory he designed at Göttingen University.

using only three observations, seemed almost superhuman. By 1806, Gauss's sponsor, the duke of Brunswick, had been killed leading his troops in battle against French general Napoléon Bonaparte (1769–1821). Gauss eventually was appointed director of the Göttingen Observatory in 1807. During his time there, he published a book based on his Ceres calculations that would become a classic in astronomy.

Family life

In 1805, Gauss married Johanna Osthoff, with whom he had a son and a daughter before she died in 1809. It is said that Gauss was happiest during these years. Although he soon married Minna Waldeck, his wife's best friend, who gave him three more children, he was never quite the same. His second wife contracted tuberculosis and was seldom well. The unhappy Gauss eventually grew to dominate his children as his own father had done; quarrels were frequent in the household. His sons would later state that Gauss had discouraged them from taking up science because he doubted their work would ever equal his and he did not want anything mediocre to be associated with his name. Gauss survived both his wives and all but one of his children, and he had a sometimes bitter and often lonely life.

Geodesic career

At Göttingen Observatory in 1817, Gauss took up geodesy (pronounced GEE-ah-duh-see) as a third career. A branch of applied mathematics, geodesy is used to determine the shape and the size of the Earth as well as to locate exact positions on its surface. Gauss had long been interested in this field. While at Göttingen, he studied geodesy seriously and invented a device called a heliotrope, which used the Sun's reflected rays to make more precise measurements of the Earth's shape.

Until 1825, Gauss did a great deal of difficult surveying work in the field, but after that year he confined himself to calculations. In 1828, he produced yet another book that became a classic in its field by using the principles of **geometry** to understand curved surfaces. This study led Gauss to consider the possibility that space itself might be curved—an idea that would become central to the ideas of German American scientist **Albert Einstein** (1879–1955), who would study space-time nearly a hundred years later.

In the 1830s, Gauss collaborated with German physicist Wilhelm Weber (1804–91) and worked on electricity and magnetism. They built a workable telegraph as early as 1833. For this work, Gauss was honored by having a unit of magnetism, a "gauss," named after him. Today's term "degauss" means demagnetizing something.

Despite some personal unhappiness and physical problems like gout (which causes painful inflammation of the joints), Gauss remained mentally active into his old age. He even taught himself Russian at the age of 62. In 1855, at the age of 77, Gauss died of a heart attack.

Throughout his life and work, Gauss had a passion for perfection and must certainly have been a difficult man with whom to live and work. Those who knew him best described him as a person who was as cold as a glacier. Sadly, in his chosen field of mathematics, he had no collaborators and could never find an intellectual friend in or out of Germany with whom he could share his best thoughts and ideas. Finally, since he published so little and kept to himself so much, his actual impact on mathematics is not as great as his reputation.

Carl Friedrich Gauss

Carl Friedrich Gauss

For More Information

Bergamini, David. *Mathematics.* Alexandria, VA: Time-Life Books, 1980.

Biographical Dictionary of Mathematicians. New York: Charles Scribner's Sons, 1991.

MacTutor History of Mathematics Archive. "Johann Carl Friedrich Gauss." http://www-groups.dcs.st-and.ac.uk/~history/Mathematicians/Gauss.html (accessed on April 19, 1999).

Simmons, George F. *Calculus Gems: Brief Lives and Memorable Mathematics.* New York: McGraw-Hill, 1992.

Young, Robyn V., ed. *Notable Mathematicians: From Ancient Times to the Present.* Detroit: Gale Research, 1998.

Geometry

G eometry is a branch of mathematics that deals with the properties—such as size, shape, and position—and relationships
of lines, surfaces, and solids in space. Knowing the principles of
geometry helps in the understanding of the characteristics and
rules of certain geometric figures, thereby making practical problems easier to solve.

Background

Geometry is most often identified with the Greeks, who made it the
logical system it is today. But well before Greek geometry there was the
very practical work of the Egyptians some five thousand years ago.
Besides using a form of geometry to build the pyramids, the Egyptians
employed geometrical techniques in many ways. The best known of
these was to reestablish land boundaries that were washed away by the
annual flooding of the Nile River. However, the geometry of both the
Egyptians and the later Babylonians could be described more as an
accumulation of practical facts than as an organized body of knowledge. The former might best be described as "knowing how but not
knowing why," while the latter contains certain rules and principles
that allow one to understand the all-important "why."

Geometry

The geometry of the Greeks was a formal system of **logic,** meaning that the system could demonstrate that something was true by using a step-by-step process in which each part was essential for the next one. The Greeks used the principles of geometry to understand the physical world as well as to construct things and make surveys and measurements.

It was Greek mathematician **Euclid of Alexandria** (c. 325–c. 270 B.C.) who turned geometry into an organized body of knowledge and provided a pattern for others to follow with his basic textbook of geometry called *Elements.* While little if any of Euclid's work was original to him, he proved to be a master at choosing the most significant mathematical axioms (things considered by everyone to be obviously true) and weaving them together in such a way as to unify 300 years of Greek mathematical thought.

Euclid's skill went beyond simple selection, since he also arranged the conclusions or theorems himself and suggested his own proofs for them. These proofs and demonstrations displayed the clarity and logic of his thinking. Although his work would influence all later thought about geometry, nowhere in his work did he use the word "geometry," which meant the narrow field of "earth measurement." Yet in the ancient world, it was in measuring the earth that the usefulness of geometry was first dramatically demonstrated. Greek astronomer Eratosthenes (c. 276–c. 194 B.C.), who was a friend of **Archimedes of Syracuse** (287–212 B.C.)and lived after Euclid, employed Euclid's theorems and was able to invent a practical method of measuring the actual circumference of the Earth itself (not to mention demonstrating that the Earth was round). (See sidebar on Eratosthenes in the **Euclid of Alexandria** entry.) Euclid's *Elements* came to the West via Arabic translations. By the sixteenth century, it was being published in languages other than Latin."

In Renaissance Europe, geometry played an important role in the development of the use of perspective by a number of great artists. Perspective is the technique that allows a painter to project a three-dimensional scene onto a two-dimensional (flat) canvas. Using a technique called projection, a painter can accurately represent a scene exactly as it is perceived by the viewer: objects close to the front are larger than those of the same size in the background. By painting with a grid, all of whose lines are projected toward a center vanishing point, the artist captures the illusion of space and

A page from Euclid's Elements.

depth. A simple example of the use of perspective is that of parallel railroad tracks that appear, when viewed head-on, to meet in the distance. By using geometry, artists could for the first time accurately represent a scene. This technique revolutionized painting.

Another major and very useful Renaissance application of geometry was in the map projections used by Flemish geographer Gerard Mercator (1512–94). He showed the world how to depict a spherical world on a flat surface by using his revolutionary projection lines.

The Rock and Roll Hall of Fame in Cleveland, Ohio, is a fine architectural example of the merging of many different geometric shapes.

Description and use

Once the axioms and theorems of geometry are learned and understood, it is unnecessary to start from scratch each time certain types of problems must be solved. Theorems can be used to answer questions about real, physical things that actually take up space (like a building) as well as something two-dimensional (like a drawing). Knowing rules for certain shapes (**circles, triangles, polygons**) allows a container's **volume**, or the **area** of a piece of land, or even the size of the Earth to be computed. Over 2,300 years ago, Eratosthenes was able to make some determinations about the Earth by knowing that when the summer sun was at its highest point and directly over the city of Alexandria, Egypt, it was at the same time seven degrees from its high point at the city of Cyrene (in North Africa). He was able to guess that the Earth was round as well as calculate its circumference by using the distance between the two cities and by knowing the properties of a circle (that it has a total of 360 degrees).

In some ways, an understanding of geometry provides a useful kind of shorthand for problem-solving. A typical example might be knowing that the area of a rectangle is simply its length times it width. A less-common example is knowing that any angle drawn inside a semicircle must be a right angle. The importance of geometry in everyday life becomes apparent when one realizes that architects, engineers, and even carpenters must understand the properties of geometric objects and shapes in order to do their jobs correctly. Ships and planes could not get where they are going or even stay on course without geometry, and space travel would be an impossibility. Although there are many types of geometry today, some more complicated than others, they all are rooted in the ancient Greek idea of "geo" (earth) "metron" (measure).

Geometry

For More Information

Burton, David M. *Burton's History of Mathematics: An Introduction.* Dubuque, IA: Wm. C. Brown Publishers, 1995.

Diggins, Julia E. *String, Straightedge, and Shadow: The Story of Geometry.* New York: Viking Press, 1965.

Kohn, Edward. *Geometry.* Lincoln, NE: Cliffs Notes, Inc., 1994.

Miller, Charles D., et al. *Mathematical Ideas.* Reading, MA: Addison-Wesley, 1997.

VanCleave, Janice Pratt. *Janice Vancleave's Geometry for Every Kid: Easy Activities That Make Learning Geometry Fun.* New York: John Wiley & Sons, 1994.

Born April 1, 1776
Paris, France

Died June 27, 1831
Paris, France

French applied mathematician,
number theorist, and mathematical physicist

Sophie Germain

Regarded by many mathematicians as France's greatest female mathematician, Sophie Germain was a creative and highly original thinker. Her contributions to the applied mathematics of acoustics and elasticity were of such quality that some scholars consider her to be one of the founders of what is called mathematical physics. Although she was entirely self-taught and worked mostly alone, she was in her time considered to be equal or superior to most of the mathematicians of her age.

Early life and education

Marie-Sophie Germain (pronounced zhur-MAN) was born April 1, 1776, in Paris, France, the middle of three daughters. Since three of the women in the Germain household had names beginning with Marie, they were each called by their second names to avoid confusion. Nothing is known about the background or the family of her mother, Marie-Madeleine Gruguelu. Her father, Ambroise-François Germain, was a wealthy silk merchant who was active in French politics and served in the Estates Général (a

> *"When a person of the sex which, according to our customs and prejudices, must encounter infinitely more difficulties than men . . ., succeeds nevertheless in surmounting these obstacles . . ., then without doubt she must have the noblest courage, quite extraordinary talents and superior genius."*
>
> —*German mathematician*
> *Carl Friedrich Gauss*

version of parliament). Later he became one of the directors of the Bank of France.

Sophie Germain

Most accounts of Sophie Germain's life begin when she was 13 years old. Her parents chose to shield her from the violence and turmoil of revolutionary France by keeping her safely in their home and not letting her go out. To pass the long hours of solitude and boredom, she eventually retreated to her father's large library and began reading. It is said that when she read the version of the death of **Archimedes of Syracuse** (287–212 B.C.), in which he is killed by a Roman soldier while absorbed studying **geometry**, she believed that mathematics must hold true wonders if it could so capture and hold a mind like Archimedes'. Supposedly she decided then and there to become a mathematician and vowed that it would become her life's work.

Although no information exists about the young Germain's elementary education, being a daughter of wealth in eighteenth-century France meant that she most likely was schooled at home by tutors. After her encounter with the story of Archimedes, however, she took charge of her own education and taught herself Latin and Greek so that she could read the classics of mathematics. Then, alone and untutored, she vowed to read every book in her father's library that had anything to do with mathematics (as well as other subjects that interested her). Her father's collection was so large that it took her until she was 18 to accomplish her goal.

During those early years when she was teaching herself geometry, **algebra,** and calculus, her parents initially felt she was too obsessed by her newfound passion for mathematics. Believing that this appetite for learning threatened her health, they decided to take extreme measures when they found that she would not stop studying. Because she usually studied while the family slept, they made her go to bed without the light of a fire or a candlelight by which to read. They even took away her clothes so she could not get out of bed. The determined young girl would first comply with her parents' wishes, but would later get up, wrap herself in blankets, light her smuggled candles, and work at her books all night. Her parents finally found her one morning asleep at her desk in a room so cold that her ink had frozen. They wisely decided to give up their efforts to make her change.

Communicates with the great mathematicians

The end of the eighteenth century was an exciting time for French mathematicians, with several of the best joining the newly opened École Polytechnique as professors. When Germain turned 18, she wanted to attend school there, but she knew it was impossible because this prestigious school did not accept women. It did, however, make the professors' lecture notes available to anyone who asked for them, and in this manner Germain was able to study on her own. Finding the notes of French mathematician **Joseph-Louis Lagrange** (1736–1813) especially interesting, she took advantage of the practice of allowing students to send professors their observations at the end of the course and included some of her own work with it. Lagrange was so impressed by this paper, which was signed "M. le Blanc," that he sought out its author. He eventually discovered "le Blanc" was a woman—Germain.

To Lagrange's credit, his respect and admiration for Germain's work was not affected by his discovery. He provided her with encouragement and support for many years to come. In 1804, Germain sent her work under another name to the great German mathematician **Carl Friedrich Gauss** (1777–1855). Germain and Gauss began an extensive correspondence. Not until three years later did Gauss discover that his colleague was a woman.

Wins grand prize and contributes to mathematical physics

Until 1808, Germain had concentrated her mathematical research on the field called number theory, the branch of mathematics that studies the properties of numbers. She worked especially hard trying to find a proof for the famous problem called Fermat's last theorem. However, in 1808 German physicist E. F. F. Chladni (1756–1827) visited Paris and exhibited the phenomenon called "Chladni figures," which were patterns produced on a plate covered with a thin layer of sand. When Chladni drew a violin bow rapidly up and down the side of the thin plate, various vibration patterns would emerge in the thin layer of sand covering the plate. Besides being fascinating and even lovely to look at, scientists were most intrigued that there was no mathematical theory to explain what the vibrations were or how they worked.

Sophie Germain

Sophie Germain

A competition was soon organized to encourage the study of the vibration problem. A prize was offered by the French Academy of Sciences to anyone who could explain this phenomenon mathematically. Germain attempted to do so, and in September 1811 when she submitted her paper anonymously, it was the competition's only entry. When the judges, one of whom was her friend Lagrange, found a serious flaw in her work, they extended the deadline and allowed her two chances to correct it. Finally, she was awarded the grand prize by the French Academy on January 8, 1816.

Winning this prize made Germain a genuine member of the French scientific community and she was then allowed to attend sessions of the Institut de France. This was the highest honor that the organization had ever bestowed upon a woman. More importantly, her work was a major contribution to the new field of mathematical physics and laid the groundwork for what is called the applied mathematics of acoustics and elasticity. The study of these vibration patterns are used today in the construction of skyscrapers.

Recognition and even collaboration with other, well-respected mathematicians would soon come, but, sadly, she developed breast cancer. She died on June 27, 1831, at the age of 55. Germain never married. Her work, however, has stood the test of time, and her life shows that she combined great natural talent with a strong will to overcome all obstacles. Despite being denied a formal education and access to other minds and the free exchange of ideas, she achieved greatness as a mathematician. As a pioneer woman in the sciences, she is remembered today in Paris by a school (L'École Sophie Germain) and a street (la rue Germain) named after her. Her home is also a historical landmark.

For More Information

Grinstein, Louise S., and Paul J. Campbell, eds. *Women of Mathematics: A Biobibliographic Sourcebook*. New York: Greenwood Press, 1987.

MacTutor History of Mathematics Archive. "Marie-Sophie Germain." http://www-groups.dcs.st-and.ac.uk/~history/Mathematicians/Germain.html (accessed on April 19, 1999).

Morrow, Charlene, and Teri Perl, eds. *Notable Women in Mathematics: A Biographical Dictionary.* Westport, CT: Greenwood Press, 1998.

Osen, Lynn M. *Women in Mathematics.* Cambridge, MA: The MIT Press, 1974.

Young, Robyn V., ed. *Notable Mathematicians: From Ancient Times to the Present.* Detroit: Gale Research, 1998.

Sophie Germain

Born April 28, 1906
Brünn, Moravia (present-day Brno, Czech Republic)

Died January 14, 1978
Princeton, New Jersey

Austrian American logician

Kurt Gödel

Called the most important logician (a person who studies reasoning) since Aristotle (384–322 B.C.), Kurt Gödel offered a radical concept that revolutionized a branch of mathematics. Gödel also had major effects in other areas of science and in philosophy as well. His ground-breaking "incompleteness theorem," which proved that absolute completeness and consistency could not exist in mathematics, is perhaps the most influential theorem in twentieth-century mathematics.

> "To the astonishment of his teachers and fellow pupils, [Kurt Gödel] had mastered university mathematics by his final [high school] years."
>
> —Rudolf Gödel, Kurt's brother

Early life and education

Born in Brünn, Moravia (then in Austria but now called Brno, as part of the Czech Republic), Kurt Friedrich Gödel (pronounced GEUH-dull) was the younger of two sons in the family of Rudolf Gödel and Marianne Handschuh. The Gödel family belonged to the German-speaking minority in Brünn, where they had lived for generations. Gödel's father had received a classical education but became a manager and a part owner of a textile factory. Gödel's mother was the daughter of a weaver but had been well-educated at a French Institute in Brünn. An upper middle class, religious family, the Gödels baptized their sons as Lutherans.

Kurt Gödel

Young Gödel was first sent to a Lutheran school in Brünn when he turned six. When he turned ten, he entered the Staats-Realgymnasium, a German-language high school where he excelled in all his subjects. At home, the family called the inquisitive youngster "Herr Varum" ("Mr. Why"), because he asked so many questions.

Despite what appeared to be a normal childhood and success in school, Gödel was always extremely shy and seemed to become easily upset. Always short and small in build, he was very serious and did not mix well with others. These traits remained with him all his life. As a scholarly teenager, he became interested first in foreign languages, then in history, and then in mathematics when he was about 14. Soon Gödel was reading very complex and difficult works of philosophy. After graduating, he entered the University of Vienna, intending to work on a degree in physics. By 1926, however, he switched subjects and decided to major in mathematics.

Landmark dissertation

In February 1929, Gödel's father died. Despite this sad distraction, Gödel was still able to complete his doctoral dissertation by that summer. With the university's approval of his proof for what would later become known as the "incompleteness theorem," Gödel received his Ph.D. in 1930. Although he presented the new ideas that were contained in his dissertation at a conference that year, the subject appeared beyond the grasp of his audience, and no one seemed to understand its meaning and implications. However, when a German mathematics journal published his paper in 1931, the revolutionary aspects of his proof soon became fully understood.

Gödel's theory (also called "Gödel's proof") seemed to turn around what mathematicians had believed about proofs. His theory showed that within every logical system, propositions or statements cannot be proved or disproved if they are based only on the axioms (self-evident truths that everyone agrees on) of that system. Stated in another way, if mathematics were a game, the consistency or rightness of its rules could not be proved by reference to its own rules. Something outside itself would be needed.

Suffers breakdowns

Gödel was only 24 when his work forever changed mathematical **logic.** Yet when he joined the faculty at the University of Vienna, he was made only a Privatdozent, which meant he was basically an unpaid lecturer. Always shy and never one to want to be the center of attention, Gödel actually taught his few students while facing the chalkboard.

In the fall of 1933, Gödel was invited to join the Institute for Advanced Study in Princeton, New Jersey, which he did. Despite meeting German American physicist and mathematician **Albert Einstein** (1879–1955) and others there, he was lonely and depressed in this new environment. He suffered a nervous breakdown after returning to Europe in June 1934. After staying briefly at the same sanatorium (a place where people with recurring diseases are treated) he had been in once in 1931, he remained in Vienna for a time. Then he returned to Princeton. There Gödel suffered from more depression and overwork. He resigned suddenly in order to return to the sanatorium.

Marriage and final return to Princeton

In September 1938, Gödel married a nightclub dancer, Adele Porkert Nimbursky, with whom he had been involved years before when he was 21. At that time, however, Gödel's father had objected to their association because of the low social standing of her profession and because she had been previously married. So the young Gödel had broken up with her. Now, however, his father was dead and Gödel was able to marry. The marriage was good for Gödel and lasted until he died.

When Gödel and his wife returned to Vienna from the United States in 1939, the political situation had changed drastically. Since Germany's dictator, Adolf Hitler (1889–1945) had forcibly taken over Austria, Gödel found that his old position at the university no longer existed. When he asked why, he was told that since he was known to have a circle of Jewish and liberal acquaintances, he was out of favor with the new order.

Two events convinced Gödel that Austria was not the place for him. First, he was called for an army physical, which he passed; this meant he could be drafted by Austria and be made to serve in

Kurt Gödel

the German army. Second, in late 1939, he was beaten by some Hitler-supporting students. Gödel wasted no time in reapplying for visas to the United States for himself and his wife. By early 1940, the efforts of his friends in America paid off and he was allowed to leave. Because travel was so restricted and difficult during the war, it took Gödel over a year to arrange passage to the United States. He would never return to Europe again.

Gödel arrived in Princeton at the beginning of 1942. He would remain a member of the Institute for Advanced Study for the rest of his life. There he was reunited with Einstein, who served as a witness when Gödel became an American citizen that year. The friendly and outgoing Einstein was often seen walking home with the shy and almost anti-social Gödel. At Princeton, Gödel had no formal duties and was free to pursue whatever research he enjoyed. As time passed, he began to turn more toward philosophy and away from mathematics. His great reputation as a mathematician always guaranteed that his philosophical ideas would always be considered. Some of the ideas he studied involved concepts of **time** travel and alternative universes.

As the years passed and the honors bestowed upon him grew, so did his mental illnesses. In 1950, he was one of two recipients of the first Einstein Award. In 1951, he received an honorary doctorate of literature degree from Yale University in New Haven, Connecticut, and in 1952 he was given an honorary doctorate of science degree from Harvard University in Cambridge, Massachusetts. More honorary awards followed, and in 1955 he was elected to the National Academy of Sciences.

As Gödel's mental state continued to decline, he often lapsed into depression and severe hypochondria (an obsession with imaginary ailments). Always introverted (keeping to one's self), he grew to distrust all doctors even as his hypochondria increased. (It was said that when contacted for an appointment, Gödel would agree to meet but then never show up.) In 1977, the last year of his life, he suffered from paranoia as well. Forced to be hospitalized, Gödel became convinced he was being poisoned. He refused all food and treatment and eventually starved himself to death. He left his widow, Adele; they had no children.

Despite his often bizarre personality, Gödel's revolutionary mathematics made him a highly respected intellectual giant of the twentieth century. The far-reaching implications of his ideas had an impact on philosophy as well as mathematics and have found applications in such areas as **computer** science and economics.

For More Information

Biographical Dictionary of Mathematicians. New York: Charles Scribner's Sons, 1991.

Hofstadter, Douglas. "Kurt Gödel." *Time,* March 29, 1999, pp. 132–34.

MacTutor History of Mathematics Archive. "Kurt Gödel." http://www-groups.dcs.st-and.ac.uk/~history/Mathematicians/Godel.html (accessed on April 19, 1999).

Pappas, Theoni. *Mathematical Scandals.* San Carlos, CA: Wide World Publishing/Tetra, 1997.

Porter, Roy, ed. *The Biographical Dictionary of Scientists.* New York: Oxford University Press, 1994.

Wang, Hao. *Reflections on Kurt Gödel.* Cambridge, MA: Bradford Books, 1990.

Young, Robyn V., ed. *Notable Mathematicians: From Ancient Times to the Present.* Detroit: Gale Research, 1998.

Kurt Gödel

Born May 1, 1924
Washington, D.C.

African American analyst, applied mathematician, and computer scientist

Evelyn Boyd Granville

In 1949, Evelyn Boyd Granville became one of the first two African American women to ever earn a Ph.D. in mathematics when she received her degree from Yale University in New Haven, Connecticut. Granville went on to a career not only as an educator but also as a distinguished applied mathematician in the field of aerospace technology. She contributed to the Vanguard, Mercury, and Apollo space projects. She also became the first African American woman mathematician to receive an honorary doctorate from an American educational institution.

> *"Fortunately for me as I was growing up, I never heard the theory that females aren't equipped mentally to succeed in mathematics. . . ."*

Early life and education

Evelyn Boyd Granville was born May 1, 1924, in Washington, D.C., the younger of two daughters of William Boyd and Julia Walker Boyd. Her father had a variety of jobs, such as janitor, messenger, and chauffeur, and her mother was an examiner with the U.S. Bureau of Engraving and Printing. When her parents separated, young Evelyn and her sister, Doris, were raised by their mother and her twin sister, Louise Walker. Granville's mother and aunt were raised in Orange, Virginia, and graduated from high school.

Evelyn Boyd Granville

Although all public schools in the nation's capital were segregated in the 1930s—resulting in two racially distinct (black and white) school systems—Granville had the opportunity to attend Dunbar High School, an especially good academic school with high standards. As an excellent student, she was able to benefit from its high quality faculty, who regularly pushed students to excel and to apply to the best colleges. This attitude toward learning was reinforced at home. Granville was taught that education was a means not only to a productive life but to overcome and rise above the discrimination of a segregated society.

At Dunbar, Granville's favorite subject was mathematics, although she did well in every subject. Graduating as the valedictorian (the person with the highest grades), she was accepted by the two Massachusetts colleges to which she applied—Smith College in Northampton and Mount Holyoke in South Hadley. Although she received no financial assistance for her freshman year, she chose Smith and was able to attend when her Aunt Louise offered to pay half her expenses. When a scholarship from Phi Delta Kappa, a national sorority of African American teachers, provided additional financial aid, she entered Smith, the largest private college for women in the United States, in the fall of 1941.

Living in a "co-op house" (in which the students waited on tables and helped the cooks) and working at summertime jobs at the National Bureau of Standards in Washington helped Granville pay her bills during her years at Smith. Academically, Granville became fascinated by astronomy but chose instead to concentrate on mathematics. Upon graduating in 1945, she actually had taken as many course hours in physics as she had in mathematics, her major.

Because of her achievements at Smith—graduating summa cum laude (highest distinction) with honors in mathematics and being elected to Phi Beta Kappa—she received a scholarship from the Smith Student Aid Society. Granville could therefore consider continuing on to graduate school. After entering Yale University in 1945 because it offered a scholarship to supplement her help from Smith, she earned a master's degree in both mathematics and physics in one year. Winning two fellowships enabled her to continue on for her Ph.D. without interruption, and in 1949 she received her doctorate degree in mathematics from Yale. That

Marjorie Lee Browne

Marjorie Lee Browne (1914–79) shares with Evelyn Boyd Granville the distinction of being the first African American woman to receive a Ph.D. in mathematics. Born in Memphis, Tennessee, to working class parents, she was a talented tennis player, singer, and avid reader as well as a gifted student in mathematics. She received her Ph.D. in mathematics from the University of Michigan in 1949.

Browne soon found that she was unable to obtain a position at any major research institution. She then decided to return to the South where she joined the mathematics department faculty at North Carolina Central University (NCCU) in 1949. She was the department chair from 1951 to 1970; she retired in 1979.

Browne dedicated her career to strengthening the mathematical preparation of secondary school mathematics teachers and to increasing the presence of minorities and women in mathematical and scientific careers. Besides the many honors and awards she received, she also earned the gratitude of the many exceptional but financially poor students whose education was paid for by Browne. After her death of a heart attack in 1979, her friends and admirers continued her charitable legacy by establishing the Marjorie Lee Browne Trust Fund at NCCU, which annually awards a scholarship.

same year, Marjorie Lee Browne (1914–79) received her Ph.D. from the University of Michigan, so together they became the first African American women to receive Ph.D.'s in mathematics. (See accompanying sidebar for more information on Browne.)

Begins career in mathematics

After graduate school, Granville spent a year at the New York University Institute of Mathematics as a research assistant and part-time instructor. There she discovered how much she enjoyed teaching. However, unable to find a full-time teaching position in New York, she accepted one at Fisk University, a historically black college in Nashville, Tennessee. Although she did not feel she had directly experienced any discrimination because of her race or her sex, only much later did she discover that she was rejected for a position in New York City because of race or sex or both.

Evelyn Boyd Granville

After a two-year stay at Fisk, she returned to Washington, D.C., in July of 1952 to take a position as a mathematician for the National Bureau of Standards. This program eventually was taken over by the Department of the Army. Granville found herself in the company of several mathematicians who were working as computer programmers. At this time, electronic **computers** were in their infancy, and Granville found the application of computers to scientific studies very interesting. Because of this experience, she joined IBM in January 1956. She was introduced to the IBM 650 magnetic drum calculator, the first mass-produced computer, which eventually became the industry workhorse.

Contributes to the American space program

After developing programs for the IBM 650, she became part of a team of IBM mathematicians and scientists who were responsible for developing computer procedures for computing and analyzing a satellite's orbit around the Earth. Working for the National Aeronautics and Space Administration (NASA) as part of IBM, she participated in Project Vanguard and the first U.S. manned space program, Project Mercury. Granville later wrote, "I can say without a doubt that this was the most interesting job of my lifetime—to be a member of a group responsible for writing computer programs to track the paths of vehicles in space." Since NASA was created only in 1958 and launched its first satellite that year, Granville was participating in and contributing to the very beginnings of the American space program.

Although she left IBM in November 1960, she remained connected to the space program by always working for companies that had contracts with NASA. In those early days of rapid growth for the aerospace industry, it was not unusual for a person to switch to a more challenging and usually better-paying job with some frequency.

Returns to teaching

By 1967, Granville was ready for a change. Her seven-year marriage to Reverend Gamaliel Collins was breaking up, and the couple soon divorced. They had no children together. When a teaching position became available in the mathematics department of California State University at Los Angeles, she accepted the post and became full professor. There she applied her experience gained working for IBM and others in the space program, and she taught classes in computer programming.

Once at Cal State, Granville was shocked by the mathematical unpreparedness of many students. So she began working to improve mathematics education at all levels. She joined the Miller Mathematics Improvement Program of the State of California and also taught at the National Science Foundation Institute for Secondary Teachers of Mathematics. Her involvement with education at all levels led her to collaborate on a college textbook, *Theory and Application of Mathematics for Teachers,* which was adopted by over 50 colleges across the country.

In 1970, Granville married Edward V. Granville, a successful real estate broker in Los Angeles who was originally from Texas. Returning to Texas with him in 1984, supposedly to retire, she instead joined the faculty of Texas College, a small, predominantly black, four-year college in Tyler. She taught there until 1988. Although retired, she continues to teach part-time, constantly rekindling her love and that of others for mathematics.

For More Information

Granville, Evelyn Boyd. "My Life as a Mathematician." *SAGE: A Scholarly Journal on Black Women,* Fall 1989, pp. 44–46.

Grinstein, Louise S., and Paul J. Campbell, eds. *Women of Mathematics: A Biobibliographic Sourcebook.* New York: Greenwood Press, 1987.

Morrow, Charlene, and Teri Perl, eds. *Notable Women in Mathematics: A Biographical Dictionary.* Westport, CT: Greenwood Press, 1998.

Young, Robyn V., ed. *Notable Mathematicians: From Ancient Times to the Present.* Detroit: Gale Research, 1998.

Evelyn Boyd Granville

Born August 4, 1805
Dublin, Ireland

Died September 2, 1865
Dublin, Ireland

Irish algebraist

William Rowan Hamilton

Without a doubt Ireland's greatest mathematician, William Rowan Hamilton was a brilliant mathematician who created an entirely new and highly complex system of **algebra** called "quaternions." He also did work in astronomy and contributed to the field of optics.

> *"On earth there is nothing great but man; in man there is nothing great but mind."*

Early life and education

Born in Dublin, Ireland, at the stroke of midnight on August 4, 1805, William Rowan Hamilton was the fourth of nine children born to Archibald Hamilton, a practicing attorney, and Sarah Hutton. When he was three years old, young Hamilton went to live with his uncle, James Hamilton, a parson (clergyman) and the head of a church school in the village of Trim. It is thought that financial conditions drove the family to send the boy to live with his uncle. Trim was 40 miles northwest of Dublin, and young Hamilton had little contact with his parents during his early childhood, although his sisters would stay with him at times. His mother died when Hamilton was 12 and his father died two years later.

From when he was first brought to his uncle in Trim, the three-year-old's rare abilities were immediately apparent. As an educator,

William Rowan Hamilton

Hamilton's uncle knew that the boy was certainly a prodigy (a child with exceptional intelligence). Because young Hamilton's father intended for his son to have some sort of commercial career in the East, Archibald Hamilton instructed his brother to teach William Oriental languages. Young Hamilton proved so smart that he learned Latin, Greek, and Hebrew at five. By nine, he had mastered such languages as Persian, Arabic, Sanskrit, Chaldee, Syriac, Hindustani, Malay, Marathi, and Bengali.

When he was 13, Hamilton encountered someone who would spark a strong interest in mathematics and change his life. In 1818, he met and competed against Zerah Colburn, the "calculating boy" of America. Colburn could give solutions to complex math problems very quickly. In an exhibition, Hamilton went against this "lightning calculator" and came out second-best.

Following his second-place finish to Colburn, Hamilton took up mathematics on his own with a fury. He began studying **Euclid of Alexandria** (c. 325–c. 270 B.C.) in Greek, **Isaac Newton** (1642–1727) in Latin, and Pierre-Simon de Laplace (1749–1827) in French. In fact, Hamilton read Newton's *Aritmetica universalis,* and after mastering analytic **geometry** and calculus, went on to read the great *Principia.* At the age of 17, he found an error in Laplace's *Mécanique celeste,* which he communicated to the president of the Royal Irish Academy. At this point, astronomer John Brinkley, said of Hamilton: "This young man, I do not say will be, but is, the first mathematician of his age." Hamilton had not yet even gone to college.

At the age of 18, Hamilton entered Trinity College in Dublin. Throughout his academic career, he consistently was the top in his class and won extraordinary honors. For example, the college awarded him two separate "Optimes," or off-the-chart grades. This was such a rare honor at Trinity that no one had even won one in the previous 20 years. While still a student, Hamilton wrote the first part of a very important paper on optics. The paper dealt with the patterns of light produced by reflection and refraction. He also predicted a phenomenon called conical refraction, a cone-shaped pattern of light that occurs when light passes through a certain type of crystal. Conical refraction was later proved experimentally by others. Hamilton, however, had used only algebraic functions to figure it out.

Becomes astronomer royal

By his final year at Trinity, Hamilton had achieved such a reputation that, while still an undergraduate, he was appointed professor of astronomy at Trinity. With this position went the titles of astronomer royal of Ireland and director of the Dunsink Observatory. Incredibly, Hamilton had not even applied for the astronomer royal position, which had become vacant when Brinkley resigned to become a bishop. Hamilton accepted the position on the understanding that he could continue to pursue mathematics. Hamilton's first love was mathematics, and he accomplished little as a practical astronomer. Besides lacking the technical training, he suffered from having inferior equipment. After his first few years, Hamilton did little actual observing and devoted himself mainly to theoretical studies. Nevertheless, he remained at the observatory for the rest of his life.

Marries and meets poets

While still at Trinity, Hamilton fell in love with a friend's sister. When the woman rejected his marriage proposal, the sensitive Hamilton became so ill and depressed that he came close to suicide. It is said that this rejection stayed with him all his life. In 1831, he was again rejected, this time by the sister of poet Aubrey De Vere (1814–1902). However, two years later, Hamilton married Helen Marie Bayly, a country preacher's daughter. Although they had three children together, his wife proved to be not only chronically ill but extremely pious, shy, and timid. Since she was also unable to run a household, Hamilton's married life was both difficult and unhappy.

Hamilton's demeanor was not all sadness, however. He was often described as an outgoing, friendly man with a good sense of humor. Always a lover of poetry and philosophy, he became good friends with two of England's greatest poets, William Wordsworth (1770–1850) and Samuel Taylor Coleridge (1772–1834). When he was young, Hamilton had considered himself a poet. His friend Wordsworth often feared that Hamilton might give up being a superior scientist to become a bad poet.

Develops quaternions

As a highly intelligent mathematician, Hamilton naturally considered the most difficult concepts. Negative and imaginary numbers

William Rowan
Hamilton

William Rowan Hamilton

were therefore part of what he thought hardest about when he considered the foundations of algebra. By 1843 Hamilton had reached a point where he could logically go no further after ten years of work. However, while taking a walk with his wife along the Royal Canal on October 16 of that year, he suddenly thought of a solution to his problem that would allow him to create an entire new system of mathematics. He later described that moment, saying, "An electric circuit seemed to close, and a spark flashed forth." All his life, Hamilton was a dedicated scribbler who always had paper and pencil ready to jot down an idea or a formula. When his flash struck suddenly on the bridge, however, he had nothing with which he could capture his idea, so he scratched the correct formula for his discovery on the stone of the Brougham Bridge. Today a plaque marks that important spot.

Hamilton believed that his discovery of what he called "quaternions" (so called, because it involved a fourth dimension) would revolutionize mathematical physics. Hamilton's quaternions involved the analysis of vectors or forces that have both size and direction (like a river flowing west at 5 miles per hour, or a 20 mile-per-hour wind blowing from the north). Since he was trying to study the rotation of a vector in space, he found he had to calculate it in four dimensions, thereby creating an entirely new type of algebra.

Hamilton spent the rest of his life working on quaternions. However, the books and articles he published in his lifetime on this subject were long, complex, and impossible for nearly everyone to understand. He was not the best advocate for his own ideas; in fact, his discoveries had none of the revolutionary impact that he foresaw. It was not until three quarters of a century later that his new kind of algebra would prove useful. By then, his quaternions (now called "noncommutative algebra") would prove essential to the formation of the basis for quantum mechanics and for understanding the internal structure of the atom.

Although Hamilton received several major awards in his life—he was the first foreign member of the National Academy of Sciences in the United States, and he was knighted by Great Britain in 1835—the last third of his life proved to be a time of personal unhappiness. During these years he suffered badly from a serious drinking problem as well as from gout. He died in Dublin on September 2, 1865. His invalid wife survived him by four years.

For More Information

Asimov, Isaac. *Asimov's Biographical Encyclopedia of Science and Technology.* Garden City, NY: Doubleday & Company, 1982.

Biographical Dictionary of Mathematicians. New York: Charles Scribner's Sons, 1991.

Burton, David M. *Burton's History of Mathematics: An Introduction.* Dubuque, IA: Wm. C. Brown Publishers, 1995.

MacTutor History of Mathematics Archive. "Sir William Rowan Hamilton." http://www-groups.dcs.st-and.ac.uk/~history/Mathematicians/Hamilton.html (accessed on April 20, 1999).

Young, Robyn V., ed. *Notable Mathematicians: From Ancient Times to the Present.* Detroit: Gale Research, 1998.

William Rowan Hamilton

Born December 9, 1906
New York, New York

Died January 1, 1992
Arlington, Virginia

American computer scientist

Grace Hopper

One of the world's foremost pioneers in the field of **computer** programming, Grace Hopper contributed to the design and development of COBOL, one of the most widely used computer languages. Because her professional career spanned the growth of modern computer science, she became an influential force and a legendary figure in the development of programming languages.

> *"A ship in port is safe, but that's not what ships are built for."*

Early life and education

Grace Brewster Murray Hopper was born December 9, 1906, in New York City, the first of three children. She had a sister, Mary, and a brother, Roger. Her parents were Walter Fletcher Murray, an insurance broker, and Mary Campbell Van Horne, whose father was an engineer. It was this grandfather who inspired Hopper's love of **geometry** and mathematics. Her family was close-knit and would spend many warm months in their summer home in Wolfeboro, New Hampshire. As a youngster, Hopper was not interested in what most other girls were playing with, and she spent a great deal of her time building things. Instead of playing with her doll house, she preferred to build furniture for it. She was especially intrigued by devices with moving parts. A family story tells how she dismantled all seven clocks in her summer home trying to figure out how to put back together the first one she had taken apart.

Grace Hopper

Besides her grandfather, her father was an important influence on her, especially on her ability not to give up on anything she did. Her father lost both his legs when his daughter was in high school. As a double amputee, he refused to feel sorry for himself and taught himself to walk using two wooden legs and a cane. More important was his strong belief that girls should be given the same educational opportunities as boys. He saw to it that his daughters were given those opportunities.

In school, Hopper was an excellent student who also participated in many different types of activities. She was so bright that she graduated from high school at age 16. Her parents wisely guided her toward a one-year preparatory school, thinking she was too young to send off to college. The following year she enrolled at Vassar College, a women's college in Poughkeepsie, New York.

At Vassar she proved to be a hard worker, taking as many courses as possible and tutoring other students as well. In 1928 she graduated from Vassar with a bachelor's degree in mathematics and physics and was elected to Phi Beta Kappa, a prestigious national collegiate honor society. After winning a fellowship, she attended Yale University in New Haven, Connecticut, and received her master of arts degree in mathematics in 1930. That year she also married Vincent Foster Hopper, an English teacher at New York University's School of Commerce, whom she had met in Wolfeboro. The couple would have no children and eventually divorced in 1945.

Grace Hopper remained at Yale to pursue her Ph.D. and began teaching at Vassar as an instructor in 1931. Working under algebraist Oystein Ore (1899–1968), she received her Ph.D. in mathematics in 1934. Yale awarded only seven Ph.D.'s in mathematics in four years (1934–37). She was the only woman to receive one of these Ph.D.'s, which made her degree an especially significant achievement.

Wartime involvement leads to early computer work

Hopper taught at Vassar College from 1931 to 1943, rising from instructor to associate professor. After World War II (1939–45) broke out, she felt the strong need to serve her country as her family had always done. One of her ancestors had been a minuteman during the Revolutionary War (1775–83), and a great-grandfather had been a rear admiral in the Civil War (1861–65). When the United States entered World War II in 1941, Hopper's husband and brother joined the Army Air Corps, her father worked for the Selective Service Board, her mother served on the Ration Board, and her sister worked in a factory making fuses for bombs. Hopper tried to join the Navy but was at first rejected because of her age (36) and low weight (121 pounds). She kept applying and finally was allowed to join the Naval Reserve in 1943. She was commissioned as a lieutenant in the U.S. Navy in 1944.

A bug in the system

While working with the Mark II, Grace Hopper and her team at Harvard University became responsible for the terms "bug" and "debug" entering the vocabulary of computer programmers. Once, when the Mark II suddenly stopped working altogether, Hopper and her team found a dead moth in an electric switch. The dead bug was removed and fixed to the page of a logbook that was given to Aiken. The page noted that the Mark II had been "debugged!"

Because of her mathematical expertise, she was assigned to the Bureau of Ordnance Computation Project at Harvard University in Cambridge, Massachusetts, where she worked with Commander Howard Aiken (1900–73). Aiken was a pioneer in computers. He was trying to build a machine that would perform long and complicated calculations very rapidly. Called the Mark I, it would become the earliest automatic sequence digital computer. This first computer was noisy and large enough to fill a room. Despite having no experience with computers, after Hopper joined the group she was given a codebook and asked to begin computations. Although she worked nearly around the clock at times, Hopper enjoyed the experience and began to write her first programs for Mark I. By the time the war ended, the Mark II, which was five times faster than the first version, had already been built. Hopper decided to remain with Aiken and not return to teaching at Vassar.

Develops "A-O" and influences COBOL

Hopper remained with Aiken and the Navy through Mark III. In 1949, she left and joined a new company formed by computer pioneers J. Presper Eckert (1919–95) and John W. Mauchly (1907–80). She became senior mathematician at the Eckert-

Grace Hopper

Grace Hopper salutes at her retirement ceremony in 1986.

Mauchly Computer Corporation. A year later she became a senior programmer, probably one of the first persons to hold what would become a common title in the computer industry. She stayed in that position as the company was absorbed by the Remington Rand Corporation, which later became the Sperry Rand Corporation.

While Hopper was at Eckert-Mauchly working on UNIVAC I—which would become the first large, commercially available, general-purpose computer—she developed the first language compiler.

Until her program, no software existed that could translate a programmer's language into machine-readable instructions. With her innovative "A-O" program, programming became easier and faster and opened a new era for programming languages.

Having demonstrated that computers were programmable and capable not only of doing arithmetic but of manipulating symbols as well, Hopper and her staff created FLOW-MATIC, the first program using English language words. This program came out at a time when the need for standardization in languages was becoming obvious to everyone. If different computer programs could all agree on certain basic standards, they could be more efficient and more widely used. When a common language called COBOL (Common Business Oriented Language) was finally developed by RCA, Hopper's FLOW-MATIC was highly influential in determining how COBOL would look. Because of her work, the English language–based COBOL was universally accepted and became the most widely used language of the 1960s and 1970s.

In 1959, Hopper was named director of automatic programming development at the UNIVAC Division of Sperry Rand, where she remained until her retirement in 1971. She returned to active duty in the Navy in 1967 and was promoted to captain in 1973 by a special act of Congress. In 1983, she was the oldest officer on active duty in the Navy. Two year later, she was promoted from commodore to rear admiral. When she left the Navy in 1986, she had served for 43 years.

Among her many awards and honors were the 1969 award as "Man of the Year" from the Data Processing Management Association and the National Medal of Technology given to her by President George Bush (1924–) in 1991. After leaving the Navy, she continued to work as a senior consultant for the Digital Equipment Corporation until her death on January 1, 1992. One of her favorite sayings, and one that typified her life, was "A ship in port is safe, but that's not what ships are built for."

For More Information

Agnes Scott College Mathematics Department. *Biographies of Women Mathematicians.* "Grace Murray Hopper." http://www.scottlan.edu/lriddle/women/hopper.html (accessed on April 20, 1999).

Grace Hopper

Grace Hopper

Cortada, James W. *Historical Dictionary of Data Processing: Biographies.* New York: Greenwood Press, 1987.

Grinstein, Louise S., and Paul J. Campbell, eds. *Women of Mathematics: A Biobibliographic Sourcebook.* New York: Greenwood Press, 1987.

MacTutor History of Mathematics Archive. "Grace Brewster Murray Hopper." http://www-groups.dcs.st-and.ac.uk/~history/Mathematicians/Hopper.html (accessed on April 20, 1999).

Maisel, Merry. "Tribute to Grace Murray Hopper." *The Systers Home Page.* http://www.sdsc.edu/Hopper/hopper.html (accessed on May 4, 1999).

Morrow, Charlene, and Teri Perl, eds. *Notable Women in Mathematics: A Biographical Dictionary.* Westport, CT: Greenwood Press, 1998.

Young, Robyn V., ed. *Notable Mathematicians: From Ancient Times to the Present.* Detroit: Gale Research, 1998.

Born April 14, 1629
The Hague, The Netherlands

Died July 8, 1695
The Hague, The Netherlands

Dutch astronomer and mathematical physicist

Christiaan Huygens

B est known for his classic work and discoveries in astronomy and physics, Christiaan Huygens might have been one of history's greatest mathematicians had he not spent so much time and energy in other fields. He made several improvements to then-existing methods of mathematical calculations, but his real contribution to mathematics was his demonstration of how mathematics could be used to solve problems in the natural sciences.

Early life and education

Christiaan Huygens (pronounced HEUY-kuns) came from a very prominent Dutch family of diplomats. Both his grandfather, after whom he was named, and his father, Constantijn, served as secretary to the monarch. The family had a strong tradition of education and culture. His grandfather took an active role in the education of his children, seeing to it that they were well-educated in both the sciences and the arts. Young Huygens's father, for example, was not only an important government official but an artist, a composer, and a poet whose work gave him a lasting place in the history of Dutch literature.

> *"The world is my country, science my religion."*

Christiaan Huygens

Both Huygens and his brother were educated at home until the age of 16 by their father and private tutors; both received a broad basic education. Huygens was especially talented. Even at age 13, he demonstrated a unique ability to excel at both theoretical and practical matters. From 1645 to 1647, Huygens studied law and mathematics at the University of Leiden. His abilities in mathematics were so strong that even at a young age he was corresponding with French number theorist Marin Mersenne (1588–1648). For the next two years, he studied law and mathematics at the newly founded Collegium Arausiacum (College of Orange) at Breda in Holland. There he studied classical mathematics as well as the most modern methods, such as those of French algebraist and philosopher **René Descartes** (1596–1650).

In August 1649 when he completed his studies, Huygens did not choose the diplomatic career of his family's tradition but decided rather to devote himself completely to what he called the study of nature, or natural science. Using an allowance given to him by his father, he was able to remain at home from 1650 to 1666 and pursue his scientific interests. These years were the most productive part of his life.

First publications

Huygens turned first to mathematics and, inspired by the work of third-century Greek mathematician Pappus of Alexandria (c. 290–c. 350 B.C.), published his first book in 1651. Another book followed in 1654. Soon, his attention turned to the new idea of **probability** after he read the work of French geometer and philosopher Blaise Pascal (1623–62). (See sidebar on Pascal in the **Probability** entry.) By 1657, he completed and published his *De Ratiociniis in Ludo Aleae,* applying the important new theory of probability to the calculation of life expectancy. This important work remained the only book on the subject of probability until the eighteenth century.

Telescopic discoveries

In 1655, Huygens and his brother discovered a way to make better lenses and incorporated them into a new, 23-foot-long telescope. That winter Huygens turned his telescope to the skies. He discovered that the planet Saturn is surrounded by a thin ring that does

not touch the planet's surface. He also discovered a huge satellite of Saturn, which he named Titan. He went on to observe both the large cloud of gas and dust known as the Orion Nebula and the surface of the planet Mars. He made the first specific guess of the distance of stars.

Christiaan Huygens used a new, 23-foot-long telescope to study the rings of the planet Saturn.

Measurement of time

As a mathematician, Huygens always tried to give his work a sound quantitative basis. One difficulty was the lack of any way of keeping really accurate **time.** To this problem, Huygens brought a special combination of theory and practice. What was needed, he knew, was a device that would keep a constant, regular motion to which a clock could be geared.

In late 1656, Huygens began adapting the work of Italian mathematician, astronomer, and physicist **Galileo** (1564–1642).

Christiaan Huygens

Galileo's work involved the use of a pendulum to measure time. Seventy-five years earlier, Galileo had observed the swinging movement of a chandelier in a church and realized that the time of each swing was *nearly* the same, no matter how long or short was its arc. Huygens then set out to build a mechanism that would make the time of each swing *exactly* the same. Mathematics was essential for him to do this.

By 1659, Huygens's intensive theoretical studies paid off. He discovered that "perfect tautochronism" (*exactly* equal time of each swing) can be obtained if the path of the pendulum's end follows a cycloid shape (a type of curve). Having solved the theoretical part of the problem, Huygens then set out to actually build a mechanism that would take advantage of this cycloid shape. His brilliant solution was a pendulum with **weight**s at its end that made it move in a cycloid arc. He then used a system of falling weights that would keep the pendulum moving despite friction and air resistance. The design of today's old-fashioned "grandfather clock" has changed little since Huygens built the first one.

Moves to Paris

During his years at home, Huygens made three trips to Paris and London, the first when he was 26. In these cities he was able to meet with many of the best scientists and scholars of the time. During his third trip to Paris, he took time in September 1663 to journey to London to become a member of the newly founded Royal Society. At the same time in France, a circle of scholars was obtaining official status and financial support from the king for their own national scientific society. When the Académie Royale des Sciences was formed in 1666, Huygens was one of its founding members. He then traveled to Paris in May 1666 and remained there until 1681.

At the age of 37, Huygens was an internationally known scholar and the most prominent member of the Academy. Because of his success, he received a salary and free living quarters. Huygens might have remained in this comfortable situation for the rest of his life, but as a Protestant in Catholic France, he was aware of the gradually increasing intolerance of Protestants on the part of King Louis XIV (1638–1715). When war finally broke out between Holland and France, Huygens was in a very uneasy situation, despite the king's assurance of protection. When he left Paris in 1681 because of an illness, he would never return.

Wave theory of light

By 1681, Huygens had already been hard at work trying to correct the theory of light held by English mathematician and physicist **Isaac Newton** (1642–1727). Newton's theory argued that light was composed of a stream of particles. Huygens disagreed and tried to prove that there were many more conditions under which light would behave as if it were a wave. In 1678, he wrote his *Traité de la Lumière,* which announced the wave or pulse theory of light. This work eventually was published in 1690. Modern physics now shows that both Newton and Huygens were in some ways correct.

Huygens never married. In many ways, he was a solitary scholar who seldom collaborated with anyone else. He was often ill and was never as financially secure as others assumed him to be. Although solitude seems to characterize him personally and professionally, his work still reaches out to others and demonstrates the great explanatory power that mathematics can have in explaining the forces of the natural world.

For More Information

Asimov, Isaac. *Asimov's Biographical Encyclopedia of Science and Technology.* Garden City, NY: Doubleday & Company, 1982.

Eves, Howard. *An Introduction to the History of Mathematics.* Philadelphia: Saunders College Publishing, 1990.

Gillispie, Charles C., ed. *Dictionary of Scientific Biography.* New York: Charles Scribner's Sons, 1990.

MacTutor History of Mathematics Archive. "Christiaan Huygens." http://www-groups.dcs.st-and.ac.uk/~history/Mathematicians/Huygens.html (accessed on April 20, 1999).

Young, Robyn V., ed. *Notable Mathematicians: From Ancient Times to the Present.* Detroit: Gale Research, 1998.

Born c. 370
Alexandria, Egypt

Died 415
Alexandria, Egypt

Greek geometer, astronomer, and philosopher

Hypatia of Alexandria

Hypatia is the earliest known female mathematician in history. She was the first woman to make a substantial contribution to the development of mathematics. Although all her writings are lost, it is known that she both lectured and wrote on some of the most advanced mathematics of her time. Hypatia lived at a time when her city of Alexandria and its institutions were in decline and were no longer the center of Greek intellectual life. It was also a time of conflict between pagans (people without a religion) and Christians, who identified learning and science with paganism. Because of this attitude, the learned Hypatia was brutally murdered by a fanatical Christian group.

> *"Reserve your right to think, for even to think wrongly is better than not to think at all."*

Early life and training

Hypatia (pronounced high-PAY-shee-uh) was born around 370 (although possibly as early as 355) and lived in Alexandria, the Egyptian city built 700 years earlier by Alexander the Great (356–323 B.C.), conqueror of Greece, Asia Minor, and Egypt. After its founding, Alexandria became a great city, with schools and libraries that attracted scholars from all over the world. By Hypatia's time, however, the Alexandrian empire had given way to the great Roman empire, and its universities and libraries were rapidly breaking up and closing down.

Hypatia of Alexandria

Hypatia's father, Theon of Alexandria, was a well-known and highly educated mathematician. He was part of the last generation of scholars who still taught at the university known as the Museum. It is believed that he educated Hypatia himself and tried to develop her into "the most perfect human being." He not only gave her the best training in arts, literature, science, and philosophy but allowed her to travel and study in Athens. He supervised her physical training as well.

Much of Hypatia's life is clouded in legend. For example, she has been described as very beautiful, charismatic, and modest, though that cannot be confirmed. What *is* known, however, is that she was an excellent pupil and shared her father's love of learning and his passion for finding answers—especially in mathematics. Most historians believe that her talents and intelligence quickly showed themselves and that she went beyond her own father's abilities at a young age. She also learned from her father the great power of words. When she began to teach, she soon became one of the university's most popular lecturers. Students came from great distances to hear her speak.

Hypatia's mathematics

Like her father, Hypatia was a strong supporter of Greek scientific rational thought, which held that nature's laws can be learned by observation and experiment. Therefore she did not believe that religion had the answers to everything. Because of this belief, she never converted to the Christianity of the Roman Empire as did many of her contemporaries. Furthermore, she always argued that the search for truth was the highest calling. To her, mathematics was one area where certain truths could be discovered, and she grew to love mathematics simply for its own sake.

Her love and enjoyment of mathematics came across not only in her lectures but in her writings as well. Although all her mathematical writings were destroyed when the libraries and temples of Alexandria were sacked, it is known that she wrote "commentaries" on the works of two highly influential Greek mathematicians, Apollonius of Perga (c. 262–c. 190 B.C.) and Diophantus of

Alexandria (c. 200–c. 284). In her time, commentaries were a way of explaining difficult mathematical classics to students in a way that made them understandable. The important early **algebra** of Diophantus is said to have survived mainly because of Hypatia. Also, she explained the landmark work on conic sections (curves) by Apollonius to her students. Her explanation would prove very important to seventeenth-century astronomers who studied the curved orbits of planets and comets. It would also be critical to the birth of modern science.

In addition to other commentaries done on the classics of astronomy, Hypatia also co-authored with her father at least one book on the **geometry** of **Euclid of Alexandria** (c. 325–c. 270 B.C.). Most historians are convinced that she assisted Theon of Alexandria (c. 335–c. 405) in producing his revised and much-improved version of Euclid's *Elements*. Theon's version eventually became the basis of all modern editions of that mathematical classic.

Admired and respected

Nearly all that is known about Hypatia comes from the writings of her contemporaries, naturally all of whom were men. One of her most distinguished pupils, Synesius of Cyrene (378–430), who went on to become bishop of Ptolemais (located on the coast of what is now Libya). He wrote letters to her in which it is very obvious how much he valued her scientific advice. Hypatia was also admired and written about by several religious historians who, despite her paganism, described her as a genius.

Not everyone thought of her in such positive terms, however. Some people (especially the more intense Christians who identified science and learning with paganism) regarded her as a real threat to their interests. Hypatia was a unique woman, especially for her time. Besides being more talented and more educated than most men of Alexandria, she was an unusually liberated person. She wore the rough, white cloak or robe called a tribon that philosophers favored. She also traveled freely and walked the streets of the city discussing ideas as only men did. Historian Socrates Scholasticus (c. 380–c. 450), who knew her well, described her as always being confident and at ease in such situations. Yet, he said, she was never a show-off and always exercised modesty, moderation, and self-control. She was so popular that some historians believe she may have held a political position.

Greek tragedy

By Hypatia's time, Christianity had become the official religion of the Roman Empire; many of the Greek temples were converted into churches. Since Christians regarded the traditional Greek religious beliefs as pagan and therefore as opposing their new religion, they considered anyone who strongly held those beliefs as a threat. Both the pagan Greeks and the Jews of Alexandria were increasingly treated as scapegoats and were blamed for anything that went wrong. During one of the more violent outbreaks of hostility between pagans and Christians, Hypatia was singled out as responsible for the trouble between the local authorities and the Church. She was killed by a crazed mob of Christians.

The great eighteenth-century historian Edward Gibbon wrote of her death in *The History of the Decline and Fall of the Roman Empire,* basing his comments on ancient accounts. He said, "On a fatal day, in the holy season of Lent, Hypatia was torn from her chariot, stripped naked, dragged to the church, and inhumanely butchered. . .; her flesh was scraped from her bones with sharp oyster shells, and her quivering limbs were delivered to the flames."

Following Hypatia's torture and terrible death, many scholars felt threatened; Alexandria became even less the center of learning that it once had been. Gibbon and others use Hypatia's death to mark the end of the great age of Greek mathematics. Much later, in 641, the city of Alexandria itself was invaded and destroyed by Arabs who used the manuscripts in the library as fuel for the city's warm baths. Hypatia's works were probably among them.

For More Information

Alec, Margaret. *Hypatia's Heritage: A History of Women in Science from Antiquity through the Nineteenth Century.* Boston: Beacon Press, 1986.

Dzielska, Maria, and F. Lyra (translator). *Hypatia of Alexandria.* Cambridge, MA: Harvard University Press, 1995.

Grinstein, Louise S., and Paul J. Campbell, eds. *Women of Mathematics: A Biobibliographic Sourcebook.* New York: Greenwood Press, 1987.

Osen, Lynn M. *Women in Mathematics.* Cambridge, MA: The MIT Press, 1974.

Perl, Teri. *Math Equals: Biographies of Women Mathematicians.* Menlo Park, CA: Addison-Wesley Publishing Company, 1978.

Young, Robyn V., ed. *Notable Mathematicians: From Ancient Times to the Present.* Detroit: Gale Research, 1997.

Hypatia of Alexandria

Selected Bibliography

General sources

Asimov, Isaac. *Realm of Numbers*. Boston: Houghton Mifflin, 1959.

Ball, W. W. Rouse. *A Short Account of the History of Mathematics*. New York: Dover Publications, 1960.

Bergamini, David. *Mathematics*. Alexandria, VA: Time-Life Books, 1980.

Borman, Jami Lynne. *Computer Dictionary for Kids—and Their Parents*. Hauppauge, NY: Barron's Educational Series, 1995.

Boyer, Carl B., and Uta C. Merzbach. *A History of Mathematics*. New York: John Wiley & Sons, 1989.

Bunt, Lucas N. H., et al. *The Historical Roots of Elementary Mathematics*. Englewood Cliffs, NJ: Prentice Hall, 1976.

Burton, David M. *Burton's History of Mathematics*. Dubuque, IA: Wm. C. Brown Publishers, 1995.

Cajori, F. *A History of Mathematics*. New York: Chelsea, 1985.

Selected Bibliography

Dictionary of Mathematics Terms. New York: Barron's Educational Series, Inc., 1987.

Duren, Peter, ed. *A Century of Mathematics in America.* 3 vols. Providence, RI: American Mathematical Society, 1989.

Eves, Howard. *An Introduction to the History of Mathematics.* Philadelphia: Saunders College Publishing, 1990.

Flegg, Graham. *Numbers: Their History and Meaning.* New York: Schocken Books, 1983.

Friedberg, Richard. *An Adventurer's Guide to Number Theory.* New York: Dover Publications, 1994.

Green, Gordon W., Jr. *Helping Your Child to Learn Math.* New York: Citadel Press, 1995.

Green, Judy, and Jeanne Laduke. *A Century of Mathematics in America.* Providence, RI: American Mathematical Society, 1989.

Groza, Vivian Shaw. *A Survey of Mathematics: Elementary Concepts and Their Historical Development.* New York: Holt, Rinehart and Winston, 1968.

Heath, T. L. *A History of Greek Mathematics.* New York: Dover Publications, 1981.

Heddens, James W. and William R. Speer. *Today's Mathematics: Concepts and Methods in Elementary School Mathematics.* Upper Saddle River, NJ: Merrill, 1997.

Hirschi, L. Edwin. *Building Mathematics Concepts in Grades Kindergarten Through Eight.* Scranton, PA: International Textbook Co., 1970.

Hoffman, Paul. *Archimedes' Revenge: The Joys and Perils of Mathematics.* New York: Ballantine, 1989.

Hogben, Lancelot T. *Mathematics in the Making.* London: Galahad Books, 1974.

Humez, Alexander, et al. *Zero to Lazy Eight: The Romance of Numbers.* New York: Simon & Schuster, 1993.

Immergut, Brita. *Arithmetic and Algebra—Again.* New York: McGraw-Hill, 1994.

Julius, Edward H. *Arithmetricks: 50 Easy Ways to Add, Subtract, Multiply, and Divide Without a Calculator.* New York: John Wiley and Sons, 1995.

Katz, Victor J. *A History of Mathematics: An Introduction.* New York: HarperCollins College Publishers, 1993.

Kline, Morris. *Mathematics for the Nonmathematician.* New York: Dover Publications, 1985.

Kline, Morris. *Mathematics in Western Culture.* New York: Oxford University Press, 1953.

Miles, Thomas J., and Douglas W. Nance. *Mathematics: One of the Liberal Arts.* Pacific Grove, CA: Brooks/Cole Publishing Co., 1997.

Miller, Charles D., et al. *Mathematical Ideas.* Reading, MA: Addison-Wesley, 1997.

Moffatt, Michael. *The Ages of Mathematics: The Origins.* Garden City, NY: Doubleday & Company, 1977.

Rogers, James T. *The Pantheon Story of Mathematics for Young People.* New York: Pantheon Books, 1966.

Slavin, Steve. *All the Math You'll Ever Need.* New York: John Wiley and Sons, 1989.

Smith, David Eugene. *Number Stories of Long Ago.* Detroit: Gale Research, 1973.

Smith, David Eugene, and Yoshio Mikami. *A History of Japanese Mathematics.* Chicago: The Open Court Publishing Company, 1914.

Smith, Karl J. *Mathematics: Its Power and Utility.* Pacific Grove, CA: Brooks/Cole, 1997.

Stillwell, John. *Mathematics and Its History.* New York: Springer-Verlag, 1989.

Temple, George. *100 Years of Mathematics.* New York: Springer-Verlag, 1981.

Selected Bibliography

Selected Bibliography

West, Beverly Henderson, et al. *The Prentice-Hall Encyclopedia of Mathematics.* Englewood Cliffs, NJ: Prentice-Hall, 1982.

Wheeler, Ruric E. *Modern Mathematics.* Pacific Grove, CA: Brooks/Cole Publishing, 1995.

Wheeler, Ruric E., and Ed R. Wheeler. *Modern Mathematics for Elementary School Teachers.* Pacific Grove, CA: Brooks/Cole Publishing, 1995.

Wulforst, Harry. *Breakthrough to the Computer Age.* New York: Charles Scribner's Sons, 1982.

General biographical sources

Abbott, David, ed. *The Biographical Dictionary of Scientists: Mathematicians.* New York: Peter Bedrick Books, 1986.

Albers, Donald J., and G. L. Alexanderson, eds. *Mathematical People: Profiles and Interviews.* Boston: Birkhauser, 1985.

Albers, Donald J., Gerald L. Alexanderson, and Constance Reid. *More Mathematical People.* New York: Harcourt, 1991.

Alec, Margaret. *Hypatia's Heritage: A History of Women in Science from Antiquity through the Nineteenth Century.* Boston: Beacon Press, 1986.

Asimov, Isaac. *Asimov's Biographical Encyclopedia of Science and Technology.* Garden City, NY: Doubleday & Company, 1982.

Bell, Eric T. *Men of Mathematics.* New York: Simon and Schuster, 1986.

Biographical Dictionary of Mathematicians. New York: Charles Scribner's Sons, 1991.

Cortada, James W. *Historical Dictionary of Data Processing: Biographies.* New York: Greenwood Press, 1987.

Daintith, John, et al. *Biographical Encyclopedia of Scientists.* London: Institute of Physics Publishing, 1994.

Dunham, W. *The Mathematical Universe: An Alphabetical Journey through the Great Proofs, Problems, and Personalities.* New York: John Wiley & Sons, 1994.

Elliott, Clark A. *Biographical Dictionary of American Science: The Seventeenth Through the Nineteenth Centuries.* Westport, CT: Greenwood Press, 1979.

Gillispie, Charles C., ed. *Dictionary of Scientific Biography.* New York: Charles Scribner's Sons, 1990.

Grinstein, Louise S., and Paul J. Campbell, eds. *Women of Mathematics: A Biobibliographic Sourcebook.* New York: Greenwood Press, 1987.

Haber, Louis. *Black Pioneers of Science and Invention.* New York: Harcourt, Brace & World, 1970.

Henderson, Harry. *Modern Mathematicians.* New York: Facts on File, 1996.

Hollingdale, Stuart. *Makers of Mathematics.* London: Penguin Books, 1989.

Hudson, Wade, and Valerie Wilson Wesley. *Afro-Bets Book of Black Heroes From A to Z: An Introduction to Important Black Achievers for Young Readers.* East Orange, NJ: Just Us Books, 1997.

Itô, Kiyosi, ed. *Encyclopedia Dictionary of Mathematics.* Cambridge, MA: MIT Press, 1987.

McGraw-Hill Modern Scientists and Engineers. New York: McGraw-Hill, 1980.

McMurray, Emily J., ed. *Notable Twentieth-Century Scientists.* Detroit: Gale Research, 1995.

Metcalf, Doris Hunter. *Portraits of Exceptional African American Scientists.* Carthage, IL: Good Apple, 1994.

Millar, David, Ian Millar, John Millar, and Margaret Millar. *The Cambridge Dictionary of Scientists.* Cambridge, England: Cambridge University Press, 1996.

Selected Bibliography

Selected Bibliography

Morgan, Bryan. *Men and Discoveries in Mathematics*. London: John Murray Publishers, 1972.

Morrow, Charlene, and Teri Perl, eds. *Notable Women in Mathematics: A Biographical Dictionary*. Westport, CT: Greenwood Press, 1998.

Muir, Jane. *Of Men and Numbers: The Story of the Great Mathematicians*. New York: Dover Publications, 1996.

Ogilvie, Marilyn Bailey. *Women in Science: Antiquity through the Nineteenth Century*. Cambridge, MA: MIT Press, 1986.

Osen, Lynn M. *Women in Mathematics*. Cambridge, MA: The MIT Press, 1974.

Pappas, Theoni. *Mathematical Scandals*. San Carlos, CA: Wide World Publishing/Tetra, 1997.

Perl, Teri. *Math Equals: Biographies of Women Mathematicians*. Menlo Park, CA: Addison-Wesley Publishing Company, 1978.

Porter, Roy, ed. *The Biographical Dictionary of Scientists*. New York: Oxford University Press, 1994.

Potter, Joan, and Constance Claytor. *African Americans Who Were First: Illustrated with Photographs*. New York: Cobblehill Books, 1997.

Reimer, Luetta, and Wilbert Reimer. *Mathematicians Are People, Too: Stories from the Lives of Great Mathematicians*. Palo Alto, CA: Dale Seymour Publications, 1995.

Ritchie, David. *The Computer Pioneers*. New York: Simon and Schuster, 1986.

Shasha, Dennis E. *Out of Their Minds: The Lives and Discoveries of 15 Great Computer Scientists*. New York: Copernicus, 1998.

Simmons, George F. *Calculus Gems: Brief Lives and Memorable Mathematics*. New York: McGraw-Hill, 1992.

Slater, Robert. *Portraits in Silicon*. Cambridge, MA: The MIT Press, 1989.

Spencer, Donald D. *Great Men and Women of Computing*. Ormond Beach, FL: Camelot, 1999.

Young, Robyn V., ed. *Notable Mathematicians: From Ancient Times to the Present.* Detroit: Gale Research, 1998.

Internet sites

Readers should be reminded that some Internet sources change frequently. All of the following web sites were accessible as of May 27, 1999, but some may have changed addresses or been removed since then.

The Abacus
http://www.ee.ryerson.ca:8080/~elf/abacus/

American Mathematical Society (AMS)
http://e-math.ams.org/

Ask Dr. Math
http://forum.swarthmore.edu/dr.math/

Biographies of Women Mathematicians
http://www.scottland.edu/lriddle.women/chronolo.htm

Brain Teasers
http://www.eduplace.com/math/brain/

Canadian Mathematical Society
http://camel.cecm.sfu.ca/CMS

Eisenhower National Clearinghouse for Mathematics and Science
http://www.enc.org/

Elementary School Student Center
http://forum.swarthmore.edu/students/students.elementary.html

Explorer
http://explorer.scrtec.org/explorer/

Flashcards for Kids
www.edu4kids.com/math/

Fraction Shapes
http://math.rice.edu/~lanius/Patterns/

Galaxy
http://galaxy.einet.net/galaxy/Science/Mathematics.html

Selected Bibliography

The Geometry Center
http://www.geom.umn.edu/

MacTutor History of Mathematics Archive
http://www-groups.dcs.st-and.ac.uk/~history/index.html

Mandelbrot Explorer
http://www.softlab.ntua.gr/mandel/mandel.html

Math-Forum: Women and Mathematics
http://forum.swarthmore.edu/social/math.women.html

Math League Help Topics
http://www.mathleague.com/help/help.htm

Math Magic!
http://forum.swarthmore.edu/mathmagic/

A Math Website for Middle School Students
http://www-personal.umd.umich.edu/~jobrown/math.html

Mathematical Association of America
http://www.maa.org/

Mathematical Programming Glossary
http://www-math.cudenver.edu/~hgreenbe/glossary/glossary.html

The Mathematics Archives
http://archives.math.utk.edu/

Mathematics Web Sites Around the World
http://www.math.psu.edu/MathLists/Contents.html

Mathematics WWW Virtual Library
http://euclid.math.fsu.edu/Science/math.html

Measure for Measure
http://www.wolinskyweb.com/measure.htm

Mega Mathematics!
http://www.c3.lanl.gov/mega-math/

Past Notable Women of Computing and Mathematics
http://www.cs.yale.edu/~tap/past-women.html

PlaneMath
http://www.planemath.com

Project Athena
http://inspire.ospi.wednet.edu:8001/

Women in Math Project
http://darkwing.uoregon.edu/~wmnmath/

The Young Mathematicians Network WWW Site
http://www.youngmath.org/

Organizations

American Mathematical Society
P.O. Box 6248
Providence, RI 02940
Internet site: http://www.ams.org

American Statistical Association
1429 Duke Street
Alexandria, VA 22314-3402
Internet site: http://www.amstat.org

Association for Women in Mathematics
4114 Computer and Space Science Building
University of Maryland
College Park, MD 20742-2461
Internet site: http://www.awm-math.org

Association of Teachers of Mathematics
7 Shaftesbury Street
Derby DE23 8YB England
Internet site: http://acorn.educ.nottingham.ac.uk/SchEd/pages/atm

Institute of Mathematical Statistics
3401 Investment Boulevard, Suite 7
Hayward, CA 94545-3819
Internet site: http://www.imstat.org

The Madison Project
c/o Robert B. Davis
Rutgers University
Graduate School of Education

Selected Bibliography

10 Seminary Place
New Brunswick, NJ 08903

Math/Science Interchange
c/o Department of Mathematics
Loyola Marymount University
Los Angeles, CA 90045

Math/Science Network
Mills College
5000 MacArthur Boulevard
Oakland, CA 94613
Internet site: http://www.elstad.com/msngoal.html

Mathematical Association of America
1529 18th Street N.W.
Washington, DC 20036
Internet site: http://www.maa.org

National Council of Supervisors of Mathematics
P.O. Box 10667
Golden, CO 80401
Internet site: http://forum.swarthmore.edu/ncsm

National Council of Teachers of Mathematics
1906 Association Drive
Reston, VA 20191-1593
Internet site: http://www.nctm.org

School Science and Mathematics Association
400 East 2nd Street
Bloomsburg, PA 17815
Internet site: http://www.ssma.org

Society for Industrial and Applied Mathematics
3600 University City Science Center
Philadelphia, PA 19104-2688
Internet site: http://www.siam.org/nnindex.htm

Study Group for Mathematical Learning
c/o Robert B. Davis
501 South 1st Avenue
Highland Park, NJ 08904

Women and Mathematics Education
c/o Charlene Morrow
Mount Holyoke College
302 Shattuck Hall
South Hadley, MA 01075

Selected Bibliography

Picture Credits

The photographs appearing in *Math and Mathematicians: The History of Math Discoveries Around the World* were reproduced by permission of the following sources:

The Library of Congress: pp. 1, 21, 31, 34, 49, 53, 59, 62, 65, 99, 110, 125, 127, 153, 164, 177, 207, 213, 219, 235, 253, 271, 285, 299, 313, 345, 348, 399, 400; **Daytona International Speedway/Dennis Winn:** p. 19; **Fisk University Library:** p. 37; **David Blackwell/Jean Libby:** p. 45; **The Wolf Foundation:** pp. 71, 119, 451; **AP/Wide World Photos, Inc.:** pp. 73, 116, 180, 195, 198, 216, 284; **The Stock Market:** p. 79; **Hans & Cassidy, reproduced by permission of The Gale Group:** pp. 80, 89, 335, 358, 363, 423, 425; **CorbisBettmann:** pp. 83, 84, 132, 133, 171, 185, 225, 305, 331, 379, 403, 419; **PhotoEdit/Anna Zuckerman:** p. 94; **The Granger Collection, New York:** pp. 102, 114, 141, 147, 189, 263, 308, 365; **The Bettmann Archive/CorbisBettmann:** p. 111; **Photo Researchers, Inc.:** pp. 131, 247, 413, 427; **U.S. Fish & Wildlife Service:** p. 139; **Archive Photos, Inc.:** pp. 163, 261, 323; **Jim Sugar Photography/Corbis:** p. 166; **Convention & Visitors Bureau of Greater Cleveland:** p. 186; **The University of Texas at Tyler:** p. 201; **U.S. National Aeronautics and Space Administra-**

Picture Credits

tion (NASA): p. 221; New York Public Library Picture Collection: p. 238; Mathematisches Forschungsinstitut Oberwolfach: pp. 259, 319, 401; Robert L. Wolke: p. 269; Photo Researchers, Inc./Hank Morgan: p. 287; The Bettmann Archive: pp. 311, 349, 351, 357; Photo Researchers/Mikki Rain: p. 314; Edward S. Ross: p. 336; UPI/CorbisBettmann: pp. 337, 445, 448; Field Mark Publications/Robert Huffman: p. 346; CorbisBettmann/P. Dupin: p. 347; Susan D. Rock: p. 359; Colorado Springs Convention & Visitors Bureau: p. 424; The Granger Collection, Ltd.: p. 428; WWF/Dan Guravich: p. 435; Photo Researchers, Inc./ Peter Goddard, p. 454.

Index

Italic type indicates volume number; **boldface** indicates main entries and their page numbers; (ill.) indicates photos and illustrations.

Index

Index

Index

Cooking with fractions, *1:* 162

Coordinate geometry, *1:* 87, 103

Coordinate graphing, *1:* **87–90**, 89 (ill.). *See also* Geometry

Copernican theory. *See* Heliocentric theory

Copernicus, Nicolas, *2:* 235

Counting, *1:* 8. *See also* Numbers

Cowcatcher, *1:* 34

Crelle, Leopold, *1:* 4

Crelle's Journal, *1:* 4

Cross-multiplication rule, *2:* 372

Cube root, *2:* 394

Cubic equations, *1:* 61

Cubit (measurement), *2:* 267

Currency, *1:* **91–94**, 94 (ill.)

Curvature of space, *2:* 382

Curves, area under, *1:* 24, 181

Customary system, *2:* 269, 438

Cybernetics, *2:* 447–48

D

Da Vinci, Leonardo, *1:* 60

Dal Ferro, Scipione, *1:* 62

Dar al-Hikma, *2:* 242

Day, *2:* 418

Debug (computer term), *1:* 215

Decibel, *2:* 278

Decimal fraction, *1:* 96, 162; *2:* 302, 344, 373, 405

Decimal point, *2:* 299, 302

Decimal system, *1:* 80, 95; *2:* 405

Decimals, *1:* **95–98**; *2:* 278

Deduction, *2:* 282

Deductive reasoning. *1:* 128; *2:* 282, 398, 415. *See also* Inductive reasoning; Logic

Degauss, *1:* 181

Degen, Ferdinand, *1:* 3

Denominator, *1:* 96, 160, 161; *2:* 372

Descartes, René, *1:* 87, **99–105**, 99 (ill.), 102 (ill.), 143; *2:* 261

Descriptive statistics, *2:* 398, 400

Diameter, *1:* 24, 78; *2:* 326, 330, 376

Difference engine, *1:* 33, 34 (ill.), 82

Difference (subtraction), *2:* 410

Differential geometry, *1:* 71, 72

Digital clock, *2:* 418

Digital computer, *1:* 82

Diophantus, *1:* 18, 226, 227

Dirichlet, Johann, *2:* 380

Dirichlet problem, *2:* 447

Discrete mathematics, *1:* 119

Distributive property, *2:* 294

Dividend, *1:* 108, 109

Division, *1:* **107–10**; *2:* 279

Division symbol, *1:* 109; *2:* 295

Divisor, *1:* 108, 109; *2:* 443

Dodgson, Charles, *2:* 284, 284 (ill.)

E

$E = mc^2$, *1:* 115

Earth, 89–90, 128–30, 181, 184; *2:* 352, 415–16, 437

Earth-centered theories. *See* Geocentric theory

Eclipses, *2:* 414

Eddington, Arthur Stanley, *1:* 117

EDVAC (computer), *2:* 309

Egyptian campaign (Napoleon Bonaparte), *1:* 155

Einstein, Albert, *1:* **111–18**, 111 (ill.), 114 (ill.), 116 (ill.), 181, 197, 198 (ill.); *2:* 275, 321, 382, 429

Einstein Award, *1:* 198, 199

Elasticity, *1:* 189

Electrical Numerical Integrator and Computer (ENIAC), *1:* 84, 84 (ill.); *2:* 331

Electronic Discrete Variable Automatic Computer (EDVAC), *2:* 309

Elements, *1:* 125, 126, 184, 185 (ill.), 227; *2:* 372

Ellipses, *2:* 237, 352

ENIAC (computer), *1:* 84, 84 (ill.); *2:* 331

Enigma (code machine), *2:* 430

Equations, *1:* 18; *2:* 282

    Algebraic, *1:* 19

    Cubic, *1:* 61

    Linear, *1:* 20

    Quadratic, *1:* 61

Index

Galois, Évariste, *1:* 171–75, 171 (ill.)

Galton, Francis, *2:* 398, 400 (ill.)

Game theory, *1:* 47

    Economics, *2:* 309

    Neumann, John von, *2:* 305–10

Gauss, Carl Friedrich, *1:* **177–82,** 177 (ill.), 180 (ill.); *2:* 272, 380, 381–82

General equation of the fifth degree, *1:* 3

General theory of relativity, *1:* 117; *2:* 319–24, 382

Genetics, *2:* 344, 373

Geodesy, *1:* 181

Geometric diagrams, *1:* 127 (ill.)

Geometrical optics, *2:* 240

Geometry, *1:* **183–87**

    Agnesi, Maria, *1:* 11–15

    Analytic, *1:* 88, 99, 141, 143

    Archimedes of Syracuse, *1:* 21–26

    Chern, Shiing-Shen, *1:* 71–75

    Coordinate geometry, *1:* 103

    Descartes, René, *1:* 99–105

    Differential geometry, *1:* 71, 72

    Egypt, *1:* 183; *2:* 415

    Euclid of Alexandria, *1:* 125

    Euler, Leonhard, *1:* 131–36

    Fiber bundles, *1:* 71

    Fractal, *2:* 287, 290

    Graphs, *1:* 144

    Hypatia of Alexandria, *1:* 227

    Imaginary geometry, *2:* 274

    Lobachevsky, Nikolay, *2:* 271–75

    Mandelbrot, Benoit B., *2:* 287–91

    Non-Euclidean, *2:* 271, 274

    Plane geometry, *1:* 128

    Pythagoras of Samos, *2:* 349–53

    Riemann, Bernhard, *2:* 379–83

    Solid geometry, *1:* 128

Thales of Miletus, *2:* 413–16

Germain, Sophie, *1:* **189–93,** 189 (ill.)

German Mathematical Society, *1:* 56

Gibbon, Edward, *1:* 228

Gödel, Kurt, *1:* **195–99,** 195 (ill.), 198 (ill.)

Gödel's proof, *1:* 196

Golden Rectangle, *2:* 362

Gordon, Paul, *2:* 320

Grand Prix, Académie Royale des Sciences, *1:* 4, 67, 192; *2:* 255

Grandfather clocks, *1:* 165

Granville, Evelyn Boyd, *1:* **201–205,** 201 (ill.)

Graphs, *1:* 87, 144

Graunt, John, *2:* 398

Great Internet Mersenne Prime Search (GIMPS), *2:* 341

Great Pyramid at Giza, *2:* 357, 359, 359 (ill.)

Grid, *1:* 88, 184

Group theory, *1:* 1, 174

    Galois, Évariste, *1:* 171–75

H

Halley, Edmond, *2:* 254, 315, 398, 399, 399 (ill.)

Hamilton, William Rowan, *1:* **207–11,** 207 (ill.)

Hand (measurement), *2:* 267

Hardware, *1:* 82, 84

Hardy, Godfrey Harold, *2:* 367

Harmonic analysis, *1:* 156

Harmonics, *2:* 351

Heat transfer, *1:* 155

Heinrich, Peter, *1:* 38

Heliocentric theory, *2:* 235, 237

Heliotrope, *1:* 181

Herodotus, *2:* 415

Herschel, John, *1:* 32

Hertz, Heinrich, *1:* 113

Hilbert, David, *2:* 321, 446

Hindu-Arabic numerals, *1:* 148; *2:* 243–44

Holmboe, Bernt Michael, *1:* 2

Index

Index

Einstein, Albert, *1:* 111–18
Euler, Leonhard, *1:* 135
Galileo, *1:* 163–69
Germain, Sophie, *1:* 189–93
Greece, *1:* 127
Huygens, Christiaan, *1:* 219–23
Japan, *2:* 385
In literature, *1:* 118
Logical method, *1:* 128
Music, *2:* 351
Neumann, John von, *2:* 305–10
Newton, Isaac, *2:* 311–18
Quaternions, *1:* 210
Riemann, Bernhard, *2:* 379–83
Stevin, Simon, *2:* 403–407
Pi, *1:* 79; *2:* 326, **329–32**, 376
Archimedes of Syracuse, *1:* 24
Babylonia, *2:* 330
China, *2:* 330
Egypt, *2:* 330
Pi symbol, *2:* 331
Pisano, Leonardo. *See* Fibonacci, Leonardo Pisano
Place value (positional notation), *1:* 8, 96; *2:* 410, 442
Planck, Max, *1:* 113
Plane geometry, *1:* 128
Planetary motion, laws of, *2:* 235, 239
Planetary orbits, *2:* 238 (ill.)
Plato, *2:* 353
Plus symbol, *1:* 8; *2:* 295
Poe, Edgar Allen, *1:* 118
Poincaré, Jules Henri, *1:* 55
Polo, Marco, *1:* 92
Polygon, *2:* 268, 326, **333–38**, 335 (ill.), 336 (ill.), 337 (ill.), 361, 362, 422
Population, *2:* 398
Positional notation, *1:* 8; *2:* 244
Positive numbers, *2:* 232
Powers of ten, *1:* 25
Prime factorization, *2:* 340–41
Prime meridian, *2:* 418, 419

Prime number, *2:* **339–41**
"Prince of Mathematics," *1:* 177
Probability, *1:* 220; *2:* **343–48**, 346 (ill.), 372
Probability, laws of, *1:* 59
Probability theory, *1:* 141, 144; *2:* 398
Product, *1:* 138; *2:* 294
Programs (computer), *2:* 309
Project Mercury, *1:* 204
Project Vanguard, *1:* 204
Projection, *1:* 184
Proper fraction, *1:* 160
Property, *1:* 9
Proportion, *2:* **371–74**
Proportional compass, *1:* 165
Proposition, *2:* 282
Pseudosphere, *2:* 274
Ptolemy, *2:* 239
"The Pulverizer," *1:* 109
Punched cards, *1:* 33
Pythagoras of Samos, *2:* **349–53**, 349 (ill.), 350, 351 (ill.), 355, 357 (ill.), 372, 395. *See also* Pythagorean theorem
Pythagorean theorem, *2:* 352, **355–59,** 358 (ill.), 395, 422. *See also* Pythagoras of Samos

Q

Quadrilateral, *2:* **361–63,** 363 (ill.)
Qualifier, *2:* 362
Quanta, *1:* 113
Quantity, *1:* 8, 17
Quantum mechanics, *1:* 174
Quantum physics, *2:* 307
Quantum theory, *1:* 113
Quaternions, *1:* 210
Queen Dido, *2:* 327
Quintic equation, *1:* 3
Quotient, *1:* 108, 109; *2:* 376

R

Radical sign, *2:* 394
Radicand, *2:* 394
Radius, *1:* 78
Rahn, Heinrich, *1:* 109, 295

Index

Index

X

Y

Z

Index

OVER NIGHT BOOK
**This book must be returned before the
first class on the following school day.**

DEMCO